The Special Education Teacher's BOOK OF LISTS

Roger Pierangelo, Ph.D.

NATIONAL UNIVERSITY
LIBRARY   SAN DIEGO

**THE CENTER FOR APPLIED
RESEARCH IN EDUCATION**
West Nyack, New York 10995

© 1995 by

THE CENTER FOR APPLIED
RESEARCH IN EDUCATION

West Nyack, NY

10 9 8 7 6 5 4 3 2 1

Library of Congress Cataloging-in-Publication Data

Pierangelo, Roger.
    The special education teacher's book of lists / Roger Pierangelo.
        p. cm.
    ISBN 0-87628-876-X (pbk.)
    1. Special education—Handbooks, manuals, etc. 2. Special education teachers—Handbooks,
    manuals, etc. I. Center for Applied Research in Education. II. Title.
    LC3965.P54   1995
    371.9—dc20   95-36912
                                                                                    CIP

ISBN 0-87628-876-X

Special thanks to Dover Publications for
permitting us to use illustrations from
their Dover Clip Art series

Winfield Huppuch, *Publisher*
Susan Kolwicz, *Acquisitions Editor*
Jacqueline Roulette, *Production Editor*
William Ruoto, *Interior Designer*
Evan Holstrom, *Developmental Editor*

**The Center for Applied Research
in Education,** Professional Publishing
West Nyack, New York 10995
A Simon & Schuster Company

Printed in the United States of America

DEDICATION

To my loving wife Jackie and my two beautiful children Jacqueline and Scott I dedicate this book and all the work that went into it; my parents, who got so much pleasure from being parents; my sister Carol, who would make any brother proud; and my brother-in law, Dr. George Giuliani, who throughout our relationship has always been there unconditionally.

ACKNOWLEDGMENTS

To all the students, parents and teachers of the Herricks Public School District, New Hyde Park, N.Y. that I have had the pleasure of meeting, knowing and helping in my 23 years in the district.

Again to Ollie Simmons, an extraordinary individual and personal friend who always helps me start the day with a smile.

Helen Firestone, one of the most instrumental individuals in my career who always believed in me.

Charlotte Podolsky, head of Pupil Personnel Services in Herricks Public Schools for many of my years in the district before her retirement, who always showed a genuine support and confidence in my work.

In memory of Bill Smyth, a truly "extraordinary ordinary" man and one of the best guidance counselors and individuals I have ever known.

To Susan Kolwicz, my editor, who makes my life of writing textbooks very easy through her organization, efficiency, manner and good humor.

ABOUT THE AUTHOR

Dr. Roger Pierangelo has over 25 years of experience as a regular classroom teacher, school psychologist in the Herricks Public School District in New Hyde Park, N.Y., administrator of special education programs, full professor in the graduate special education department at Long Island University, private practitioner in psychology, member of Committees on Special Education, evaluator for the N.Y. State Education Department, director of a private clinic, and consultant to numerous private and public schools, PTA and SEPTA groups.

Dr. Pierangelo earned his B.S. from St. John's University, M.S. from Queens College, Professional Diploma from Queens College, and Ph.D. From Yeshiva University. Currently he is working as a psychologist both in the schools and in private practice, teaching at the college level, and serving as director of a private clinic.

Dr. Pierangelo is a member of the American Psychological Association, New York State Psychological Association, Nassau County Psychological Association, New York State Union of Teachers, and Phi Delta Kappa.

ABOUT THIS BOOK

The world of special education is changing rapidly and more is expected and demanded from the educator of this exceptional population. Today's special education teacher must be familiar with the academic, legal, medical, psychological, social, environmental, and perceptual aspects of an exceptional child's life. Without this knowledge or quick access to resources that hold it, teachers are at a disadvantage. Having the right "tool" at the right time can only enhance teaching and result in success.

The *Special Education Teacher's Book of Lists* is such a tool. This unique information source and time saver for preK–12 special education teachers contains 194 ready-to-use lists to help you make important decisions about your students and to assist you in every phase of the special education process.

Included are a broad range of lists conveniently organized into seven sections which contain the most current research on all types of disabilities, including identification, assessment, and remediation . . . simplified explanations of special education practices and procedures, laws, regulations, and rights . . . and numerous definitions, organizations, journal publications, parent resources, and practical parenting tools. This is an all-inclusive reference guide for special and regular educators, administrators, professors, college students, parents, and anyone else interested in or involved with the field of special education.

HOW TO USE THIS BOOK

This resource offers guidance through every phase of development and can be referred to by anyone seeking assistance with children from birth to adulthood. All of the sections will enable you to feel more secure and aware about the sometimes overwhelming process of special education.

The first section, **Foundational Issues**, presents an overall summary of preventive and diagnostic measures and procedures to help identify special students more quickly. It contains descriptions of signs and characteristics to look for, and offers tips on what to do when presented with high-risk symptoms.

Evaluation Measures and Assessment Procedures takes you through the list of methods used in the diagnosis of special education students. This section also provides you with a wealth of resources that cover hundreds of specific tools used to assess strengths and weaknesses in all areas.

The section on **Special Education Procedures** includes all of the information necessary in understanding the overall special education process. In a time when understanding the laws and proper procedures is crucial, you will find the examples of forms, explanations of laws, and IEP information indispensable in making professional decisions.

Specific Disabilities contains facts about 12 different exceptionalities and suggestions on how to handle them. From causality and diagnosis to behavior management and treatment, this section gives you a good base of information on each category.

You will find practical tips and materials in **Classroom Instruction Techniques for Various Exceptionalities**. This section also includes lists of computer software companies that specialize in educational tools for exceptional children, as well as suggested readings and a review of medications that may be prescribed for students with special needs.

The **Parent Education** section provides numerous lists of practical parenting suggestions on helping children with homework, improving self-esteem, using discipline effectively, communicating better, and spotting possible signs of learning disabilities. When both teachers and parents have this knowledge, they can discuss diagnosis, behavior management techniques, and remediation, and help children in school and at home.

The last section of this resource—**Definitions, Terminology, and Abbreviations**—features definitions and terms associated with special education, psychology, medicine, and occupational therapy plus 68 key abbreviations.

The Special Education Teacher's Book of Lists places in your hands an unparalleled reference packed with valuable information and materials that might otherwise take years and much effort to acquire! And any of the lists, such as the "Sample IEP Form," "Childhood Immunization Checklist," and "Structured Observation Report Form" are ready for immediate use as on-the-job working tools.

Roger Pierangelo

UNIQUE FEATURES

This book, which contains the most up-to-date information possible, is a unique guide for special education teachers because of several features:

1. Provides special educators with a variety of practical lists, charts, tables, references, and forms that can be used on a daily basis in all areas involving disabled children.

2. Gives special educators with legal, medical, and psychological facts, tables, forms, references, and lists that can enhance their understanding of the many factors that affect disabled children.

3. Contains useful and reproducible forms that can save time, enhance instruction, and reinforce concepts.

4. Includes practical and step-by-step lists for identification, assessment, and practical remediation of all disabilities.

5. Puts at your fingertips vast references, forms, lists, charts, and tables that can be reproduced and handed out to assist parents in their everyday activities with their disabled children.

CONTENTS

PART I

Foundational Issues for Special Educators

1-1. PUPIL PERSONNEL OR CHILD STUDY TEAM GUIDELINES

Questions for the PPT or Child Study Team to Consider

When a PPT first receives a referral from a teacher the team must consider many issues. These may include the following:

1. Has this child ever been referred to the PPT?

Prior referral may indicate a *historical disturbance* or long-term problem and therefore a more serious situation, especially if the same pattern exists. *Situational disturbances,* with no prior problems, usually have a better prognosis.

2. Do we have any prior psychological, educational, language, or other evaluations?

This information is very important, so the child is not put through unnecessary testing. The reports also offer the team another perspective on the problem.

3. Is anyone familiar with other family members?

Family patterns of behavior may help define contributing factors to the child's problem, and offer the team some experience on the best approach to take with this family.

4. Are there any medical issues that might impact on this case?

These issues are crucial; the existence of medical problems should always be determined first. Difficulties with hearing, eyesight, taking medication, severe allergies, etc., may be significant contributors to poor performance and may be masked by terms like "unmotivated," "lazy," "stubborn," and so on.

5. What do his or her report cards look like? What patterns are exhibited?

Some children have trouble starting off in a new situation and play catch-up the entire year. Others do well the first marking period and slowly decline to a pattern of poor grades. Others exhibit the "roller coaster effect"—consistently receiving grades from failing to passing and back again. Knowing the child's report card "style" may help determine the type of support, remediation, and program offered.

6. What are the child's group achievement test score patterns?

Achievement test scores can offer a great deal of useful information about a child's patterns. If the team suspects a learning disability, then the areas affected should be consistently low from year to year. Many fluctuations of scores and wide ranges of results may indicate more emotional involvement than a learning disability.

7. If no prior testing is available, is there any group IQ test information to give us some general idea of ability?

While group IQ tests should never be used to determine a high-risk child's true intellectual potential, they may offer a general idea of ability.

3

1-1. Continued

8. **Has anyone observed this child?**

This piece of information is required if the team plans to refer the child to the CSE. In any case, observation should always be a piece of the contributing information presented to the PPT. It is very important for the team to know how this child functions in structured and unstructured settings.

9. **Do we have samples of his or her classwork?**

Samples of classwork over a period of time offer a clearer overview of the child's abilities and attitude toward class work.

10. **Has the parent been notified of the teacher's concerns?**

It is the responsibility of the classroom teacher to alert the parents that he or she is concerned and would like a closer look by the PPT. A parent does not have a legal right to refuse such a request, since it is considered a normal school procedure.

4

1-2. SUGGESTED INTERVENTION OPTIONS USED PRIOR TO EVALUATION

Pupil Personnel Team (PPT) discussions: This procedure should be used so that several staff members are able to view the symptoms and provide a variety of preventive suggestions prior to evaluation.

Team meeting with teachers: Sometimes a group meeting with all the child's teachers can prevent the need for further involvement. Once a pattern is identified, it may be handled in a variety of ways without the need for more serious intervention.

Parent interviews: Meeting with the parent(s) is always recommended when a child is having some difficulty in school. This initial meeting can be informal and may be just for the purpose of clarifying certain issues and gathering pertinent information that may help in the classroom.

Classroom management techniques: There are times when the real issue may not be the child, but the style of the classroom teacher. If that is the case, then help for the teacher can come in the form of classroom management techniques to be tried before taking more serious steps.

Help classes: Some schools provide extra nonspecial education services, such as help classes that may be held during lunch or after school. They assist a child by clarifying academic confusion, which could lead to more serious problems if not addressed.

Resource room assistance: This option can be tried prior to any CSE (Committee on Special Education) review only when the school district offers such services for nonspecial education students. If this option is available, then the school may want to try it first.

Remedial reading or math services: These types of services do not require a review by the CSE. Remedial reading or math classes are not special education services and can be instituted as a means of alleviating the child's academic problems.

Speech and language services: There are times when children who have not been classified by the CSE as disabled encounter mild developmental speech or language difficulties that can be remediated with this type of intervention.

Recommendation for in-school counseling: When a pattern occurs that temporarily interferes with a child's ability to concentrate, remember, or attend to tasks, the school psychologist may want to institute in-school counseling with the parent's involvement and permission. This recommendation should be instituted only with issues that can resolved in a relatively short period of time. More serious issues may have to be referred to outside agencies or professionals for longer treatment.

Daily/weekly progress reports: Sometimes children who have fallen behind academically "hide" from the real issues by avoiding reality. The use of daily progress reports for a week or two at first—and then weekly reports—may provide the child with the kinds of immediate gratification needed to get back on track.

1-2. Continued

Disciplinary action: This recommendation is usually made when the child in question needs a structured boundary set because of inappropriate behavior. It is usually used in conjunction with other recommendations if a pattern exists, since such patternal behavior may be symptomatic of a more serious problem.

Medical exam: Try to rule out any possibility of a medical condition's causing or contributing to the existing problems. If the **PPT** sees any possibility of such involvement, then a recommendation should be made to the parents that the PPT's concerns be discussed with the child's pediatrician.

Change of program: This recommendation usually occurs when a student is placed in a course that is not suited to his or her ability or needs. If a student is found to have a low IQ and is in an advanced class and failing, then the program should be changed.

Consolidation of program: If a child's available energy level is extremely low, a temporary consolidation or condensing of the program allows for the possibility of salvaging some courses, since his or her available energy does not have to be spread so thin.

PINS petition: A PINS petition (Person in Need of Supervision) is a family court referral. This referral can be made by either the school or the parent and is usually made when a child under the age of 16 is out of control in terms of attendance, behavior, or some socially inappropriate or destructive pattern.

Referral to Child Protective Services: A referral to Child Protective Services is mandated for all educators if there is a suspicion of abuse or neglect. Referrals to this service may result from physical, sexual, or emotional abuse, or from educational, environmental, or medical neglect.

1-3. EVALUATION OPTIONS OF THE PUPIL PERSONNEL TEAM

To make an accurate diagnosis of a child's situation a Child Study Team or Pupil Personnel Team must gather a great deal of information, which may include:

- evaluations
- observations
- rating scales
- parent intake
- work samples
- academic records
- group achievement scores
- medical records
- past teacher reports

Several directions and recommendations can be instituted during this process by the PPT:

Psychoeducational evaluation: The team may resort to this when a child's academic skill levels (reading, math, writing, and spelling) are unknown or inconsistent, learning process shows gaps (i.e., memory or expression) or when making a referral to the CSE.

Some symptoms that might suggest this recommendation are

- consistently low test scores on group achievement tests
- indications of delayed processing when faced with academic skills
- labored handwriting after grade 3
- poor word recall
- poor decoding (word attack) skills
- discrepancy between achievement and ability
- consistently low achievement despite remediation

Language evaluation: This recommendation usually occurs when the child is experiencing significant delays in speech or language development, problems in articulation, or problems in receptive or expressive language. Some symptoms that might warrant such an evaluation are

7

1-3. Continued

- difficulty pronouncing words through grade 3
- immature or delayed speech patterns
- difficulty labeling thoughts or objects
- difficulty putting thoughts into words

Psychological evaluation: Use this recommendation when the child's intellectual ability is unknown or there is a questionable factor in his or her inability to learn. Also use this recommendation when referring to the CSE for a potential learning, emotional, or intellectual problem. The psychological evaluation can rule out or rule in emotionality as a primary cause of a child's problem. Ruling this factor out is required before the diagnosis of LD can be determined. Some symptoms that might signal the need for such an evaluation are

- high levels of tension and anxiety exhibited in behavior
- aggressive behavior
- lack of motivation or indications of low energy levels
- patterns of denial
- oppositional behavior
- despondency
- inconsistent academic performance ranging from very low to very high
- history of inappropriate judgment
- lack of impulse control
- extreme and consistent attention-seeking behavior
- pattern of provocative behavior

Reading evaluation: This evaluation can be recommended when reading is the specific area of concern and the need for a complete and comprehensive reading diagnostic battery is called for by the team. Some symptoms that may necessitate this type of evaluation are

- inability to develop a sight word vocabulary by grade 2
- consistent inability to remember what is read
- constant loss of place while reading
- inadequate development of word attack skills

Intellectual evaluation: This evaluation may be a first step in determining whether or not the child's present problems reflect a severe discrepancy between ability and achievement. It should also be used if group intelligence test scores are questionably lower than the ability observed by the teacher(s). This option may also place unrealistic expectations on the part of the parents, child, or teachers in better perspective.

1-3. Continued

Hearing test: This evaluation should be one of the first factors recommended by the team if one has not been accomplished within the last six months to one year. Be aware of inconsistencies in test patterns from year to year that might indicate a chronic pattern. Some symptoms that might indicate an updated audiological examination are

- child turns head when listening
- child asks you to repeat frequently
- child consistently misinterprets what he or she hears
- child does not respond to auditory stimuli
- child slurs speech, speaks in a monotone, or articulates poorly

Vision test: As with the hearing exam, results of the vision screening should also be considered first by the PPT. Again, if a vision screening has not been done within six months to a year, then request this immediately. Possible symptoms that may necessitate such an evaluation are

- turning head when looking at board or objects
- excessive squinting
- frequent rubbing of eyes
- holding books and materials close to face or at unusual angles
- frequent headaches
- avoiding close work of any type
- covering an eye when reading

Referral to CSE for a meeting to discuss the recommendation for evaluation denied by parent(s): If a parent refuses to sign a release for testing and the school feels strongly that such a procedure is in the best interests of the child, a review by the CSE is possible to resolve this dispute.

Whatever the recommendation instituted by the Pupil Personnel Team, it should be done with all the most recent information available on a child. Such recommendations may have tremendous implications and should never be taken lightly.

1-4. HOW TO DEAL WITH PARENT INTAKES AND INTERVIEWS

An important step in the referral process involves a complete social history that can be regarded as a description of the family life situation. In some cases this part of the process may not be possible to obtain because of a number of variables, such as parent's work restrictions, inability to obtain coverage for younger siblings, resistance, or apathy.

While the intake in many schools is performed by the social worker or psychologist, it is important that you understand the process in case you are called upon to do the intake. If you are able to arrange for a parent intake there are several things to consider before the meeting.

1. **Always make the parent(s) feel comfortable and at ease by setting up a receptive environment.** If possible, hold the meeting in a pleasant setting, use a round table or any table instead of a desk, and offer some type of refreshment to ease tension.

2. **Never view the parent(s) as adversaries even if they are angry or hostile.** Keep in mind that the anger or hostility is a defense because they may not be aware of what you will be asking, or they may have experienced a series of negative school meetings over the years. Since this may be an opportunity for parents to "vent," listen to their concerns, do not get defensive, and be understanding without taking sides.

3. **Inform them every step of the way as to the purpose of the meeting and the steps involved in the referral process.** Reassure them that no recommendation will be made without their input and permission.

4. **Tell them the purpose of testing and what you hope to gain from the process.** Be solution oriented and offer realistic hope even if past experiences have resulted in frustration. Remind the parent that children can be more motivated, resilient, and successful at different stages.

5. **Make sure the parents know that if the testing reveals a significant discrepancy between ability and achievement, the case must be reviewed by the CSE.** This is an important piece of information to convey to the parents, since it involves their rights to due process.

6. **Go over the release form and explain each test and its purpose.** The more information parents have, the less fearful they will be. Explain that the testing must be completed 30 days from the date signed and that it will not take months before they are made aware of the findings.

7. **You may want to offer them a pad and pen so that they can write down information, terms, or notes on the meeting.** Further indicate that they should feel free to call you with any questions or concerns they may have.

8. **Reassure the parents about the confidentiality of the information gathered.** Indicate the individuals on the team who will be seeing the information and the purpose for their review of the facts.

1-5. RESPONSIBILITIES AND VARIOUS ROLES OF THE SPECIAL EDUCATION TEACHER

The special education teacher in today's schools plays a very critical role in the proper education of exceptional students. The teacher is unique in that he or she can fit many different roles in the educational environment. For instance the special education teacher can be assigned as

1. **Teacher in a self-contained special education classroom in a regular school.** This role involves working with a certain number of disabled students in a special education setting. This type of setting also allows for the use of *mainstreaming,* the involvement of a disabled child in a regular classroom for a part of the school day—when a student is ready for this type of transitional technique. The teacher in a self-contained classroom is usually assisted by a teaching assistant.

2. **Resource teacher in a categorical resource room.** This resource room, in a special school, deals with only one type of exceptionality.

3. **Teacher in a noncategorical resource room.** This resource room is usually found in the regular mainstream school, where many exceptionalities are educated at one time. This role necessitates close involvement with each child's homeroom teacher and the transfer of practical techniques and suggestions to facilitate the child's success while in the regular setting.

4. **Educational evaluator on the Child Study Team or Pupil Personnel Team, the school-based support team that discusses and makes recommendations on high-risk students.** This role requires a complete and professional understanding of testing and evaluation procedures, and diagnosis and interpretation of test results.

5. **Member of the Committee on Special Education.** This is a district-based committee, mandated by Federal law, whose responsibilities include the classification, placement, and evaluation of all disabled children within the district. This role involves interpreting educational test results, making recommendations, and diagnosing strengths and weaknesses for the *Individual Educational Plan*—a list of goals, needs, and objectives required for every disabled student.

6. **Member of a multidisciplinary team.** This type of team is responsible for educating secondary students in a departmentalized program.

7. **Consultant teacher.** This position requires a special education teacher to work with a disabled child right in the mainstreamed class.

8. **Itinerant teacher.** In this type of arrangement, a special education teacher is hired to visit various schools in several districts and work with special children, providing the children with the required auxiliary services and a district to meet requirements without having a program of its own.

9. **Private practitioner.** This role deals with the evaluation and remediation of children as an auxiliary service after school.

1-5. Continued

Whatever the role, you will always encounter a variety of situations that require practical decisions and relevant suggestions. No matter what role you play in special education, there is always a need to fully understand symptomatology, causality, evaluation, diagnosis, prescription, and remediation as well as to communicate vital information to professionals, parents, and students.

1-6. SCHOOL SYMPTOMS EXHIBITED BY HIGH-RISK STUDENTS

A high-risk student is usually experiencing severe emotional, social, environmental, or academic stress. As a result of this intense turmoil, many symptoms are generated in a dynamic attempt to alleviate the anxiety. They can show up in many different behavior patterns. Some of the more common patterns exhibited by either elementary or secondary students while in school are

- a history of adequate or high first quarter grades followed by a downward trend leading to failures in the final quarter
- a history of excessive absences
- a history of excessive lateness
- frequent inability to separate from parent at the start of the school day—normal behavior in very young children, but a more serious symptom after age 6 or 7
- high achievement scores and high school abilities index with a history of low academic performance
- consistent failure in two or more quarters of at least two subjects
- a history of parent "coverage" for inappropriate behavior, poor work performance, poor attitude, failures, or absences
- wandering the halls after school with no direction or purpose
- history of constant projection onto others a reason for lack of performance, handing in late work, failures, or cutting
- history of feeling powerless in the student's approach to problems
- recent stress-related experiences—divorce, separation, death of a parent, or parent's loss of employment
- history of constant visits to the nurse
- social withdrawal from peers with an emphasis on developing relationships with adults

1-7. HOW TO DETERMINE THE SEVERITY OF A PROBLEM

While many symptoms may indicate a problem, several guidelines should be used to determine the severity of the situation:

1. **Frequency of Symptoms.** Consider how often the symptoms occur; the greater the frequency, the greater the chance of a serious problem.

2. **Duration of Symptoms.** Consider how long the symptoms last. The longer the duration the more serious the problem

3. **Intensity of Symptoms.** Consider how serious the reactions are at the time of occurrence. The more intense the symptom, the more serious the problem.

Dynamic problems—conflicts, fears, insecurities—create tension. The more serious the problem, or the greater number of problems experienced by a child, the greater the level of tension. When tension is present, behavior is used to relieve the tension. When serious problems exist, the behavior required to relieve this tension becomes more immediate. As a result, the behavior may be inappropriate and impulsive rather than well thought out.

When tension is very high it may require a variety of behaviors to relieve the dynamic stress. These behaviors then become symptoms of the seriousness of the problem, so the frequency and intensity of the symptomatic behavior reflects the seriousness of the underlying problem(s).

As the child becomes more confident or learns to work out problems, for example, through therapy, the underlying problems become smaller, generate less tension, and produce fewer inappropriate, impulsive, or self-destructive behavior patterns.

1-8. SYMPTOMATIC BEHAVIOR POSSIBLY INDICATING MORE SERIOUS PROBLEMS

Examples of typical symptomatic behavior that may be indicative of more serious concerns may include the following:

—is impulsive
—frequently hands in incomplete work
—gives excuses for inappropriate behavior
—constantly blames others for problems
—panics easily
—is distractible
—has short attention span
—overreacts
—is physical with others
—is intrusive
—is unable to focus on task
—procrastinates
—squints
—turns head while listening
—is disorganized
—is inflexible
—is irresponsible
—uses poor judgment
—exhibits denial
—daydreams
—is unwilling to venture a guess
—is unwilling to reason
—withdraws socially
—constantly uses self-criticism
—bullies other children
—needs constant reassurance
—reads poorly

—lies constantly
—is awkward
—is fearful of adults
—is fearful of new situations
—is verbally hesitant
—is hypoactive
—is hyperactive
—fears criticism
—rarely takes chances
—is moody
—defies authority
—is anxious
—cannot generalize
—is insecure
—has trouble starting work
—tires easily
—is controlling
—is overly critical
—is forgetful
—is painfully shy
—is overly social
—is a slow starter
—is argumentative
—destroys property
—is lazy
—exhibits inconsistency
—spells poorly

1-9. COMMON AVOIDANCE BEHAVIORS

Avoidance behaviors are common tools used by children who are experiencing problems in learning. Children will often exhibit these symptoms at home and at school to avoid loss of parental approval, peer humiliation, or feelings of failure. Examples include the following:

Selectively forgets

The selectivity of the forgetfulness usually centers around areas of learning that may be creating frustration.

Forgets to write down assignments day after day

The avoidance of a perceived failure experience is accomplished through the use of this behavior.

Takes hours to complete homework

This symptom also occurs if a child is under tension and cannot concentrate for long periods of time. He or she will tend to "burn out" quickly and daydream the night away.

Finishes homework very quickly

With this type of symptom, the child's major objective is to get the ego-threatening situation (homework) over as quickly as possible. Every attempt is made to rush through the assignments with little care or patience.

Can't seem to get started with homework

When a child's anxiety level is very high it is very difficult to "start the engine." This child may spend a great deal of time "getting ready" for the homework by arranging books, sharpening pencils, getting the paper out, opening the textbooks, getting a glass of water, going to the bathroom and so on, but never really starting assignments.

© 1995 by The Center for Applied Research in Education

16

1-9. Continued

Frequently brings home unfinished classwork

This symptom is exhibited by students for three reasons:

- One reason is a low energy level, and therefore problems dealing with tasks involving sustained concentration.
- The second reason may involve the concept of learned helplessness, and may arise when a parent constantly sits next to a child while he or she is doing homework. The child becomes conditioned to this assistance and is helpless without it.
- The third reason may involve the child's need for attention. Bringing home unfinished classwork necessitates having a parent sit with the child until the work is completed. This "captive audience" aspect of parent attention is reinforced when a parent tries to leave.

Consistently leaves long-term assignments until the last minute

Avoidance of school-related tasks, especially long-term ones, is a frequent symptom of children with low energy levels

Complains of headaches, stomachaches and other physical ailments before or after school

Very high tension levels over an extended period of time may result in somatic (bodily) complaints. These complaints, while real to the child, may indicate an avoidance of an uncomfortable or ego-deflating situation. When a child has a pattern of these types of complaints, the teacher must see this signal as a symptom of a more serious problem.

Exhibits "spotlight" behaviors

"Spotlight" behaviors are any behaviors that bring the focus of attention to the child—calling out, laughing out loud, getting up out of the seat, annoying other children. When this occurs it is usually a release of tension.

- Some children use spotlight behaviors to alleviate the tension of academic inadequacy and may even hope to get into trouble to leave the room.
- Another reason for spotlight behaviors is control; however, keep in mind that the more controlling a child is, the more out of control he or she feels.
- The third reason for spotlight behaviors is to gain the teacher's attention; however, in this way the child is determining when he or she gets attention, not the teacher.

17

1-10. ENERGY DRAIN AND ITS EFFECT ON BEHAVIOR AND LEARNING

Normal Development—Division of Energy

Everyone has a certain amount of psychic energy to use in dealing with the everyday stresses of life. In normal development there is a certain amount of stress but because of an absence of major conflicts that tend to drain energy, the individual has more than enough to keep things in perspective. Consequently, the division of energy and the symptoms that result (more often than not) when a child is relatively conflict free may look like this:

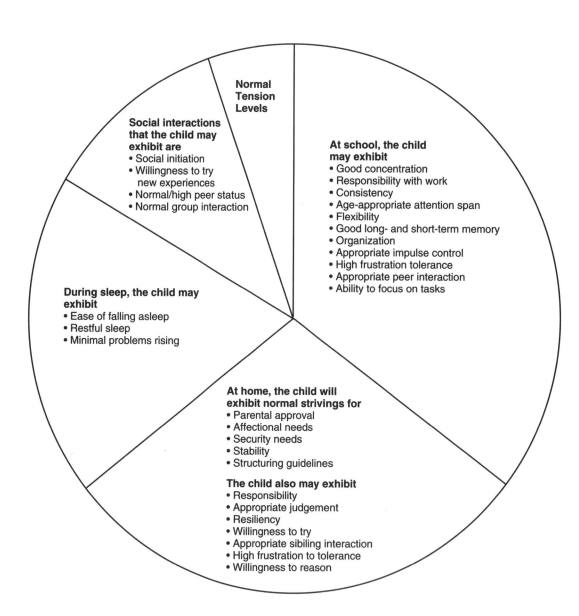

Normal Tension Levels

Social interactions that the child may exhibit are
- Social initiation
- Willingness to try new experiences
- Normal/high peer status
- Normal group interaction

At school, the child may exhibit
- Good concentration
- Responsibility with work
- Consistency
- Age-appropriate attention span
- Flexibility
- Good long- and short-term memory
- Organization
- Appropriate impulse control
- High frustration tolerance
- Appropriate peer interaction
- Ability to focus on tasks

During sleep, the child may exhibit
- Ease of falling asleep
- Restful sleep
- Minimal problems rising

At home, the child will exhibit normal strivings for
- Parental approval
- Affectional needs
- Security needs
- Stability
- Structuring guidelines

The child also may exhibit
- Responsibility
- Appropriate judgement
- Resiliency
- Willingness to try
- Appropriate sibling interaction
- High frustration to tolerance
- Willingness to reason

© 1995 by The Center for Applied Research in Education

18

1-10. Continued

High Tension Level—Division of Energy

When serious conflicts arise, the available energy must be "pulled" to deal with the conflicts—like white blood cells to an infection. Since energy must be drained away, there is less available energy to keep things in perspective. In this case the resulting symptoms and behaviors take on a different look. When a parent or teacher observes a pattern of behaviors similar to these, he or she should automatically become aware that some serious problem may exist. These symptoms are not the problems but an outgrowth of a serious problem. It is therefore very important for the teacher or team to try to identify what the problem or problems are so that treatment can take place.

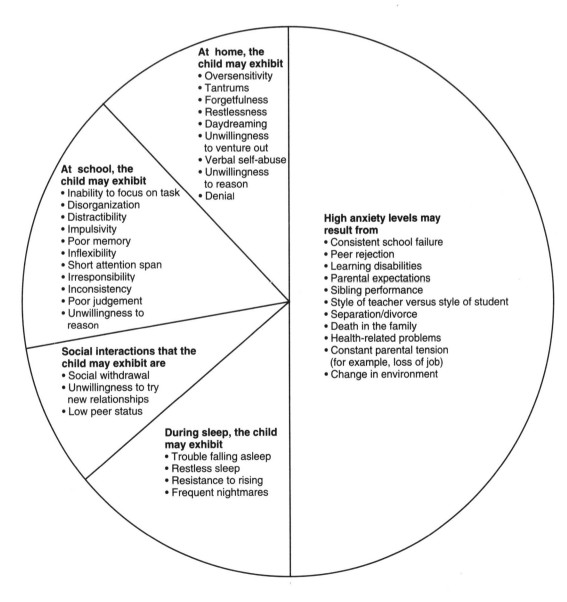

19

1-11. EXAMPLES OF STRUCTURED REFERRAL FORMS

Many schools utilize a referral form that teachers submit, indicating the possibility of a high-risk student. This is usually the first step in the referral process. The form then goes to the Pupil Personnel Team for discussion and future direction. The initial section of these forms is usually the same, containing basic identifying information. The differences are usually in the body of the form. Following are several examples of these forms.

Student Name

Grade Level

Teacher Name

Parent(s) Names

Date of Referral

Date of Birth

Chronological Age

Phone

1-11. Continued

Example A

Please answer the following questions using behavioral terms:

What symptoms is the child exhibiting that are of concern at this time? _____

_____

_____

What have you tried that has worked? _____

_____

_____

What have you tried that does not seem to work towards alleviating these symptoms? __

_____

_____

What are the child's present academic levels of functioning? _____

_____   _____

What is the child's social behavior like? _____

_____

_____

Have the parent(s) been contacted ? yes _____ no _____ If no, why not? _____

_____

Further comments? _____

_____

_____

1-11. Continued

Example B

Grades Repeated (if any): _____

Current Academic Performance Levels: _____

Math: _____ Reading: _____ Spelling: _____

Any observable behavioral or physical limitations: _____

_____

Reasons for referral: _____

_____

List specific academic and behavioral strengths _____

_____

List academic and behavioral weaknesses: _____

_____

What have you tried to remedy the problem? _____

_____

Has the parent(s) been notified of this referral? yes ____ no ____ _____

_____

What was their reaction? _____

_____

_____

1-11. Continued

Example C

Why is this pupil being referred? _____

_____

_____

How have you attempted to deal with these problems? _____

_____

_____

Have you discussed this referral with the student? What was his or her reaction? _____

_____

_____

What is the child's perception of the situation?_____

_____

_____

Current performance estimates (below, on, or above grade level)

Reading _____ Math _____ Spelling _____

Describe the child's current social behavior with peers: _____

_____

_____

_____

1-11. Continued

Any relevant history that may assist in the understanding of this child? _____

_____

_____

Have the parent(s) been contacted about this referral? yes ____ no ____ _____

_____

_____

What was their reaction? _____

_____

_____

1-12. EXAMPLES OF STUDENT RATING SCALES

Some schools will use a student rating scale along with or instead of a referral form. The purpose of a rating scale is to get a more objective measure of a student's behavior, performance, and characteristics. Such forms do not force the referring teacher to generalize comments, but instead allow for a more accurate appraisal of the student. The teacher is usually asked to rate the student along some continuum determined by the frequency and intensity of the behavior being rated. Following are some examples of such scales.

Student Rating Scale—Example A

Never Seldom Sometimes Most of the time Always

Academic Behavior

1. Has trouble comprehending what he or she reads
2. Uses adequate word attack skills
3. Loses his or her place while reading
4. Slows down when reading aloud
5. Exhibits good sight word vocabulary
6. Shows adequate math computational skills
7. Understands word problems
8. Applies mathematical skills in solving problems
9. Exhibits appropriate handwriting for age
10. Exhibits adequate spelling skills

Classroom Behavior

1. Exhibits impulsivity
2. Exhibits distractibility
3. Gets along with peers
4. Follows rules of a game
5. Is willing to reason
6. Conforms to boundaries and rules in the classroom
7. Attends to task
8. Completes homework
9. Completes classwork in allotted time
10. Listens carefully
11. Becomes easily frustrated
12. Cooperates with others

Language Behavior

1. Exhibits adequate vocabulary
2. Exhibits limited verbal fluency
3. Exhibits faulty articulation

1-12. Continued

Pupil Behavior Rating Scale—Example B

Please rate the following behaviors according to the following scale:

RATING

1. The behavior does not apply to this child and is never observed
2. The behavior is rarely exhibited
3. The behavior occurs some of the time
4. The behavior occurs most of the time
5. The behavior always occurs

____ Anxious

____ Disruptive

____ Fights frequently

____ Unhappy

____ Withdrawn

____ Moody

____ Distractible

____ Impulsive

____ Does not complete work

____ Short attention span

____ Daydreams

____ Argumentative

____ Disorganized

____ Easily confused

____ Poor speller

____ Poor reader

____ Limited reading comprehension

____ Faulty articulation

____ Poor grammar

____ Problems judging time

____ Poor fine motor skills

____ Slow in completing tasks

____ Poor logical reasoning and thinking

____ Poor number concepts

____ Tires easily

____ Defies authority

____ Fears criticism

____ Critical to others

____ Controlling

____ Painfully shy

____ Slow starter

____ Inconsistent

____ Hyperactive

____ Hypoactive

____ Fearful of new situations

____ Procrastinates

____ Rarely takes chances

____ Overreactive

____ Problems with writing

____ Problems with math

____ Poor vocabulary usage

____ Poor expressive language ability

____ Inadequate word attack skills

____ Poor balance and coordination

____ Poor gross motor skills

____ Tracing and drawing difficulties

____ Difficulty with abstract concepts

____ Problems with auditory memory tasks

1-13. PROCEDURES TO FOLLOW IF YOU SUSPECT ABUSE OR NEGLECT

Remember you need only suspect abuse or neglect to report the case. If you suspect possible abuse or neglect follow the following steps:

1. Gather all the information you can about the suspected incident or incidents and write it up in *factual and behavioral terminology*. (This means no opinions, interpretations, assumptions or guesses—just factual observations or information, that is, The child said . . . I directly observed . . . There were black and blue marks on his or her legs.)

2. Notify your direct administrator (usually a building principal) of the information you have that caused you to suspect abuse or neglect. Here again, verbalize only facts. At this point, the administrator will usually call the Child Abuse Hotline or assign someone to call.

If the administrator listens to the facts and does not see it as a reportable case, you should ask the reasons why and suggest that the case be presented to the Child Abuse Counselor. If the administrator continues to indicate that he or she does not think it needs to go any further, inform the administrator that as a mandated reporter, you feel a responsibility to call the Child Abuse Hotline and ask the counselor on call if she or he sees this as a reportable case. If an administrator does not want to report a case, and you agree with this decision—and it is later determined that abuse or neglect was taking place—you may find yourself in very serious trouble. It is not acceptable to use the excuse, "I told my administrator." Remember, you are a mandated reporter and directly responsible for actions taken or not taken.

If you are assigned to call, keep the following in mind:

- Make sure you call the mandated reporters' hotline. Many state have two lines—one for the public to report cases and one for mandated reporters. The numbers can be found in the phone book or by calling 800-555-1212 and asking for the State Child Abuse and Neglect Hotline for Mandated Reporters, since most of these hotlines are 800 numbers.

- Once you have a counselor on the phone, immediately ask for his or her name and note the time and date of your call.

- Inform the counselor that you have a suspected case of abuse or neglect. He or she will ask you some basic questions for the records and then ask you what evidence you have.

- Again, report only facts and direct observations. At this point, the counselor may indicate that it is either reportable or not a reportable case.

- If the case is reportable, the counselor will ask you more questions, so be prepared with the following information: the child's full name, the address of the child, the child's birthdate, the parent or guardian's first and last names (if different), the child's telephone number, the parent or guardian's work number if known, other siblings in the house and their ages, the grade of the child, the school and school district of the child, and the number and nature of any previous reports.

1-13. Continued

3. After the counselor gathers all the information, he or she may assign a case number; jot this down. The counselor will inform you that the case will be passed on to a local case worker who will be in touch with the school.

4. Ask the counselor if he or she thinks that the child can go home or if the school should retain the child until the case worker appears. The school has this right if the child's health or safety will be compromised in any way by returning home after school. Many times the case worker will come immediately if it is deemed a serious case and will speak with the child before the end of the school day. A home visit is usually made within 24 hours or less if the case is considered serious.

5. The school nurse, under the direction of the building administrator, may photograph any obvious marks or contusions for evidence.

6. Once the case is reported, you will probably receive a Report of Suspected Child Abuse or Maltreatment form from the Department of Social Services. The school must fill this out and return it within 24 hours. Here again, the person who made the original contact with the state counselor may be the one who fills out the form. An example of this type of form appears at the end of this section. Keep in mind that this is a legal requirement.

7. In some instances, the counselor may indicate that a case does not sound reportable as abuse or neglect. He or she may indicate that it does represent poor judgment on the part of parents but does not constitute abuse or neglect. At this point you can ask why and ask the counselor's advice for the next step. However, if it is not reportable, write your administrator a letter indicating the time, the date, and the name of the counselor to whom you spoke, and the reasons why the case was not accepted as reportable. Your legal responsibilities are now covered; however, your moral responsibilities have just begun.

1-14. CLINICAL AND BEHAVIORAL CLUES TO POSSIBLE CHILD ABUSE OR NEGLECT

Since special education teachers are mandated reporters, you should be aware of clinical and behavioral clues to possible abuse. Try to keep in mind that you should use common sense and proper judgment prior to reporting suspected abuse. Such reports are a serious matter. On the other hand, never hesitate if you suspect abuse because "such a family could never do such things." Remember that, as a mandated reporter, you are really an advocate for children in cases of suspected abuse or neglect; never assume that something is so obvious that someone must have called it in. It is always better to be safe than sorry.

Physical Abuse

SOME POSSIBLE BEHAVIORAL SIGNS OF PHYSICAL ABUSE

1. Fear of, or resistance to, going home

2. Past history of self-injurious behavior

3. Extreme neurotic conditions, that is, obsessions, compulsions, phobias

4. Wears clothing that is inappropriate for the season, for example, long sleeves in the summertime—possibly to cover up bruises

5. Extreme mood changes and periods of aggressive behavior

6. Seems apprehensive or afraid of adults

7. Flinches or reacts defensively to adult gestures or behavior that is not generally considered dangerous

8. Communicates that he or she is constantly falling or running into things as an excuse for bruises

SOME POSSIBLE PHYSICAL SIGNS OF PHYSICAL ABUSE

1. Unexplained marks, welts, bites, or bruises on the body

2. Unexplained burns

3. Unexplained injuries to the head area

Sexual Abuse

SOME POSSIBLE BEHAVIORAL SIGNS OF SEXUAL ABUSE

1. Acts in an infantile manner and exhibits frequent withdrawal and fantasy

1-14. Continued

2. Has difficulties maintaining peer relationships

3. Engages in sexual activities with other children

4. Is frequently late or absent from school

5. Resists physical examinations

6. Has a history of running away

7. Has a history of self-injurious behavior

8. Expresses sophisticated, bizarre, or unusual knowledge of sexual acts or behavior to other children or adults

SOME POSSIBLE PHYSICAL SIGNS OF SEXUAL ABUSE

1. Talks about or exhibits bruises in genital areas

2. Has difficulty walking or sitting for long periods of time because of pain

3. Exhibits bruises to the mouth area

4. Exhibits extreme pain, itching, or discomfort in the genital area

5. Has a history of urinary tract infections

6. Has developed sexually transmitted diseases, especially in the preadolescent period

Neglect or Maltreatment

SOME POSSIBLE BEHAVIORAL SIGNS OF NEGLECT

1. Is frequently caught taking food from other children

2. Arrives at school much earlier than the other children

3. Resists going home at the end of the day and is seen wandering the halls

4. Exhibits constant fatigue

5. Frequently falls asleep in class

6. Develops habit disorders: tics or other signs of tension

7. Exhibits symptoms typical of conduct disorders, that is, antisocial behavior

8. Frequently uses drugs or alcohol

9. Develops clinging behavior patterns with other adults

1-14. Continued

SOME POSSIBLE PHYSICAL SIGNS OF NEGLECT

1. Seems to have medical or physical conditions that go untreated

2. Severe lags in physical development as a result of malnutrition

3. Expresses constant hunger

4. Comes to school exhibiting poor hygiene

5. Comes to school inappropriately dressed for the particular weather conditions

6. Mentions that he or she is left home alone a great deal

7. Exhibits chronic absences from school

8. Has a history of lateness to school

1-15. EXAMPLE OF A REPORT FORM FOR SUSPECTED CHILD ABUSE OR MALTREATMENT

SUBJECTS OF REPORT

List all children in household, adults responsible for household, and alleged perpetrators.

Last Name	First Name	M.I.	Aliases	Sex M or F	Birthdate or Age	Ethnic Code	Suspect or Relationship Code	Check if alleged Perpetrator Code
1.								
2.								
3.								
4.								
5.								
6.								
7.								

If known, list addresses and telephone numbers:

BASIS OF SUSPICIONS

Alleged consequences or evidence of abuse or maltreatment. Place the above line numbers next to the appropriate area. If all children, write "ALL."

_____ Sexual Abuse   _____ Drug Withdrawal

_____ Emotional Neglect   _____ Child's Drug/Alcohol

_____ Abandonment   _____ Lack of Medical Care

_____ Lack of Supervision   _____ Malnutrition

_____ DOA/Fatality   _____ Failure to Thrive

_____ Fractures   _____ Educational Neglect

_____ Lacerations, Bruises, Welts _____ Lack of Food, Clothing, Shelter

_____ Excessive Corporal Punishment _____ Internal Injuries

_____ Other   Specify _____

State reason for suspicion. If possible, include type and extent of the child's injury or abuse. If known, give time and date of maltreatment in each case. Further, if known, list any evidence of prior injuries, abuse, or alleged incident: maltreatment of the child or any siblings. Also list suspicions of any behavior on the part of the parent(s) that may contribute to the problem.

Month _____ Date _____ Year ____   Time _____ A.M. ____ P.M. ____

1-15. Continued

SOURCES FOR THE REPORT

Person Making This Report

Name   Telephone

Address

Agency/Institution

Source of This Report if Different

Name   Telephone

Address

Agency/Institution

Relationship (Mark X for Reporter and * for Source)

___ Medical Examiner/Coroner   ___ Physician   ___ Hospital Staff   ___ Law Enforcement

___ Neighbor   ___ Relative   ___ Social Services   ___ Public Health

___ Mental Health   ___ School Staff   ___ Other (Specify) _____
    (Specify) _____

THIS SECTION FOR PHYSICIANS ONLY

Medical Diagnosis on Child:

Signature of Physician Who Examined or Treated Child:

Telephone Number:

Hospitalization Required: ___ None   ___ Under One Week   ___ 1–2 Weeks   ___ Over 2 Weeks

---

Actions Taken or About to Be Taken:

___ Medical Examination   ___ Hospitalization   ___ Notified D.A   ___ Notified Medical Examiner

___ Notified Coroner   ___ Returned Home   ___ Removal/Keeping   ___ X-Ray

___ Photographs

Signature of Person Making This Report: Title: Date Submitted

PART 2

Evaluation Measures and Assessment Procedures

2-1. WECHSLER INTELLIGENCE SCALES

The most widely used individual intelligence tests in education are the Wechsler Scales. There are three Wechsler Scales, Wechsler Preschool and Primary Scale of Intelligence (WPPSI)—ages 4 1/2–6 1/2; Wechsler Intelligence Scale for Children-III (WISC-III)—ages 6 1/2–16 1/2; and the Wechsler Adult Intelligence Scale–Revised (WAIS-R)—ages 16 1/2 and over. All three scales result in three IQ measures: Verbal IQ, Performance IQ, and Full-scale IQ. The resulting IQ scores fall into several classification ranges:

The WPPSI consists of 11 subtests, the WISC-III has 13 and the WAIS-R has 11. A description of all the subtests found on the three scales is as follows:

Verbal and Performance Subtests

VERBAL TESTS

- **Information:** Measures general information acquired from experience and education, remote verbal memory, understanding, and associative thinking. The socioeconomic background and reading ability of the student may influence the subtest score. This subtest is part of the WPPSI, WISC-III and WAIS-R.

- **Similarities:** Measures abstract and concrete reasoning, logical thought processes, associative thinking, and remote memory. This subtest is part of the WPPSI, WISC-III, and WAIS-R.

- **Arithmetic:** Measures mental alertness, concentration, attention, arithmetic reasoning, reaction to time pressure, and practical knowledge of computational facts. This is the only subtest directly related to the school curriculum. Greatly affected by anxiety. This subtest is part of the WPPSI, WISC-III, and WAIS-R.

- **Vocabulary:** Measures understanding of spoken words, learning ability, general range of ideas, verbal information acquired from experience and education, and kind and quality of expressive language. Relatively unaffected by emotional disturbance, but highly susceptible to cultural background and level of education. It is also the best single measure of intelligence in the entire battery. This subtest is part of the WPPSI, WISC-III, and WAIS-R.

- **Comprehension:** Measures social judgment, common sense reasoning based on past experience, and practical intelligence. This subtest is part of the WPPSI, WISC-III, and WAIS-R.

- **Digit Span:** Measures attention, concentration, immediate auditory memory, auditory attention, and behavior in a learning situation. This subtest correlates poorly with general intelligence. This subtest is part of the WPPSI, WISC-III, and WAIS-R.

- **Sentences:** Measures attention, concentration, immediate auditory memory, auditory attention, and behavior in a learning situation. This subtest is part of the WPPSI.

2-1. Continued

PERFORMANCE SUBTESTS

- **Picture Completion:** Measures visual alertness to surroundings, remote visual memory, attention to detail, and ability to isolate essential from nonessential detail. This subtest is part of the WPPSI, WISC-III, and WAIS-R.
- **Picture Arrangement:** Measures visual perception, logical sequencing of events, attention to detail, and ability to see cause-effect relationships. This subtest is part of the WISC-III and WAIS-R.
- **Block Design:** Measures ability to perceive, analyze, synthesize, and reproduce abstract forms; visual motor coordination; spatial relationships; and general ability to plan and organize. This subtest is part of the WPPSI, WISC-III, and WAIS-R.
- **Object Assembly:** Measures immediate perception of a total configuration, part-whole relationships, and visual motor spatial coordination. This subtest is part of the WISC-III and WAIS-R.
- **Coding:** Measures ability to associate meaning with symbol, visual motor dexterity (pencil manipulation) flexibility and speed in learning tasks. This subtest is part of the WISC-III.
- **Digit Symbol:** Measures ability to associate meaning with symbol, visual motor dexterity (pencil manipulation), flexibility and speed in learning tasks. This subtest is part of the WAIS-R.
- **Symbol Search:** Measures visual discrimination. This subtest is part of the WISC-III.
- **Mazes:** Measures ability to formulate and execute a visual-motor plan, pencil control and visual-motor coordination, speed and accuracy, and planning capability. This subtest is part of the WPPSI and WISC-III.
- **Animal House:** Measures ability to associate meaning with symbol, visual motor dexterity, and flexibility and speed in learning tasks. This subtest is part of the WPPSI.
- **Geometric Design:** Measures pencil control and visual-motor coordination, speed and accuracy, and planning capability. This subtest is part of the WPPSI.

2-2. INTELLIGENCE CLASSIFICATIONS AND IQ RANGES

IQ Range Included	Classification	Percent
130 and above	Very Superior	2.2
120–129	Superior	6.7
110–119	High Average	16.1
90–109	Average	50.0
80–89	Low Average	16.1
70–79	Borderline	6.7
69 and below	Intellectually Deficient	2.2

2-3. INDICATIONS OF GREATER POTENTIAL ON THE WECHSLER SCALES

Once a child has finished taking an IQ test and received a score, it is crucial to determine whether that score is truly reflective of his or her potential ability or is an underestimate of that ability. To determine expectations, educational plans, and placement on this child, his or her true intellectual potential must be considered a very important factor. At this point, you, the special education teacher, may want to secure a copy of the *protocol* (the booklet or sheet on which the answers to a test are written) from the psychologist. Having this information may facilitate calculations and diagnosis.

Once you have the protocol in front of you, you will notice many things about the test. The first thing we want to look at is the pattern of *Scaled Scores* (scores converted from raw scores for purposes of interpretation and a common standard) that appear next to the *Raw Score* (the number of correct responses on a given test) on the front of the protocol. The scaled scores can range from a low of 1 to a high of 19 with 10 considered the midpoint; however, several scaled scores may constitute a specific range (i.e., scaled scores of 8, 9, 10, and 11 are considered average).

To get a better idea of the value of a scaled score, simply multiply it by 10; that will give you a rough idea of the correlated IQ value. Our investigation of greater potential begins from these scaled scores.

To determine if the resulting scores are valid indicators of an individual's true ability, use the following guidelines.

1. **Check for Intertest Scatter**—scatter or variability between subtests. Check for verbal intertest scatter and performance intertest scatter by first finding the range of scores from low to high. If the range is greater than 3 points, the possibility of intertest scatter exists.

Example:

Information-8
Similarities-15
Arithmetic-6
Vocabulary-13
Comprehension-10
Digit Span-5

In the above illustration, the range of scores is from 5 (Digit Span) to 15 (Similarities). Since the range is greater than 3 points, intertest scatter may exist. When intertest scatter is present it may indicate an unevenness of performance. In order for a resulting IQ score to be considered valid, the pattern should reflect subtest scores with a range of 3 or less. The reason for this scatter can be varied, including emotional factors, processing problems, and neurological factors. Intertest scatter is only one signal, but if it exists jot it down on your work sheet.

2-3. Continued

2. **Check for Intratest Scatter**—variability in performance within a subtest. You will need to see the test protocol to establish this type of scatter. Since IQ tests are made with questions increasing in difficulty, one would expect a subject to answer easier ones and miss the more difficult questions. Sometimes the opposite occurs, where a subject will continuously miss easier questions and be able to respond correctly to harder ones. When this occurs in several subtests, intratest scatter may exist—indicating greater potential. The more subtests that reflect intratest scatter, the greater the potential.

3. **Check for Verbal/Performance Scatter**—the normal range difference of scores between the two levels should be under 12–15 points. Such a pattern indicates a more consistent pattern of performance. More than a 15-point difference between Verbal IQ and Performance IQ is an indicator of scatter and uneven performance, possibility resulting from one or several factors, such as emotionality or processing difficulties.

4. **Check for Vocabulary/Similarities Scatter**—find the *Verbal Mean Scaled Score* (the average of all the verbal scaled scores added together). First add up *all* the Verbal Scaled Scores given and divide by the number of subtests. This will provide you with the *Mean Scaled Score*. If the Vocabulary and/or Similarities scaled scores are more than 3 points higher than this mean, then another type of scatter may exist. *Vocabulary* and *Similarities* have the greatest correlation with intelligence on the Wechsler Scales. If an individual is able to score significantly higher on these subtests than the others, the possibility of greater potential is present, regardless of the scores on other subtests.

41

2-4. RELATIONSHIP OF IQ SCORES TO PERCENTILES

IQ	Range	Scaled Score	Percentile
145	Very Superior	19	99.9
140	Very Superior	18	99.6
135	Very Superior	17	99
130	Very Superior	16	98
125	Superior	15	95
120	Superior	14	91
115	Above Average	13	84
110	Above Average	12	75
105	Average	11	63
100	Average	10	50
95	Average	9	37
90	Average	8	25
85	Low Average	7	16
80	Low Average	6	9
75	Borderline	5	5
70	Borderline	4	2
65	Mentally Deficient	3	1
60	Mentally Deficient	2	0.4
55	Mentally Deficient	1	0.1

2-5. STANFORD-BINET INTELLIGENCE SCALE (4TH EDITION)

The Stanford-Binet attempts to serve the following purposes:

- To help differentiate between children who have a mental disability and those who have a specific learning disability
- To help teachers and psychologists understand why a particular child is having trouble learning in school
- To help in the identification of gifted children
- To study the development of cognitive skills of individuals from ages 2 to adult

There are 15 tests divided according to four areas presumed to be measured by the various tests. The four areas are:

Verbal Reasoning: four types of tests

- **Vocabulary:** This test requires the child to name pictures of common objects.
- **Comprehension:** This test requires the child to point to body parts on a picture of a child.
- **Absurdities:** This test requires the child to point to which of three pictures shows something "wrong" or "silly."
- **Verbal Relations:** In this test, the child is read four words and is required to tell how three words are alike and which of the four is different

.Quantitative Reasoning: three types of tests

- **Quantitative:** This test requires the child to use dice to match, count, add, subtract, or form logical series of numbers.
- **Number Series:** This test requires the child to find the next two numbers that would be consistent according to a certain rule.
- **Equation Building:** This test requires the child to build mathematical statements from a list containing several numbers and operational symbols.

Abstract/Visual Reasoning: four tests

- **Pattern Analysis:** This test requires the child to complete a three-hole formboard with a circle, square, and triangle and then with combinations of pieces that together fit into the holes.
- **Copying:** This test requires the child to arrange blocks or draw copies of designs.
- **Matrices:** This test requires the child to choose from four or five options the symbol or picture that completes the pattern.

2-5. Continued

■ **Paper Folding and Cutting:** This test requires the child to choose which of five drawings would look like a paper design if it were unfolded.

Short-term Memory: four tests

■ **Bead Memory:** This test requires the child to identify beads or patterns of beads from memory.

■ **Memory for Sentences:** This test requires the child to correctly repeat a sentence spoken by the examiner.

■ **Memory for Digits:** This test requires the child to repeat a series of digits spoken by the examiner.

■ **Memory for Objects:** This test requires the child to identify the correct order of pictures presented in a series.

Stanford-Binet uses the following standard for interpretation:

132 and above	Very Superior
121–131	Superior
111–120	High Average
89–110	Average
79–88	Low Average
68–78	Slow Learner
67 and below	Mentally Retarded

2-6. KAUFMAN ASSESSMENT BATTERY FOR CHILDREN (K-ABC)

The Kaufman is an individually administered intelligence test that contains 10 subtests divided into two areas.

Sequential Processing Scale:

- **Hand Movements:** The child (ages 2 1/2 to 12 1/2) is to perform a series of hand movements presented by the examiner.
- **Number Recall:** The child (ages 2 1/2 to 12 1/2) is to repeat a series of digits in the same sequence as presented by the examiner.
- **Word Order:** The child (ages 4 to 12 1/2) is asked to touch a series of silhouettes of objects in the same order as presented verbally by the examiner.

Simultaneous Processing Scale:

- **Magic Windows:** The child (ages 2 1/2 to 5) is to identify a picture that the examiner exposes slowly through a window so that only a small part is exposed at a time.
- **Face Recognition:** The child (ages 2 1/2 to 5) is to choose from a group photo the one or two faces that were exposed briefly.
- **Gestalt Closure:** The child (ages 2 1/2 to 12 1/2) is to name an object or scene from a partially constructed inkblot.
- **Triangles:** The child (ages 4 to 12 1/2) is to assemble several identical triangles into an abstract pattern.
- **Matrix Analogies:** The child (ages 5 to 12 1/2) is to choose a meaningful picture or abstract design that best completes a visual analogy.
- **Spatial Memory:** The child (ages 5 to 12 1/2) is to recall the placement of a picture on a page that was briefly exposed.
- **Photo Series:** The child (ages 6 to 12 1/2) is to place photographs of an event in the proper order.

This test uses the following standard score ranges for interpretation:

130 and above	Upper Extreme
120–129	Well Above Average
110–119	Above Average
90–109	Average
80–89	Below Average
70–79	Well Below Average
69 and below	Lower Extreme

2-7. OTHER INTELLIGENCE TESTS

- Advanced Progressive Matrices (APM)—ages 11 and older

- Bayley Scales of Infant Development (Mental Scale)—1 month–42 months

- Cattell Infant Intelligence Scale—ages 3–30 months

- Cognitive Abilities Test—grades K–12

- Coloured Progressive Matrices (CPM)—ages to 11 and selected populations

- Columbia Mental Maturity Scale (CMMS)—ages 3.5–10

- Henmon-Nelson Tests of Mental Ability—grades K–12

- Kaufman Adolescent and Adult Intelligence Test (KAIT)—ages 11–85

- Kaufman Brief Intelligence Test (K-BIT)—ages 4–90

- Leiter International Performance Scale (LIPS)—ages 3 and older

- McCarthy Scales of Children's Abilities—ages 2.6–8.6

- Otis-Lennon School Ability Test—grades K–12

- Peabody Picture Vocabulary Test–Revised (PPVT-R)—ages 2.5–40

- Pictorial Test of Intelligence—ages 3–8

- Slosson Full-Range Intelligence Test (SF-RIT)—ages 5–21

- Slosson Intelligence Test–Revised (SIT-R)—ages 4–adult

- Standard Progressive Matrices (SPM)—ages 6–adult

- Test of Nonverbal Intelligence-2 (TONI-2)—ages 5–85

2-8. LANGUAGE TESTS

- Adolescent Language Screening Test (ALST)—ages 11–17
- Assessment for Children's Language Development—ages 3–8
- Assessment of Fluency in School-age Children—ages 5–18
- Bankson Language Test (BLT-2)—ages 3–7
- Boehm Test of Basic Concepts—kindergarten–grade 2
- Boston Assessment of Severe Aphasia—all ages
- Clark-Madison Test of Oral Language—ages 4–8
- Communicative Abilities in Daily Living—adults
- Comprehensive Receptive and Expressive Vocabulary Test (CREVT)—ages 4–17
- Early Language Milestone Scale (ELM-Scale-2)—birth–36 months
- Examining for Aphasia (Third Edition (EFA)—all ages
- Expressive One-Word Picture Vocabulary Tests—ages 2–12
- Figurative Language Interpretation Test (FLIT)—ages 9–16
- Goldman-Fristoe Test of Articulation—ages 2–16
- Goldman-Fristoe-Woodcock Auditory Skills Test Battery—ages 3–adult
- Goldman-Fristoe-Woodcock Test of Auditory Discrimination G-F-WTAD)—ages 3.8–70
- Illinois Tests of Psycholinguistic Abilities (ITPA)—ages 3–11
- Kaufman Survey of Early Academic and Language Skills—ages 3–7
- Khan-Lewis Phonological Analysis (KLPA)—ages 2–6
- Kindergarten Language Screening Test (KLST)—kindergarten
- Language Structured Auditory Retention Span–Revised (LARS)—ages 3 1/2–adult
- Minnesota Test for Differential Diagnosis of Aphasia—adult
- Peabody Picture Vocabulary Test–Revised (PPVT-R)—ages 2.5–40
- Photo Articulation Test (PAT)—all ages
- Picture Articulation and Language Screening Test (PALST)—grade 1
- Preverbal Assessment Intervention Profile (PAIP)—all ages
- Receptive-Expressive Emergent Language Test (REEL-2)—infants and toddlers
- Receptive-One-Word Picture Vocabulary Test—ages 2–12
- Screening Test for Developmental Apraxia of Speech—ages 4–12
- Speech Ease Screening—grades K–1
- Stuttering Prediction Instrument for Young Children—ages 3–8
- Stuttering Severity Instrument for Children and Adults (SSI-3)—ages 8–adult
- Test for Auditory Comprehension of Language (TACL)—ages 3–9
- Test of Adolescent and Adult Language (TOAL-3)—ages 13–25

2-8. Continued

- Test of Awareness of Language Segments (TALS)—ages 4.6–7
- Test of Early Language Development (TELD-2)—ages 2–8
- Test of Language Development (TOLD-2)—ages 4–13
- Test of Pragmatic Language (TOPL)—ages 5–13
- Test of Word Knowledge (TOWK)—ages 5–17
- The Assessment of Phonological Processes–Revised (APP-R)—all ages
- The Speech and Language Evaluation Scale (SLES)—ages 4.5–18
- Utah Test of Language Development (UTLD-3)—ages 3–9.11
- Voice Assessment Protocol for Children and Adults (VAP)—all ages

2-9. TESTS FOR THE HEARING IMPAIRED

- Auditory Perception Test for the Hearing Impaired (APT/HI)—ages 5 and up
- Carolina Picture Vocabulary Test (CPVT)—ages 4–11.5
- Goodenough-Draw-A-Person Test—all ages
- Hiskey-Nebraska Test of Learning Aptitude—ages 3–18
- Leiter International Performance Scale—ages 2–17
- Rhode Island Test of Language Structure (RITLS)—ages 3–20
- Screening Instrument for Targeting Educational Risk (SIFTER)—for children with identified hearing loss
- Test of Early Reading Ability—Deaf or Hard of Hearing (TERA-D/HH)—primary grades

2-10. STANDARDIZED TESTS USED BY OCCUPATIONAL THERAPISTS

Certain tests are used by occupational therapists in their evaluation. Such measures may include:

- **Bruninks-Oseretsky Test of Motor Proficiency (BOT)**—ages 4.6–14.6. Gross and fine motor subtests on running speed, balance, bilateral coordination, strength, upper limb coordination, response speed, visual-motor control and upper limb speed and dexterity.

- **Degangi-Berk Test of Sensory Integration**—ages 3–5. Test of sensory integration (postural control, reflex integration, bilateral, motor integration, muscle tone, ocular-motor control, and vestibular function).

- **Denver Developmental Screening Test**—ages birth–6. Individual formalized observations of normal developmental behavior of infants and children used as a screening tool for detecting developmental delays. Areas evaluated: gross motor, fine motor, language, and personal-social development.

- **Developmental Programming for Infants and Young Children**—ages birth –3. Low-volume profile designed to reduce the gap between evaluation and programs for children between the birth and three-year level of development. Areas formally evaluated include perceptual/fine motor skills, cognition, language, social/emotional level, self-care and gross motor skills. The educator/therapist develops individualized developmental programs by translating comprehensive evaluation data into short-term behavioral objectives that form the basis of daily activities planned to facilitate emerging skills.

- **Developmental Test of Visual-Motor Integration (VMI or the BEERY)**— There are two forms based on age: (A) ages 2–8; (B) ages 2–15. Test of integration of visual perception and motor behavior in young children. Subject is presented with 24 geometric forms, arranged in order of increasing difficulty, that are then copied into a test booklet.

- **Frostig Developmental Test of Visual Perception**—ages 3–8. Test of eye-motor coordination, figure-ground discrimination, form constancy, position in space, and spatial relation.

- **Early-Lap**—ages birth–3. The early learning accomplishment profile for developmentally young children that assesses gross motor, fine motor, cognitive, language, self-help, and social-emotional development.

- **Jordan Left-Right Reversal Test (Jordan Test)**—ages 5–12. An individual or group-administered instrument designed to measure letter and number reversals in the area of children's visual receptive functioning.

- **McCarthy Scales of Children's Abilities (MSCA)**—ages 2.6–8.6. Tests of the general level of intellectual functioning, the General Cognitive Index (GCI), and profile of abilities. The profile includes six scales: verbal, perceptual performance, quantitative, general cognition, memory and motor. Several items also assess hand dominance.

2-10. Continued

■ **Milani-Comparetti Motor Development Test**—ages birth–2. A basic neurodevelopmental screening test designed to assess a child's physical development. Administered several times over a period of months by a physician, nurse or therapist, the test indicates trends in a child's motor development and may be employed to detect problems in this area.

■ **Miller Assessment or Preschoolers (MAP)**—ages 2.9–5.8. Screenings test a child's developmental status with respect to other children his/her age. Once completed, the examiner has a comprehensive overview of the developmental status in each of five indices; foundations, coordination, verbal, nonverbal and complex task. Specifically, areas tested include basic motor and sensory abilities, complex, fine and oral-motor sensory abilities, cognitive language abilities, cognitive abilities not requiring spoken language and skills requiring the interaction of sensory motor and cognitive abilities.

■ **Motor Free Visual Perception Test**—ages 4–8. Overall/visual-perception processing ability is tested while avoiding motor involvement. Areas tested include spatial relationships, visual discrimination, figure ground, visual closure, and visual memory.

■ **Quick Neurological Screening Test (QNST)**—ages 5–adult. Individual neurological screening for maturity of motor development; skill in controlling large and small muscles, motor planning and sequencing, sense of rate on rhythm, spatial organization, visual and auditory perceptual skills, balance, and cerebellar-vestibular function and disorders of attention.

■ **Riley Motor Problems Inventory (RMPI)**—ages 4–9. A ten-item test to evaluate motor performance in the following areas: oral-motor, fine-motor, and gross-motor tasks.

■ **Southern California Sensory Integration Test (SCIST)**—ages 4–10. Series of tests for perceptual-motor development that include figure ground, somesthetic perception, motor accuracy, perceptual motor function, and postrotary nystagmus.

■ **The Purdue Perceptual-Motor Survey (PPMS)**—ages 4–10. Sometimes referred to as the "Kephart Scale," the PPMS is an instrument designed to provide qualitative information regarding the degree to which children demonstrate adequately developed perceptual-motor skills. Items are grouped into five basic areas: balance and posture, body image and differentiation, perceptual-motor match, ocular control, and form perception.

51

2-11. PSYCHOLOGICAL TESTS

- Adjustment Scales for Children and Adolescents (ASCA)—ages 5–17
- Anxiety Scale for Children and Adults (ASCA)—all ages
- Assessment of Interpersonal Relations (AIR)—grades 5–12
- Assessment of Interpersonal Relations (AIR)—ages 10–19
- Beck Anxiety Inventory (BAI)—ages 17–80
- Beck Depression Scale—ages 17–80
- Beck Hopelessness Scale (BHS)—ages 13–80
- Beck Scale for Suicide Ideation—ages 17 and up
- Behavior Assessment System for Children (BASC)—ages 4–18
- Behavior Rating Profile (BRP-2)—ages 6.6–18.6
- Children's Apperception Test (CAT)—ages 5–10
- Children's Apperceptive Story-telling Test (CAST)—ages 3–10
- Children's Depression Inventory (CDI)—ages 7–17
- Conners' Rating Scales (CRS)—ages 3–17
- Culture-Free Self-Esteem Inventories (CFSEI-2)—ages 5–adult
- Depression and Anxiety in Youth Scale (DAYS)—children and adolescents
- Differential Test of Conduct and Emotional Problems (DT/CEP)—grades K–high school
- Draw a Person Test (DAP)—ages 6–17
- Emotional and Behavioral Problem Scale (EBPS)—ages 4.5–21
- Goodenough-Harris Drawing Test—ages 5–15
- Holtzman Inkblot Technique—ages 5–adult
- Index of Personality Characteristics (IPC)—ages 8–17.11
- Kinetic Family Drawing—ages 6–17
- Million Index of Personality Styles (MIPS)—ages 18–65
- Personality Assessment Inventory—ages 18 and older
- Reynolds Adolescent Depression Scale (RADS)—ages 13–18
- Rorschach Technique—ages 5–adult
- Self Esteem Index (SEI)—ages 7–18
- Sentence Completion Test—all ages
- Social Emotional Dimension Scale (SEDS)—ages 5.5–18.5
- Social Skills Rating System (SSRS)—ages 3–18
- Student Self Concept Scale (SSCS)—grades 3–12
- Test of Early Socioemotional Development (TOESD)—ages 3–7.11
- The Mooney Problem Check Lists—junior high–college
- Thematic Apperception Test (TAT)—children and adults

2-12. PERCEPTUAL TESTS

- Beery-Buktenica Developmental Test of Visual Motor Integration—ages 4–18
- Bender Gestalt Visual Motor Test (BGVMT)—children and adults
- Bruininks-Oserestsky Test of Motor Proficiency—ages 4.5–14.5
- Cognitive Abilities Scale (CAS)—grades K–12
- Comprehensive Scales of Student Abilities (CSSA)—ages 6–16
- Detroit Tests of Learning Aptitude-3 (DTLA-3)—ages 6–17
- Developmental Activities Screening Inventory-II—ages birth–60 months
- Developmental Test of Visual-Motor Integration (VMI)—ages 3–18
- Early Screening Profiles (EPS)—ages 2–7
- Frostig Developmental Test of Visual Perception—elementary age children
- Frostig Movement Skills Test Battery—elementary age children
- Goldman-Fristoe Woodcock Test of Auditory Discrimination—ages 3.8–70
- Jordan Left-Right Reversal Test–Revised (JLRRT)—ages 5–12
- K-ABC: Kaufman Assessment Battery for Children—ages 2.5–12.5
- Learning Efficiency Test II–Revised (LET-II)—ages 5–adult
- Lindamood Auditory Conceptualization Test—all ages
- Malcomesius Specific Language Disability Test—grades 6,7,8
- McCarthy Screening Test (MST)—ages 4–6.6
- Motor-Free Visual Perception Test (MVPT)—ages 4–8
- Mullen Scales of Early Learning (MSEL)—infant scale—birth–39 months
- Mullen Scales of Early Learning (MSEL)—preschool—ages 24–69 months
- Quick Neurological Screening Test (QNST)—ages 5–18
- Slingerland Screening Tests for Identifying Children with Specific Language Disabilities—grades K–5
- Test of Auditory Analysis Skills (TAAS)—ages 5–8
- Test of Auditory Perceptual Skills (TAPS)—ages 4–12
- Test of Auditory Perceptual Skills (TAPS: Upper Level)—ages 12–18
- Test of Gross Motor Development (TGMD)—ages 3–10
- Test of Memory and Learning (TOMAL)—ages 5–19
- Test of Pictures/Forms/Letters/Numbers Spatial Orientation and Sequencing Skills (TPFLNOSS)—ages 5–8
- Test of Visual Analysis Skills (TVAS)—ages 5–8
- Test of Visual Motor Skills (TVMS)—ages 2–13
- Test of Visual Motor Skills (TVMS: Upper Level)—ages 12–40
- Test of Visual Perceptual Skills (Non Motor)-(TVPS n-m:UL)—ages 12–19
- Test of Visual Perceptual Skills (Non Motor)-(TVPS)—ages 4–13

2-12. Continued

- Tests of Auditory-Perceptual Skills (TAPS)—ages 4–12
- Tests of Auditory-Perceptual Skills (TAPS: Upper Level)—ages 12–18
- Visual Skills Appraisal (VSA)—ages 5–9
- Vulpe Assessment Battery–Revised (VAB-R)—ages birth–6
- Wepman Auditory Discrimination Test—ages 3–8
- Woodcock Johnson Psychoeducational Battery—all ages

2-13. RATING SCALES AND ADAPTIVE BEHAVIOR SCALES

- AAMR Adaptive Behavior Scales—Residential and Community
- AAMR Adaptive Behavior Scales—School—school-age children
- Adaptive Behavior Inventory (ABI)—school-age children
- Barsch Learning Style Inventory—ages 14–adult
- Career Inventories for the Learning Disabled (CILD)—ages 6–adult
- Comprehensive Behavior Rating Scale for Children (CBRSC)—ages 6–14
- Comprehensive Test of Adaptive Behavior (CTAB)—ages birth–60 months
- Conners Rating Scales—ages 3–17
- Developmental Assessment for the Severely Handicapped (DASH)—ages birth–60 months
- Devereux Behavior Rating Scale—School Form—ages 5–18
- Devereux Scales of Mental Disorders—ages 5–18
- Gardner Social Maturity Scale (GSDS)—ages birth to 9
- Learning Disability Rating Procedure (LDRP)—ages 6–18
- Light's Retention Scale (LRS)—ages 6–18
- Normative Adaptive Behavior Checklist (NABC)—birth–21
- Preschool Behavior Checklist (PBCL)—ages 2–5
- Pupil Rating Scale Revised: Screening for Learning Disabilities—ages 5–14
- Screen:Senf-Comrey Ratings of Extra Educational Need—ages 5–7
- Syracuse Social Maturity Scale—all ages
- The Adaptive Behavior Evaluation Scale (ABES)—grades K–12
- The Attention Deficit Disorders Evaluation Scale (ADDES)—ages 4.5–18
- The Behavior Disorders Identification Scale (BDIS)—ages 4.5–21
- The Learning Disability Evaluation Scale (LDES)—grades K–12
- Vineland Adaptive Behavior Scale—Classroom Edition—ages 3–13
- Vineland Adaptive Behavior Scale—Interview Edition—ages 0–18
- Weller-Strawser Scales of Adaptive Behavior for the Learning Disabled (WSSAB)—ages 6–18
- Woodcock Johnson Psychoeducational Battery—all ages

2-14. READING TESTS

- Brigance Diagnostic Inventory of Basic Skills—grades K–6
- Diagnostic Achievement Test for Adolescents—grades 7–12
- Doren Diagnostic Reading Test of Word Recognition Skills—grades K–4
- DRS-81: Diagnostic Reading Scales—grades 1–7
- Durrell Analysis of Reading Difficulty—grades 1–6
- Durrell Listening-Reading Series—grades 1–9
- Formal Reading Inventory (FRI)—grades 1–12
- Gates-MacGinitie Silent Reading Tests—grades 1–12
- Gates-McKillop Reading Diagnostic Tests—grades 1–6
- Gilmore Oral Reading Test—grades 1–8
- Gray Oral Reading Test (GORT-3)—grades 1–college
- Language Arts Assessment Portfolio (LAAP)—grades 1–6
- Nelson Reading Skills Test—grades 3–9
- Nelson-Denny Reading Test—grades 9–16
- Slosson Oral Reading Test (SORT-R)—ages preschool–adult
- Spache Diagnostic Reading Scales—grades 1–8 and 9–12 (students with reading deficiencies)
- Spadafore Diagnostic Reading Test (SDRT)—ages 6–adult
- Standardized Reading Inventory (SRI)—grades preprimer–8
- Stanford Diagnostic Reading Test—ages 1–adult
- Test of Early Reading Ability (TERA-2)—ages 3–10
- Test of Phonological Awareness (TOPA)—kindergarten–grade 2
- Test of Reading Comprehension (TORC)—ages 7–17
- Wide Range Achievement Tests–Revised—ages 5–adult
- Woodcock Reading Mastery Tests–Revised (WRMT-R)—grades K–12

2-15. ARITHMETIC TESTS

- Diagnostic Test of Arithmetic Strategies (DTAS)—elementary school–age children
- Key Math Diagnostic Arithmetic Tests–Revised—preschool to grade 6
- Sequential Assessment of Mathematics Inventories (SAMI)—grades K–8
- SRA Achievement Series in Arithmetic—grades 1–10
- Stanford Achievement Series in Arithmetic—grades 1–10
- Steenburgen Diagnostic Quick Math Screening Test—ages 6–11
- Test of Early Mathematics Ability (TEMA-2)—ages 3–9
- Test of Mathematical Ability (TOMA)—ages 8–19
- Wide Range Achievement Test—ages 5–adult

2-16. SPELLING AND WRITING TESTS

Written: Phonic Words, Irregular Words

- Wide Range Achievement Test–Revised—ages 5–adult
- Diagnostic Word Patterns—grade 2–college
- Mykelbust Picture Story Language Test—elementary grades
- The Spellmaster Assessment and Teaching System—all grades
- Diagnostic Spelling Potential Test (DSPT)—ages 7–adult
- Test of Written Spelling (TWS-3)—grades 1–12
- Larsen Hammill Test of Written Spelling—ages 5–15

Visual: Recognition of Sight Words

- Kauffman Individual Achievement Test—ages 5–18
- Peabody Individual Achievement Test—ages 5–adult
- Wechsler Individual Achievement Test—ages 5–18

Writing Tests

- Denver Handwriting Analysis (DHA)—ages 8–13
- Diagnostic Achievement Test for Adolescents—grades 7–12
- Myklebust Picture Story Language Test—ages 7–17
- Test of Early Written Language TEWL—ages 3–7
- Test of Written English (TWE)—ages 6–11+
- Test of Written Language-2 (TOWL-2)—grades 1–6
- Writing Process Test—grades 2–12
- Writing Supplement to the Iowa Tests of Basic Skills—grades 3–8
- Writing Supplement to the Tests of Achievement and Proficiency—grades 9–12
- Written Language Assessment (WLA)—ages 8–18+

2-17. COMPREHENSIVE ACADEMIC SKILLS TESTS

- Basic Achievement Skills Individual Screener (BASIS)—grades 1–12
- Brigance Diagnostic Inventory of Basic Skills—grades K–6
- California Achievement Test—grades1–9
- Criterion Test of Basic Skills (CBS)—ages 6–11
- Diagnostic Achievement Battery (DAB-2)—ages 6–14
- Diagnostic Achievement Test for Adolescents—grades 7–12
- Differential Ability Scales (DAS)—ages 2.6–18
- Hudson Educational Skills Inventory—grades K–12
- Iowa Test of Basic Abilities—grades 1–9
- Kaufman Survey of Early Academic and Language Skills—ages 3–7
- Kaufman Test of Educational Achievement (KTEA)—ages 5–18
- Metropolitan Achievement Test—grades 3–9
- Multilevel Academic Survey Tests (MAST)—grades K–12
- Peabody Individual Achievement Test–Revised (PIAT-R)—grades K–12
- Quick Cognitive Inventory (QCI)—ages 6–8
- Quick Score Achievement Test—grades 1–12
- Riley Inventory of Basic Learning Skills (RIBLS)—Upper—ages 8–14+
- Riley Inventory of Basic Learning Skills (RIBLS)—Primary—ages 6–7
- Scholastic Abilities Test for Adults—ages 16–70
- Test of Academic Achievement Skills: Reading, Arithmetic and Spelling (TAAS-RAS)—ages 4–12
- Test of Academic Performance—grades K–12
- Wechsler Individual Achievement Test (WIAT)—grades K–12
- Wide Range Achievement Test-3 (WRAT-3)—ages 5–adult

2-18. BILINGUAL ASSESSMENT INSTRUMENTS

- Austin Spanish Articulation Test
- Culture-Free Self-Esteem Inventories-2 (CFSEI-2)—ages 5–adult
- Developmental Assessment of Spanish Grammar
- Dos Amigos Verbal Language Scales (DAVLS)—ages 5–13
- ESL/Literacy Scale (ELS)—ages 16–adult
- James Language Dominance Test
- Language Proficiency Test (LPT)—ages 15–adult
- Matrix Analogies Test—ages 3–17
- Peabody Picture Vocabulary Test–Revised (PPVT-R)—ages 2.5–40
- Screening Test of Spanish Grammar
- Spanish Accent Auditory Discrimination Test
- System of Multicultural Pluralistic Assessment (SOMPA)—ages 5–11
- Test de Vocabulario en Imagenes Peabody (TVIP)—ages 2 1/2–18
- Test for Auditory Comprehension of Language (TACL)

2-19. EARLY CHILDHOOD AND INFANT ASSESSMENT SCALES

- AGS Early Screening Profiles—ages 2–6.11
- Bayley Infant Neurodevelopmental Screen (BINS)—ages 1 month–42 months
- Bayley Scales of Infant Development—ages 1–42 months
- Boehm Test of Basic Concepts–Revised—K–grade 2
- Bracken Basic Concept Scale (BBCS)—ages 2.6–8
- Bracken Concept Development Program (BCDP)—ages 2.6–8
- Cattell Infant Intelligence Scale—ages 3–30 months
- Child Development Inventory (CDI)—ages 15 months–6 years
- Children's Early Intervention for Speech-Language-Reading (CEI)—preK–early elementary
- FirstSTPE:Screening Test for Evaluating Preschoolers—ages 2.9–6.2
- Gardner Social Maturity Scale (GSDS)—ages birth–9
- Kindergarten Readiness Test (KRT)—kindergarten
- Metropolitan Readiness Tests (MRT)—preK–grade 1
- Miller Assessment for Preschoolers—ages 29 months–5.8 years
- Mullen Scales of Early Learning—ages birth–69 months
- Neurobehavioral Assessment of the Preterm Infant (NAPI)—ages 32 weeks conceptual age–term
- Preschool Language Scale-3 (PLS-3)—birth–6
- Screen:Senf-Comrey Ratings of Extra Educational Need—ages 5–7
- Stuttering Severity Instrument for Young Children (SPI)—ages 3–8
- Survey of Early Childhood Abilities (SECA)—ages 3–7
- Test of Gross Motor Development (TGMD)—ages 3–10
- Test of Kindergarten/First Grade Readiness Skills (TKFGRS)—ages 3.6–7
- Test of Phonological Awareness (TOPA)—grades K–2
- Tests of Early Reading Ability (TERA-2)—ages 3–9
- The Early Childhood Behavior Scale (ECBS)—ages 36–72 months
- The Preschool Evaluation Scale (PES)—birth–72 months
- Visual Skills Appraisal (VSA)—grades K–4
- Vulpe Assessment Battery–Revised (VAB-R)—birth–6 years

2-20. READING COMPREHENSION SKILLS

There are several general areas relating to reading comprehension.

The Literal Level: Occurs when the student understands the primary or direct meaning of words, sentences, or passages. Examples of this include:

- recognition of main ideas
- recognition of details
- recognition of a sequence
- recognition of comparisons
- recognition of cause-and-effect relationships
- recognition of character traits
- recall of details
- recall of main ideas
- recall of a sequence
- recall of comparisons
- recall of cause-and-effect relationships
- recall of character traits

2-20. Continued

The Inferential Level: Occurs when the student understands the deeper meanings that are not literally stated in the passage. Examples include

- inferring the main idea
- inferring comparisons
- inferring character traits
- inferring cause-and-effect relationships
- inferring supporting details
- inferring sequence
- predicting outcomes

The Reorganization Level: Occurs when the student is able to analyze, synthesize, and/or organize ideas or information gleaned from a passage or selection. Examples include

- classifying
- outlining
- summarizing
- synthesizing

The Evaluation Level: Occurs when the student is able to make an evaluative judgment by comparing and contrasting ideas presented in the selection while drawing upon outside criteria provided by the teacher or other sources, or with internal criteria provided by the student himself or herself. Examples include

- judgment of reality or fantasy
- judgment of fact or opinion
- judgment of adequacy and validity
- judgment of appropriateness
- judgment of worth, desirability, and acceptability

The Appreciation Level: Occurs when the student senses a reaction or internal response to a selection. Examples include

- emotional response to the content
- identification with characters or incidents
- reaction to the author's use of language
- imagery

2-21. GUIDELINES FOR WRITING AN EDUCATIONAL REPORT

The special education teacher may be called upon to evaluate a child and write up a comprehensive report based on the findings. This report may be presented to the parent, sent to an outside doctor or agency or presented to the CSE. Some guidelines include the following:

1. Present the report in the most professional, comprehensive, and practical manner possible.

2. Do not allow a report to run on forever. An 18-page report too comprehensive; you will lose your reader by the fifth page.

3. Try to write the report in the third person: "According to the examiner," or "It was felt that," or "There seems to be." Never write "I think" or "If it were up to me."

4. Single-space your report to condense the length.

5. Separate your recommendation section into three parts—one for the school, one for the classroom teacher, and one for the parents.

6. Write the report in the past tense as often as possible.

7. Double-space between sections for purposes of clarity.

8. Underline paragraph headings so that they stand out and are easy to locate.

9. Write reports using complete sentences. A report should never read like a telegram.

10. Try to avoid the use of too much jargon since it will confuse the reader. Never assume that the person reading the report is aware of terminology. If necessary, define confusing terms in parentheses to assist the reader.

2-22. CRITERIA REQUIRED IN AN EDUCATIONAL REPORT

Psychoeducational reports can take many forms and it is usually up to the personal choice of the examiner; however, it is important that certain information not be overlooked. The following sample outline meets all the criteria for a comprehensive report.

I. Identifying Data

Name: _____   Parent(s) Names: _____

Address: _____   Teacher: _____

Phone: _____   Referred by: _____

Date of Birth: _____   Date(s) of Testing: _____

Grade: _____   Date of Report: _____

School: _____   Examiner: _____

Chronological age at time of testing: _____

II. Reason for Referral

The second section explains to the reader the specific reasons why an evaluation is taking place. It should not be more than two to three sentences, but should be comprehensive enough to clarify the purpose. Following are some examples of this section:

John was referred by his teacher for evaluation as a result of inconsistent academic performance and poor social skills.

Mary was referred by her parents for evaluation to determine if a learning disability was interfering with her ability to learn.

Benjamin is being tested as part of the triennial evaluation.

III. Background History

This section contains a very thorough description of the child's family history, developmental history, academic history, and social history.

IV. Behavioral Observations

The fourth section includes a description of the child's behavior during the testing sessions. This can be a very important section since it may either reinforce what is seen in the class or be very different. If it is different, the structure of the testing environment should be explored for clues to learning style.

2-22. Continued

V. Tests and Procedures Administered

The next section provides a simple list of the individual tests included in the test battery and any procedures used to enhance the report—classroom observation, review of records, parent intake.

Test Results

The sixth section is a crucial section in that it analyzes the results of each test and looks at the child's individual performance on each measure. There are several approaches to this section, but the two most widely used approaches are the Test-by-Test analysis and the Content-Area-by-Content-Area analysis. The approach chosen is the personal choice of the examiner.

A **test-by-test approach** analyzes the child's performance on each test separately. It analyzes the results of the different subtests and provides indications of strengths and weaknesses, manner of approach, and indications of whether the scores on the specific test should be considered valid.

A **content-area-by-content-area approach** takes all the reading subtests, math subtests, spelling subtests and writing subtests from each evaluation measure and analyzes the results separately by content area.

VII. Conclusions

In this section the examiner indicates in very simple terms to the reader the trends in the child's testing results that may indicate academic strengths and weaknesses, modality strengths and weaknesses, process strengths and weaknesses, and overall diagnosis and level of severity of the problems areas indicated.

Recommendations

The last section of the report is probably the most valuable section for the reader. It should contain practical recommendations that will bring some hope and direction for the identified problem areas. Try to separate the recommendations into the following subsections:

Recommendations to the school. This section might contain suggestions like further testing from other professionals on staff, vision or hearing tests by the school nurse, recommendation for a review by the CSE, remedial reading assistance, or an ESL evaluation.

Recommendations to the teacher. This section should contain useful information for the teacher, including an indication of the conditions under which the child learns best.

Recommendations to the parent. This part should be very practical, direct, and diplomatic. The suggestions should also be inclusive enough to answer the questions "why" and "how" so that parents do not have to interpret them.

© 1995 by The Center for Applied Research in Education

2-23. ACADEMIC SKILL AREAS

I—Reading

■ Decoding
   Phonic skills

   Sight word recognition

   Oral paragraph reading

■ Comprehension
   Oral reading

   Silent reading

   Listening

   Comprehension in specific content areas

II—Writing

■ Penmanship
   Manuscript

   Cursive

■ Written Expression
   Fluency

   Syntax

   Mechanics

   Content

III—Spelling

■ Written
   Phonic words

   Irregular words

■ Recognition of Sight Words

■ Oral

2-23. Continued

IV—Arithmetic

- Concepts

- Computation
  Addition

  Subtraction

  Multiplication

  Division

- Word Problems
  Oral

  Written

V—Oral Language

- Receptive
  Vocabulary

  Listening Comprehension

- Expressive
  Articulation

  Morphology

  Syntax

  Semantics

2-24. HOW TO REPORT TEST RESULTS TO PARENTS

An important skill for special education teachers is their ability to report test results to other professionals or to parents in such a way that these people walk away with an understanding of the causes, specific areas of strength and weakness, and practical recommendations to alleviate the situation. Many times parents will leave a conference having been bombarded with jargon and statistics—and understand nothing. Reporting results so that they are understood may be accomplished in the following ways

1. When setting up the appointment with a parent never allow yourself to begin the explanation of the results over the phone, even if the parent requests a "quick" idea of how the child performed. If the parent does request this, gently say that the type of information that you have is better explained and understood in person. If you sense further anxiety, try to reassure the parent that you will meet as soon as possible. It is important to see the parent(s) so that you can further explain areas in which they seem confused or uncomfortable. The face-to-face contact also makes the conference a more human approach. Hearing results from our doctor over the phone may not be as comforting as in person.

2. Again, as with an intake, make the parent(s) feel comfortable and at ease by setting up a receptive environment. If possible, hold the meeting in a pleasant setting, use a round table, or any table instead of a desk, and offer some type of refreshment to ease tension.

3. It may be helpful to refresh the parent's memory about the reasons for the evaluation and the symptoms that brought the child to the attention of the team. Explain the tests that constituted your test battery, why they were used, and what specific types of information you hoped to arrive at by using these measures.

4. Go over strength areas first, no matter how few there may be. You can also report positive classroom comments, and any other information that may help set the tone for acceptance of problem areas.

5. Provide a typed outline of the tests and scores for the parent to take with them if the report is not ready. If possible, have the report typed and ready to hand them. It looks more professional and may help when reports are sent home and the parents read them without a professional present.

6. Explain any statistical terms you may be using, for example, percentiles, stanines, and mental ages. In fact, it may be a good idea to define these on the same sheet with the scores so that parents have a key when they go back and review the scores.

7. Again, as with the intake, you should offer them a pad and pen so that they can write down information, terms, or notes on the meeting. Further indicate that they should feel free to call you with any questions or concerns they may have.

8. Put aside a sufficient amount of time for difficult conferences. This is not the kind of situation in which you want to run out of time. The parents should leave in a natural manner, not be rushed.

2-24. Continued

9. Take time to explain the differences between symptoms and problems. This explanation can go a long way in alleviating parents' frustration.

10. It is helpful for parents to hear how the problems or deficiencies you found were contributing to the symptoms in the classroom and at home. It is reassuring for parents to know that what they were seeing were only symptoms, even though they may have been quite intense, and that the problems have been identified and recommendations are available. Offer them as much realistic hope as possible.

11. Be practical and specific when offering suggestions on how parents can help at home. Offer them printed sheets with step-by-step procedures for any recommendation that you make. Parents should not be teachers and should never be given general recommendations that require their interpretation; this may aggravate an already tense situation at home. Offer them supportive materials that they can use with the child. While having a parent working with a child can be positive, in some cases (e.g., low parental frustration levels) you may want to shy away from this type of interaction.

12. If the case is going to be reviewed by the Committee on Special Education, take some time to allay their fears by explaining the process and what they can expect. Indicate that your report is part of the packet that will be presented and that they are entitled to a copy of all materials. Some school districts charge for copies, so tell them if it is a policy.

13. Again, reassure the parent about the confidentiality of the information gathered. Indicate the individuals on the team who will be seeing the information and the purpose for their review of the facts. Also advise parents that, to send out this information, you would always need permission from them in the form of a signed release.

2-25. HOW TO EXAMINE SCHOOL RECORDS

The school usually has a wealth of information about all children, distributed among a number of people and a number of records. Gathering this information after a referral and prior to evaluation may reduce the need for testing and will provide a very thorough picture of the child and his or her abilities and patterns. Investigating the following areas will contribute to the overall picture of the child:

Prior teacher reports: Comments written on report cards or in permanent record folders may provide a different view of the child under a different style of teaching. Successful years with positive comments may be a clue to the child's learning style and may provide you with information about the conditions under which the child responds best.

Reports of prior parent-teacher interviews: Prior conferences between previous teachers and parents may provide you with important information for understanding the child's patterns and history.

Cumulative school record: This particular file may contain information from standardized achievement test results, group IQ results, teacher comments dating back to kindergarten, records from previous schools, individual reading test results, and family information.

Group IQ test information: This information is usually found in the permanent record folder. Many schools administer this type of test, for example, Otis Lennon or Henmon Nelson in grades 3, 6, and 9, so look carefully. Within the past year or so the term *School Abilities Index* has replaced the term *IQ* or *Intelligence Quotient*.

Standardized test scores: These scores should be analyzed for patterns of strengths and deficiencies. The older the child, the greater the number of scores that can be compared.

Report card grades: These materials can be reviewed for comments, and for patterns of productive and difficult years.

Attendance records: These records should be reviewed for patterns of lateness or absence. If such patterns exist the reasons should be investigated to rule out medical causes (hospital stays, illnesses) or psychological causes (dysfunctional family patterns, school phobia, etc.), or social causes (peer rejection or isolation).

Number of schools attended: There are times when a child will be enrolled in several schools in several years. The reasons for the many moves should be investigated and may add to the child's adjustment difficulties.

Prior teacher referrals: Investigate school records for prior referrals from teachers. There are times when a teacher will refer but no action is taken because of time of year, parent resistance, or delay in evaluation procedures. These referrals may still be on file and may reveal useful information.

71

2-25. Continued

Medical history in the school nurse's office: Investigate these records for indications of visual or hearing difficulties, prescribed medication that may have an effect on the child's behavior (e.g., antihistamines), or medical conditions in need of attention or that can be contributing to the child's present situation.

Whatever the situation, the special education teacher should review the vast amount of available records in the school building.

2-26. UNDERSTANDING THE LEARNING PROCESS

The Learning Process

The perceptual evaluation is theoretically based upon the concept of the *learning process* (the process by which information is received and the manner in which it is processed). In very simple terms, the learning process can be described in the following way:

INPUT OF INFORMATION

ORGANIZATION OF INFORMATION

EXPRESSION OF INFORMATION

To understand how learning takes place, we must first understand the specific parts that make up the learning process. There are six *modalities* or *channels* (avenues through which information is received). They include:

- **Auditory Modality**—the delivery of information through sound
- **Visual Modality**—the delivery of information through sight
- **Tactile Modality**—the delivery of information through touching
- **Kinesthetic Modality**—the delivery of information through movement
- **Gustatory Modality**—the delivery of information through taste
- **Olfactory Modality**—the delivery of information through smell

Information is delivered to the senses through one or several of the above channels. Once it is received, the information goes through a series of processes that attempt to give meaning to the material received. There are several processes that make up the learning process. They may include

- **Reception**—the initial receiving of information
- **Perception**—the initial organization of information
- **Association or Organization**—relating new information to other information and giving meaning to the information received
- **Memory**—the storage or retrieval process that facilitates the associational process in giving meaning to information or help in relating new concepts to other information that might have been learned already
- **Expression**—the output of information through vocal, motoric, or written responses

2-27. UNDERSTANDING A SUBJECT'S BEHAVIOR DURING TESTING

There are many behaviors that should be observed when administering tests. Recording these observations will greatly facilitate report writing. Some suggestions of behaviors to be observed as follows:

Adjustment to the Testing Situation

- What was the child's initial reaction?
- How did the child react to the examiner?
- Were there any initial signs of overt tension?

Several factors must be considered when the child first encounters the testing situation. These include:

1. Children's initial adjustment to the testing situation can vary greatly. The key to any adjustment period is not necessarily the initial reactions but the duration of the period of maladjustment. Children are usually initially nervous and uptight but relax as time goes on with the reassurance of the examiner. Children who maintain a high level of discomfort throughout the sessions may be harboring more serious problems that need to be explored.

2. **Examiner variables** (conditions directly related to the examiner, e.g., examiner style or gender, examiner tension, examiner expectations, etc., that may affect test outcome) may need to be considered, especially if test results vary greatly from examiner to examiner.

3. Be aware of **overt signs of tension** (observable behaviors indicative of underlying tension) that may affect the outcome of the test results. Some overt signs of behavior often manifested by children include constant leg motion, little or no eye contact with the examiner, consistent finger or pencil tapping, *oppositional behaviors* (behaviors that test the limits and guidelines of the examiner) singing or making noises while being tested, keeping a jacket on, or a hat almost covering his or her face. If this type of tension is extreme, the results may be minimal indications of ability.

© 1995 by The Center for Applied Research in Education

2-27. Continued

Reaction Time

▪ Were responses delayed, blocked, irregular?

▪ Was there any indication of negativism?

▪ Were responses impulsive or well thought out?

The speed in which a child answers questions on a test can indicate several things.

1. The child who impulsively answers incorrectly without thinking may be a child with high levels of anxiety that interfere with his or her ability to delay and concentrate.

2. The child who is negative or self defeating (e.g., I'm so stupid, I'll never get any of these right) may be exhibiting a very low level of self-confidence or hiding a learning problem.

3. The child who blocks or delays may be a child who is afraid of reaction or criticism and uses these techniques to ward off what he or she perceives as an ego-deflating situation.

Nature of Responses

▪ Are some nonsensical, immature, childlike?

▪ Are they inconsistent?

▪ Does subject ask to have questions repeated?

▪ Is the subject critical of his responses?

The types of response a child gives during an evaluation may indicate the following:

1. A child who continuously asks to have questions repeated may have hearing difficulties. This should always be ruled out first, along with vision problems, prior to a testing situation.

2. The child who asks to have questions repeated may be having problems processing information and may need more time to understand what is being asked.

Verbalizations

▪ Is the student verbose?

▪ Is he or she spontaneous in responding?

▪ Does he or she have peculiarities of speech?

The verbal interaction with the examiner during an evaluation can be very telling.

2-27. Continued

1. Some children with high levels of anxiety may tend to vent this through constant verbalizations, which begin to interfere, so that the child has to be constantly reminded to focus on the task at hand.

2. Verbal hesitations may be due to immature speech patterns, expressive language problems, poor self-esteem or lack of understanding of the question due to limited intellectual capacity.

Organizational Approach Used During Testing

- Does subject plan and work systematically?
- Does he or she make false starts?
- Does he or she use trial and error?

The manner in which a child handles individual tasks and organizes his or her approach may indicate the following:

1. A child who sizes up a situation and systematically approaches a task using trial and error may be a child with excellent internal organization, the ability to delay, and low levels of tension and anxiety. However, some children with emotional problems may also perform well on a short-term task because they see it as a challenge and can organize themselves to perform over a relatively short period of time. Their particular problems in organization and consistency may come when they are asked to perform this way over an extended period.

2. Children with chaotic internal organization may appear as if they know what they are doing, but the overall outcome of a task indicates a great deal of energy input with very low production. It's almost like "spinning wheels"; the energy output is a cover for not knowing what to do.

3. Some children may become less organized under the stress of a time constraint. The factor of style under time restrictions is one aspect in determining the child's overall learning style.

4. Children with attention deficit hyperactive disorder may also exhibit a confused sense of organization; however, there are other factors as well as the attentional that go into the diagnosis of this disorder.

Adaptability During Testing

- Does student make a smooth transition from one test to the next?
- Is interest sustained in all types of test items?

2-27. Continued

The ability of a child, or an adult for that matter, to adapt or shift from one task to another without difficulty is a very important factor in determining learning style and may be one predictor for successful outcome of a task. Other factors include the following:

1. Adaptability in life is one crucial aspect to good adjustment. The ability to shift without expending a great deal of energy offers the person more available resources for the next task. A child who is rigid or does not adapt well is using up much of his or her available energy, thus reducing the chances of success on the subsequent task.

2. Sustaining interest may also be a direct result of available energy. A child who loses interest quickly may be immature, overwhelmed, or preoccupied. Some of these reactions may be normal for the early ages; however, as the child gets older such reactions may be symptomatic of other factors—learning problems, emotional issues, or limited intellectual capacity.

Effort During Testing

- Is student cooperative?
- Does he or she give evidence of trying hard?
- Does child become frustrated easily?

The effort that a child puts into a testing situation may be reflective of the effort exhibited within the classroom and may indicate the following:

1. A child who is oppositional or uncooperative may be a child who needs to control. Always keep in mind that the more controlling a child is, the more out of control he or she feels. Control on the part of a child is aimed at securing predictability so that he or she can deal with a situation even though energy levels may be lowered by conflict and tension.

2. A child who tries hard to succeed may do so for several reasons. He or she may enjoy success and find the tasks challenging. This type of child is normally not thrown by a mistake and can easily move to the next task without difficulty.

In conclusion, always keep in mind that *all behavior is a message,* and the way a child interacts with the examiner may offer clues to learning style or problem areas. If you can "hear" a child's behavior by being aware of significant signs, you may come to a better understanding of the child's needs.

2-28. HOW TO INTERPRET AND WHAT TO LOOK FOR IN GROUP ACHIEVEMENT TEST RESULTS

A great deal of information can be gleaned from group achievement test results. While individual tests should be administered only when evaluating a child's suspected disability, group achievement results may reflect certain very important patterns. Most schools administer group achievement tests or group intelligence tests yearly or every few years. If these results are available on a student you may want to explore the various patterns that exist. It is helpful if you have several years of results to analyze. This pattern over time can be more reliable for interpretation.

The first thing you may need to know is the interpretation of the many abbreviations that exist on group achievement test results. These include:

NP or NPE—National percentile

LP or LPE—Local percentile

S—Stanine

GE—Grade equivalent

RS—Raw score

SS—Standard score

SAI—School abilities index- new term for IQ

GP—Grade percentile

AP—Age percentile

Normal Pattern

JOHN: AGE 14, GRADE 8, SAI-115 (80TH PERCENTILE)

Grade 3

	Reading Comprehension	Vocabulary	Applications	Computation	Total Reading	Total Math
RS	32	24	35	36	56	36
NP	**75**	**68**	**76**	**87**	**72**	**82**
LP	56	53	65	76	61	75
GE	4-3	3-9	4-3	4-9	4-5	4-8
S	7	6	7	8	7	8

© 1995 by The Center for Applied Research in Education

2-28. Continued

Grade 5

	Reading Comprehension	Vocabulary	Applications	Computation	Total Reading	Total Math
RS	37	28	39	39	58	38
NP	**73**	**65**	**72**	**84**	**70**	**79**
LP	58	56	66	78	64	72
GE	6-3	5-9	6-3	6-9	6-5	6-8
S	7	6	7	8	7	8

Grade 7

	Reading Comprehension	Vocabulary	Applications	Computation	Total Reading	Total Math
RS	32	24	35	36	56	36
NP	79	69	78	88	75	86
LP	60	58	66	79	68	77
GE	8-3	7-9	8-3	8-9	7-1	8-8
S	8	7	8	8	7	8

PROFILE INTERPRETATION

■ Look at the consistency of scores from year to year in the same test area. In this profile there is very little scatter and the test results parallel the child's intellectual ability level (approximately 80th percentile).

■ There is no discrepancy between ability and achievement.

Possible LD Pattern

MARY: AGE 11, GRADE 5, SAI-102 (51ST PERCENTILE)

Grade 2

	Reading Comprehension	Vocabulary	Applications	Computation	Total Reading	Total Math
RS	12	14	26	26	26	36
NP	**18**	**12**	**48**	**51**	**16**	**52**
LP	6	3	39	41	6	45
GE	K-5	K-5	2-3	2-6	K-5	2-4
S	1	1	4	4	1	4

2-28. Continued

Grade 3

	Reading Comprehension	Vocabulary	Applications	Computation	Total Reading	Total Math
RS	12	13	25	27	23	34
NP	**14**	**11**	**49**	**52**	**14**	**54**
LP	5	2	35	43	5	46
GE	1-1	1-0	3-3	3-4	1-0	2-5
S	1	1	4	5	1	4

Grade 4

	Reading Comprehension	Vocabulary	Applications	Computation	Total Reading	Total Math
RS	12	14	35	36	16	36
NP	**15**	**18**	**46**	**50**	**16**	**52**
LP	11	13	35	46	11	45
GE	2-3	1-9	4-3	4-4	1-9	4-5
S	1	1	4	5	1	5

PROFILE INTERPRETATION

▪ In this profile we notice that Mary is consistently and severely below expected level in the areas of comprehension, vocabulary, and total reading.

▪ This consistency is a pattern over the years and never shows any scatter.

▪ The results in reading show a severe discrepancy from ability (approximately 51st percentile).

Possible Emotional Pattern

BILLY: AGE 15, GRADE 8, SAI-120 (90TH PERCENTILE)

Grade 3

	Reading Comprehension	Vocabulary	Applications	Computation	Total Reading	Total Math
RS	18	34	45	16	46	36
NP	**25**	**68**	**76**	**27**	**72**	**52**
LP	16	53	65	22	61	45
GE	2-3	4-2	4-7	2-9	4-5	3-5
S	7	6	7	2	7	5

2-28. Continued

Grade 5

	Reading Comprehension	Vocabulary	Applications	Computation	Total Reading	Total Math
RS	37	18	39	39	18	38
NP	**73**	**22**	**72**	**84**	**30**	**79**
LP	58	16	66	78	24	72
GE	6-4	2-9	6-3	6-9	2-6	6-8
S	7	2	7	8	3	8

Grade 7

	Reading Comprehension	Vocabulary	Applications	Computation	Total Reading	Total Math
RS	12	39	15	36	16	36
NP	**29**	**89**	**28**	**88**	**35**	**46**
LP	20	68	16	79	28	37
GE	5-3	9-9	5-3	9-9	4-5	6-8
S	3	8	2	8	3	4

PROFILE INTERPRETATION

- This profile presents a possible emotional pattern in that there is a great deal of scatter within the same skill area over the three years.
- The pattern presents a "roller coaster" pattern.
- There is no clear consistent deficit area and the child's true ability, while not consistent, is observed in specific years.

2-29. OBJECTIVES OF INTELLECTUAL, ACADEMIC, AND PERCEPTUAL EVALUATIONS

Intellectual Evaluation Objectives

- To determine the child's present overall levels of intellectual ability
- To determine the child's present verbal intellectual ability
- To determine the child's nonlanguage intellectual ability
- To explore indications of greater potential
- To find possible patterns involving learning style—verbal comprehension, concentration
- To ascertain possible influences of tension and anxiety on testing results
- To determine the child's intellectual ability to deal with present grade level academic demands
- To explore the influence of intellectual ability on a child's past and present school difficulties, for example, limited intellectual ability found in retardation

Educational Evaluation Objectives

- To help determine the child's stronger and weaker academic skill areas, which is useful when making practical recommendations to teachers about academic expectations, areas in need of remediation, and best ways to input information to enhance the child's ability to learn.
- To help the teacher gear the materials to the learning capacity of the individual child. A child reading two years below grade level may require modified textbooks or greater explanations prior to a lesson.
- To develop a learning profile that can help the classroom teacher understand the best way to present information to the child and therefore increase his or her chances of success.
- Along with other information and test results, to help determine if the child's academic skills are suitable for a regular class or so severe that he or she may require a *restrictive educational setting* (an educational setting or situation—other than a full time regular class placement—that is best suited to the present needs of the student: resource room, self-contained class, or special school).

Whatever achievement battery the special educator chooses, it should be one that covers enough skill areas to make an adequate diagnosis of academic strengths and weaknesses.

2-29. Continued

Perceptual Evaluation Objectives

■ To help determine the child's stronger and weaker modalities for learning. Some children are visual learners, some are auditory, and some learn through any form of input. If a child is a strong visual learner in a class where the teacher relies on auditory lectures, his or her ability to process information may be hampered. This information is useful when making practical recommendations to teachers.

■ To help determine a child's stronger and weaker process areas. A child having problems in memory and expression will fall behind the rest of the class very quickly. The longer these processing difficulties continue the greater the chance that *secondary emotional problems* (emotional problems resulting from continued frustration with the ability to learn) will develop.

■ To develop a learning profile that can help the classroom teacher understand the best way to present information to the child, and therefore increase his or her chances of success.

■ Along with other information and test results, to help determine if the child's learning process deficits are suitable for a regular class or so severe that he or she may require a restrictive educational setting.

2-30. STATISTICAL TERMINOLOGY

- **Mean:** The arithmetic average and most commonly used measure of central tendency.
- **Median:** The point with the same number of scores above and below it in the distribution.
- **Mode:** The score among a set of scores that occurs most often.
- **Range:** The numerical difference between the high and low scores.
- **Semi-interquartile range:** This term refers to one-half the range of the middle 50% of the scores.
- **Standard deviation:** Indicates variation within a total set of scores.
- **Normal curve:** A theoretical representation of the manner in which an infinite number of scores will vary by chance. Also referred to as the bell-shaped curve.
- **Percentile:** Represents points on a scale of measurement that divide the scale into 100 equal units.
- **Percentile rank:** Indicates the percentage of persons tested who had scores equal to or lower than the specified score.
- **Deciles:** May be used to divide the scale of measurement into 10 larger units. The first decile is the same as the 10th percentile and so on.
- **Quartiles:** May be used to divide the scale of measurement into 4 larger units. The first quartile is the same as the 25th percentile.
- **Stanine:** A weighted scale divided into 9 equal segments that represent 9 levels of performance on any specific testing instrument.
- **Population:** Describes or refers to an entire group from which samples are taken for a particular purpose.
- **Parameters:** The characteristics or descriptions of the population in terms of a particular property or properties.
- **Sampling:** A relatively small sample of a much larger population whose results should resemble those of the larger population.
- **Statistical significance:** The significance of the results in predicting how a population feels or how it will act.
- **Correlation:** Describes a relationship between variables.
- **Coefficient of correlation:** Describes the degree of relationship between characteristics and scores or sets of scores.
- **Grade equivalent:** A very general score that is used to compare the performance of children in the same grade with one another.
- **Validity:** The ability of a test to measure effectively what it is designed to measure.
- **Content validity:** Indicates whether the test covers a sufficiently representative sample of the behavior domain being considered for study.

2-30. Continued

- **Predictive validity:** Involves testing the effectiveness of a test against future performance in the areas measured by the test.
- **Concurrent validity:** Determined by comparing test performance and some criterion data that are available at the time of testing.
- **Standard error of measurement:** Indicates the extent to which chance errors may cause variations in the scores that might be obtained by an individual if the test were administered an infinite number of times. The smaller the standard error, the more reliable the test.
- **Reliability:** The stability or consistency of scores obtained by a given individual when successive measures are taken with the same instrument.
- **Test-retest reliability:** Refers to the readministration of the same test and the degree of correlation between the scores.
- **Equivalent form reliability:** Refers to the use of two equivalent or parallel forms of the test and the correlation between the two sets of scores obtained.
- **Split-half reliability:** Involves the division of a test into two comparable halves; the correlation between the two halves is determined.
- **Item analysis:** The analysis of individual items on a test, for example, level of difficulty.
- **Nominal scale:** The lowest, or simplest, level of measurement characterized by the use of numbers to classify or identify.
- **Ordinal scale:** Used to rank according to some characteristic that must be measured but cannot be measured accurately in a manner to indicate the exact amount of difference between those in different ranks.
- **Interval scale:** At this level there are equal intervals, or distances, between each number and the next higher or lower number, but no known zero point.
- **Ratio scale:** This is the highest level of measurement. This scale has a zero point but is otherwise like an interval scale.

85

2-31. NAMES AND ADDRESSES OF TEST PUBLISHERS

Academic Therapy Publications
Fourth St.
San Rafael, CA 94901

American Association for Health,
Physical, Education, and Recreation
Sixteenth St., NW
Washington, DC 20036

American Foundation for the Blind
West 16th St.
New York, NY 10011

American Guidance Service
Publisher's Building
Circle Pines, MN 55014

American Printing House for the Blind
Frankfort Ave.
Louisville, KY 40206

Bobbs Merrill Co.
West 62nd St.
Indianapolis, IN 46268

Charles Merrill Pub. Co.
Alum Creek Drive
Columbus, OH 43216

Consulting Psychologists Press
College Ave.
Brandon, VT 05733

Crippled Children and Adults of Rhode Island
Meeting Street School
Grotto Ave.
Providence, RI 02906

Denver Public Schools
Fourteenth St.
Denver, CO 80202

2-31. Continued

Educational Performance Associates
Westview Ave.
Ridgefield, NJ 07657

Educational Testing Service
Princeton, NJ 08540

Educators Publication Service
Moulton St.
Cambridge, MA 02138

Follett Publishing Co.
W. Washington Blvd.
Chicago, IL 60607

Harcourt Brace Jovanovich
Third Ave.
New York, NY 10017

Houghton Mifflin Co.
Tremont St.
Boston, MA 02107

Ladoca Program & Publishing Foundation
East 51st Ave. & Lincoln St.
Denver, CO 80216

Marshall Hiskey
Baldwin
Lincoln, NE 68508

McGraw-Hill
Del Monte Research Park
Monterey, CA 93940

Personnel Press
Educational Center
P.O. Box 2649
Columbus, OH 43216

2-31. Continued

Psychological Corp.
East 45th St.
New York, NY 10017

Research Concepts
E. Airport Road
Muskegon, MI 49444

Science Research Associates
East Erie St.
Chicago, IL 60611

Stanwix House
Chartiers Ave.
Pittsburgh, PA 15204

Stoelting Co.
South Kostner Ave.
Chicago, IL 60623

Teachers College Press
Amsterdam Ave.
New York, NY 10027

University of Illinois Press
Urbana, IL 61801

Webster Div./McGraw-Hill
Avenue of the Americas
New York, NY 10020

Western Psychological Services
Wilshire Blvd.
Los Angeles, CA 90025

PART 3

Special Education Procedures

3-1. CSE PRESENTATION CHECKLIST

Name of Student _____ School _____ Grade _____

Type of Meeting: Initial _____ Special _____ Annual Review _____

Initial Referral

REQUIRED FORMS

- Initial Referral to CSE from School Staff or
- Initial Referral to CSE from Parent/Guardian
- Parent Consent for Evaluation

EVALUATIONS

- Medical Report
- Classroom Observation
- Psychological Report
- Educational Report
  Speech/Language Report
- Vocational (Secondary Level Only)
- Other (i.e., Occupational Therapist, Physical Therapist, ESL, Reading)—
  Specify:

GUIDANCE MATERIALS

- Child's Schedule
- Transcript of Past Grades
- Latest Report Card
- Teacher Reports

OTHER

- Social Developmental History Form
- Discipline Information
- PPT-related Documents (i.e., Minutes)
- Standardized Achievement Test Scores
- Report Cards
- Needs (Levels of Development: Social, Physical, Academic, Management)
- Recommended Goals and Objectives (Draft)

3-1. **Continued**

- Attendance Records
- Other

Special Meeting

- Name of Current/Contact Teacher:
- Special Meeting Referral Form ____
- Current Teacher Report ____
- Recommended Goals and Objectives ____
- New Evaluations if Completed ____
- Other Documents—Specify:

Annual Review

- Prep Sheet
- Current IEP
- Evaluations Completed—Specify:
- Needs (Social, Physical, etc.)
- Recommended Goals/Objectives
- Other Documents—Specify:

Triennial Evaluation Documents

- Parent Notice of Triennial
- Evaluation Form
- Psychological
- Educational
- Speech/Language
- Medical Report
- Social History Update
- Transcript of Grades
- Child's Schedule
- Recent Report Cards
- Teacher Reports
- Other—Specify:

92

3-1. Continued

Recommended CSE Participants: _____

_____

Case Manager: _____

Date: _____

3-2. CSE PRESENTATION COVER SHEET

This form gives the CSE office all the necessary identifying data on a child with a potential disability. It can also serve as a work sheet for the CSE chairperson during the meeting.

Goals submitted and attached to packet _____ yes _____ no   Student ID No.: _____

Goals changed (re-review) _____ yes _____ no   Student Date of Birth: _____

FOR CSE USE ONLY

CSE DATE _____

COMMITTEE _____

Also Present _____

Case Presented by _____

Student Name _____

Parent's Name(s) _____ Status: Married _____ Single _____ Divorced _____ Widowed _____

Address _____

All correspondence and information should be sent to: Mother ____ Father ____ Both ____ Legal Guardian _____

Current School _____ Current Teacher (Elem. Level Only) _____

Current Grade _____ Current Contact Teacher if Previously Classified (Mid. Sch. & H.S. Only) _____

Guidance Counselor _____

Dominant Language—Student _____

Dominant Language—Home _____

Ethnicity _____

Reason for the Meeting:

(Check one) Initial Review _____ Review of Present Classification ____ Declassification _____ Review of Placement _____

Pendency _____ Annual Review _____ Triennial Review_____

Date Entered Program (for a review case only)_____

Diploma Type _____

Other _____

3-2. Continued

Evaluation Information (Test names and score type—G.E., %)

IQ Test Information

Test _____ VIQ _____ % Rank _____ PIQ _____ % Rank _____

FSIQ _____ % Rank _____

Psychoeducational Test Information

<u>Area Measured (e.g., Reading)</u>

Test Name _____ Test Date _____ Percentile _____ Test Date _____

Test Name _____ Test Date _____ Percentile _____ Test Date _____

Test Name _____ Test Date _____ Percentile _____ Test Date _____

Examiner: Psychological _____ Educational _____ Speech/Language _____

STUDENT NAME _____ CSE DATE _____ STUDENT ID _____

STUDENT DOB _____ SCHOOL _____

FOR CSE USE ONLY

Recommended:

1. Classification _____ Sec. Con. _____

2. Placement _____ Staff Ratio _____

3. Related Service _____ Times/wk _____

   Related Service _____ Times/wk_____

   Related Service _____ Times/wk_____

4. Adaptive Devices _____

5. Mainstreamed Classes _____

6. Test Modifications _____

7. Transportation Y _____ N _____ Triennial Date_____

8. Special Trans. Needs _____

9. Foreign Language Exempt Yes _____ No _____ NA_____

10. Service Start Date for Placement _____ For Related Service _____

11. Related Service Provider/s_____

12. Recommended Teacher or Contact Teacher _____

13. Least Restrictive Statement

95

3-3. ANNUAL REVIEW PROCEDURES

Parent Notice: Parents will be notified of date, time, and location of meeting by the Pupil Personnel Office five school days prior to the meeting.

Annual Review CSE Membership: The following school/community personnel will constitute the Annual Review Committee: Director of Pupil Personnel Services, Parent, Special Education Teacher, Psychologist, and optional members as needed—Social Worker, Guidance Counselor, Speech Therapist.

Sequence of Discussion:

- Review of current IEP
- Evaluation of progress (demonstration based on recent tests, grades, observations, etc.)
- Identification of goals and objectives for the upcoming year
- Determination of the continuation of the child's classification (if a triennial year)
- Determination of program for upcoming year (type of instructional program—resource room, self-contained classes, etc.)
- Location of program
- Related services required for upcoming year (e.g., counseling, speech, therapy, etc.)
- Determination of related service provider
- Testing modifications for upcoming year

Secondary Students: Besides the above sequence of discussion, the following areas should be discussed when the annual review involves a student at the secondary level:

- Appropriateness of having the student in attendance at the meeting
- Credits
- Diploma requirements, including sequences
- Competency test requirements (if your state requires these tests)
- Transitional IEP for any student 15 years or older

Transportation: The child's transportation needs must be determined by the Annual Review Committee. Any special considerations should be noted—matrons, wheelchair, two-way radio—as well as necessary information relating to disabilities that would affect the child if an accident occurred (for example, child has no speech, child is a bleeder). This category should be noted with a special alert on the necessary forms.

3-3. Continued

Adaptive Devices/Special Needs: Any device that is required by the child should be discussed and noted.

Levels of Development: The child's academic, social, physical, and management goal areas must be discussed for the coming year.

3-4. TRIENNIAL REVIEW PROCEDURES

One of the responsibilities for the special education teacher may be involvement in the *triennial evaluation* (a complete and updated evaluation required every three years for all children classified as having a disability by the Committee on Special Education). This is a very important phase of the special education process because it reviews the factors that accounted for the child's classification and placement.

There are several phases to the triennial evaluation that may involve many staff members from a variety of disciplines. The objectives for the special education teacher in the triennial evaluation include the following:

1. To retest the child's achievement skill areas.

2. To retest the child's perceptual skill areas.

3. To analyze the results and compare the patterns with past evaluation results.

4. To write a detailed and comprehensive, updated report of the findings, which will be shared with the Committee on Special Education as well as the staff and parents.

5. To participate in the *annual review meeting* (a required yearly meeting for all classified students at which time the child's classification and educational placement are reviewed). Discuss the results, to help the Committee on Special Education make a decision on continuation of classification and services or *declassification*. The CSE may choose to declassify when the classified child no longer requires special education services to maintain success in mainstream classes.

6. To share the results with parents.

7. To help interpret and analyze achievement and perceptual test results that may be submitted from outside agencies or professionals pertinent to the triennial evaluation of a specific child. This can occur if the parent chooses an independent evaluation.

It should be noted that a new release for testing involving a triennial evaluation is not required by law. The school may proceed with this process without a new release but must inform the parents that the process will be taking place. An example of that communication to parents might look like the letter shown in List 3-5.

3-5. PARENT NOTICE OF TRIENNIAL EVALUATION

To Parents/Guardian of:_____

Date:_____

Dear Parents,

Please be advised that the Committee on Special Education has arranged for a comprehensive reevaluation of your child, which, according to state regulations, is required every three years.

The school psychologist will be available to review all the results with you when the reevaluation is completed. If you have any questions, please don't hesitate to call the school psychologist or me.

A **Statement of Parents' Rights** is enclosed for your information.

Sincerely,

The reevaluations to be performed are: _____

_____

_____

_____

3-6. STATEMENT OF PARENT'S RIGHTS

Dear Parent(s):

It is important that you be aware of, and understand, your rights in accordance with Section _____ of the Regulations of the Commissioner of Education:

1. To inspect all school files, records, and reports pertaining to your child. Such reports shall be available for duplication at reasonable cost.

2. To obtain an independent educational evaluation at public expense if you disagree with the evaluation obtained by the school district. The school district, however, may initiate a hearing to show that its evaluation is appropriate. Such services may be obtained at

_____

_____

3. To obtain free or low-cost legal services at no cost to the school district. Such services may be obtained at the following low cost/no cost agencies:

_____

_____

4. To appeal the recommendations of the Committee on Special Education and request, in writing, an impartial formal hearing to determine the appropriateness of the proposed placement or to change the program.

The impartial formal hearing will be conducted in accordance with the following rules:

- The board of education or trustees shall appoint an impartial hearing officer to conduct the hearing. The hearing officer shall be authorized to administer oaths and to issue subpoenas in connection with the administrative proceedings before him or her.

- A written or electronic verbatim record of the proceedings before the hearing officer shall be maintained and made available to the parties.

- At all stages of the proceeding, where required, interpreters for the deaf, or interpreters fluent in the dominant language of pupil's home shall be provided at district expense.

- The impartial hearing officer shall preside at the hearing and shall provide all parties with an opportunity to present evidence and testimony.

- The parties to the proceeding may be represented by legal counsel or individuals with special knowledge or training with respect to the problems of children with disabilities, and may be accompanied by other persons of their choice.

3-6. Continued

- Unless a surrogate parent shall have previously been assigned, the impartial hearing officer shall determine whether the interests of the parent are opposed to or inconsistent with those of the child, or whether for any other reason the interests of the child would best be protected by assignment of a surrogate parent. Where he or she so determines, the impartial hearing officer shall designate a surrogate parent to protect the interests of such child.

- The hearing shall be closed to the public unless the parent requests an open hearing.

- The parents, school authorities, and their respective counsel or representative, shall have an opportunity to present evidence and to confront and question all witnesses at that hearing. Each party shall have the right to prohibit the introduction of any evidence the substance of which has not been disclosed to such party at least five days before the hearing.

- The parents shall have the right to determine whether the child shall attend the hearing.

- The impartial hearing officer shall render a decision, and mail a copy of the decision to the parents and to the board of education, not later than 45 calendar days after the receipt by the board of education of a request for a hearing or after the initiation of such hearing by the board. The decision of the impartial hearing officer shall be based solely upon the record of the proceeding before the impartial hearing officer, and shall set forth the reasons and the factual basis for the determination. The decision shall also include a statement of such a decision by the commissioner in accordance with subdivision _____ of the hearing officer. The board of education shall mail a copy of such decision, after deleting any personally identifiable information, to the Office of Children with Handicapping Conditions, State Education Department, for the use of the state advisory panel.

- A review of the decision of a hearing officer rendered in accordance with subdivision _____ of this section may be obtained by an appeal to the commissioner. The written decision of the commissioner, a copy of which will be mailed to the parent and board of education, shall be final.

3-7. TRIENNIAL REVIEW—REQUIRED MATERIALS

Evaluations

- New Psychological Evaluation(s)
- New Educational Evaluation
- New Speech and Language Evaluation—if applicable
- Outside Reports—if applicable
- Medical Report—if applicable

Academic Data

- Classroom Teachers' Reports
- Student Schedule
- Copy of Most Recent Report Card

Developmental Data

- New Social and Developmental History Form

Other Required Information and Procedures

- Parent Letter of Triennial Review
- Medical Update
- Classroom Observation

3-8. REFERRAL TO THE CSE FROM THE SCHOOL STAFF

This form is used to alert the CSE that a case of a child with a suspected disability may be coming up for a review—depending on the outcome of evaluations. When the school suspects a disability, this form is forwarded with or without a signed parent consent for evaluation. If it is not sent with the signed consent, the CSE chairperson will send one to the parent, requesting that it be signed and returned. Again, local policy may differ and many schools try to have the parents sign this consent when they meet with them initially to discuss the reasons for the referral.

REFERRAL TO THE CSE FROM SCHOOL STAFF

From: _____ School _____ Date _____
        Name/Title

The following student is being referred to the CSE for suspicion of a disability.

Student Name _____ Grade _____

Parent/Guardian Name _____

Address _____

_____

State _____ ZIP _____

Telephone (   ) _____ Date of Birth _____

Current Program Placement _____

Teacher (Elem) _____ Guidance Counselor (Secondary)_____

Is there an attendance problem? Yes ____ No ____ Language spoken at home? _____

Did student repeat a grade? Yes ___ No ___ If yes, when? _____

Is an interpreter needed? Yes ___ No ___ Deaf _____

TEST SCORES WITHIN LAST YEAR (Standardized Achievement, Regents Competency, etc.)

TEST	PERCENTILE SCORE	COMMENT
_____	_____	_____
_____	_____	_____
_____	_____	_____
_____	_____	_____

Prior Parent Contact: _____

_____

3-8. Continued

Reasons for Referral: Describe the specific reason and/or situations indicating that a referral to the CSE is needed. Also, describe attempts to resolve problems within the current educational program.

SPECIFIC REASONS FOR REFERRAL

_____

_____

_____

_____

_____

ATTEMPTS TO RESOLVE

_____

_____

_____

_____

_____

Principal's signature _____ Date _____

Date forwarded to CSE Chairperson _____

3-9. INITIAL REFERRAL TO THE CSE FROM A PARENT OR GUARDIAN

DATE: _____

TO: _____

Principal or CSE Chairperson

I am writing to refer my child _____, age _____, to the Committee on Special Education. I am asking you to conduct an individual evaluation to determine whether a handicapping condition exists that would make my child eligible for Special Education Services.

I am concerned about my child's educational difficulties in the following areas:

_____

_____

_____

Please contact me as soon as possible to discuss my referral.

Sincerely,

Parent/Guardian _____ Phone _____

Address _____

State _____ ZIP _____

Child's Birthdate _____ School _____ Grade _____

Date received by CSE _____

3-10. PARENT CONSENT FOR EVALUATION

State laws or district policies usually mandate that parent(s) sign a consent form allowing the school to administer an evaluation on their child. As previously mentioned, the school usually obtains this form at the initial meeting with the parent to discuss the reasons for the referral or through the mail. Either way, this consent is required before any evaluation can take place. An example of such a form may look like the following.

PARENT CONSENT FOR EVALUATION

To the Parent/Guardian of: _____ Birth Date _____

School _____ Grade _____

We would like to inform you that your child _____ has been referred for individual testing because of the suspicion of a disability. Testing results will help us in determining your child's educational needs and in planning the most appropriate program. The evaluation procedures and/or tests may include the following:

Intelligence

Communication/Language/Speech

Physical

Behavior/Emotional

Academic

Vocational

Other

Before we can begin testing, it is necessary that the School District CSE have your written permission to evaluate your child. You have had the opportunity to discuss the need for this testing and the possibilities for special educational services with the school principal/designee. The evaluation(s) will be conducted by the multidisciplinary team, who will share the results of said evaluation with you at a building level meeting. Both this meeting and a CSE meeting will be held within 30 school days of receipt of this notice.

I grant permission for the evaluation(s) mentioned above _____

I do not grant permission for the evaluation(s) mentioned above _____

Date _____ Parent's Signature _____

Date _____ Administrator/Designee _____

3-11. QUESTIONS TO CONSIDER WHEN DOING A CLASSROOM OBSERVATION

Basic behaviors must be observed when doing a classroom observation, for example, attention, focus, aggressiveness, compliance, flexibility, rigidity, oppositional behavior, shyness, controlling behavior, distractibility, impulsivity, and social interaction.

Questions to Consider

1. Is there a difference between behaviors in a structured setting (i.e., classroom) and an unstructured setting (i.e., playground)?

This factor may shed light on the child's need for a more structured environment in which to learn. Children who do not have well-developed internal control systems need a highly structured environment to maintain focus and appropriate behavior. Some children cannot shift between structured and unstructured settings. They may not possess the internal monitor that regulates conformity and logical attendance to rules. These children may be more successful in a structured play setting arranged by teachers during the lunch hour.

2. Does the child seem to respond to external boundaries?

This factor is important to the teacher since it is a monitor of potential learning style. If a child who lacks internal controls does conform to external boundaries (e.g., time out or teacher proximity during worktime), this factor must be taken into consideration when prescribing classroom management techniques. When the child conforms to such boundaries, his or her behavior is a message about what works for him or her.

3. What is the child's attention span during academic tasks?

Attention span at different ages is measured normally in minutes or hours. You should become aware of the normal attention span for children of all ages and compare the child over several activities and days to see if a pattern of inattention is present. If the attention span is very short for someone of his or her age, modifications to work load (i.e., shorter but more frequent assignments) may have to be included.

4. Does the child require constant teacher supervision or assistance?

A child who requires constant teacher supervision or assistance may be exhibiting a wide variety of symptomatic behavior that may result from, but not be limited to, attention deficit disorder; processing problems; emotional difficulties involving need for attention, need for control, high anxiety, or internal stress; limited intellectual capacity; hearing problems, or other problems. All of these areas must be checked out and a good evaluation should determine the root of such behavior; however, the key is always the frequency, intensity, and duration of such symptoms.

5. Does the child interact appropriately with peers?

Observing children at play can tell us a great deal about self-esteem, tension levels, social maturity, physical development, and many other factors. Social interaction is more common in children over the age of 6 or 7, while parallel play is still common in younger children.

107

3-11. Continued

Appropriate social interaction gives us insight into the child's own internal boundaries and organization. A child who always needs to control may really be masking high levels of tension. The more controlling a child is, the more out of control he or she is feeling. A child who can appropriately conform to group rules, delay his or her needs for the good of the team, conform to rules and various changes or inconsistencies in rules, may be a very self-assured child—one who has low anxiety levels. The opposite is most always typical of children at risk. One should always consider developmental stages, however, since certain behaviors, such as control, may be more typical at early ages.

6. Is the child a high- or low-status child?

Observing a child in different settings allows us the opportunity to see the social status of the child and its impact on his or her behavior. Low-status children—as is often seen in children with learning disabilities—are more apt to feel insignificant and therefore fail to receive positive social cues that help reinforce feelings of self-esteem. Having the psychologist begin a counseling group of five or six low-status children enables them to feel empowered with feelings of connection

3-12. UNSTRUCTURED OBSERVATION SCALES

This type of unstructured observation scale checklist allows the observer to fill in any information that he or she feels is important. Any of a number of general areas can, and should be, observed. It can also serve to fulfill the Committee on Special Education's requirement for a classroom observation, which must be part of the packet when a review for classification is required.

Name of Student Observed: _____ Observer: _____

Date of Observation: _____ Place of Observation _____

Behaviors to Observe	Classroom	Playground	Lunchroom	Gym
• Impulsivity	_____	_____	_____	_____
• Attention to task	_____	_____	_____	_____
• Attention span	_____	_____	_____	_____
• Conformity to rules	_____	_____	_____	_____
• Social interaction with peers	_____	_____	_____	_____
• Aggressiveness	_____	_____	_____	_____
• Level of teacher assistance required	_____	_____	_____	_____
• Frustration levels	_____	_____	_____	_____
• Reaction to authority	_____	_____	_____	_____
• Verbal interaction	_____	_____	_____	_____
• Procrastination	_____	_____	_____	_____
• Organizational skills	_____	_____	_____	_____
• Developmental motor skills	_____	_____	_____	_____

3-13. STRUCTURED OBSERVATION REPORT FORM

Student's Name/ID# _____

Date of Birth _____ Dominant Language _____

Dates of Observation _____ Length of Observation _____

Observer _____ Position _____

Classroom Observed _____ Location _____

Teacher's Name _____

Subject area being taught _____

Task-Individual

WHEN ASSIGNED TASK, THE STUDENT:

- Initiates task without need for teacher's verbal encouragement
- Requests help in order to start task
- Complains before getting started on a task
- Demands help in order to start on a task
- Actively refuses to do task despite teacher's encouragement
- Passively retreats from task despite teacher's encouragement

WHILE WORKING ON TASK, THE STUDENT:

- Works independently
- Performs assigned task without complaints
- Needs teacher's verbal encouragement to keep working
- Needs teacher in close proximity to keep working
- Needs physical contact from teacher to keep working
- Seeks constant reassurance to keep working
- Is reluctant to have work inspected
- Belittles own work

AT THE END OF ASSIGNED TIME, THE STUDENT:

- Completes task
- Takes pride in completed task

© 1995 by The Center for Applied Research in Education

3-13. Continued

■ Goes on to next task
■ Refuses to complete task

IN SOCIAL INTERACTION, THE STUDENT:

■ Establishes a relationship to one or two peers
■ Shares materials with peers
■ Respects property of peers
■ Gives help to peers when needed
■ Accepts help from peers when needed
■ Establishes a relationship with most peers
■ Teases or ridicules peers
■ Expresses prejudiced attitudes toward peers
■ Physically provokes peers
■ Physically hurts peers
■ Seeks to be attacked by peers
■ Participates appropriately in group activities
■ Postpones own needs for group objectives
■ Withdraws from group
■ Is overly assertive in group
■ Disrupts group activities (i.e., calling out, provocative language, etc.)
■ Exhibits aggressive behavior within group—not amenable to teacher intervention

IN RELATIONSHIP TO THE TEACHER, THE STUDENT:

■ Tries to meet teacher's expectations
■ Functions adequately without constant teacher encouragement
■ Interacts with teacher in nondemanding manner
■ Responds to teacher without haggling
■ Tests limits, tries to see how much teacher will allow
■ Seeks special treatment from teacher
■ Responds to teacher's criticism without fear
■ Responds to teacher's criticism without verbal anger
■ Responds to teacher's criticism without physical outbursts (i.e., temper tantrums)
■ Defies teacher's requirement
■ Scorns or ridicules teacher's support

3-13. Continued

- Responds with anger when demands are thwarted by teacher
- Blames and accuses teacher ("not helping," "not liking me")
- Abuses teacher verbally (no apparent cause)
- Abuses teacher physically (no apparent cause)
- Requires close and constant supervision because behavioral controls are so limited

Comments:

_____

_____

_____

_____

3-14. MEDICAL FORM FOR THE CSE

To be completed by the Nurse-Teacher and included in the CSE Packet.

Date: _____

Student's Name: _____ Grade _____

Address: _____

_____ State _____ ZIP _____

Date of last medical examination _____

Name and address of physician _____

_____

_____

Medical findings (attach copy if pertinent) _____

_____

Last vision exam _____ Results _____

Last hearing exam _____ Results _____

Speech _____

Additional information that might have implications in determining the outcome of this case:

_____

_____

_____

3-15. AGREEMENT TO WITHDRAW CSE REFERRAL

There may be times when the parent and school agree that the evaluation and findings do not seem to substantiate the suspected disability that was originally considered. When this occurs, the school and parent must meet and discuss other methods to remediate the problem. At the time of the meeting, an Agreement to Withdraw CSE Referral form must be filled out and forwarded to the principal and then to the CSE chairperson. This will officially withdraw the original referral and stop the CSE process.

There are usually time requirements and constraints with this procedure, so check your district and state policies.

AGREEMENT TO WITHDRAW CSE REFERRAL

INITIAL CONFERENCE

Student Name _____ Date of Agreement _____

Date of Birth _____ Date of Referral Current _____

Current Program _____ Name of Referring Party _____

Position of Referring Party _____

Persons Present at Conference _____
_____
_____

The following method(s) will be used to attempt to resolve identified learning difficulties (attach additional sheets, as needed):
_____
_____
_____

If necessary, a follow-up conference to review the student's progress will be held on
_____

We agree to the above conditions. The referral is hereby withdrawn.

Referring Party Signature _____ Date _____

Parent/Guardian Signature _____ Date _____

cc: Student's Cumulative Educational Record

3-16. SOCIAL AND DEVELOPMENTAL HISTORY FORM

Parent/Guardian _____

Referring Party _____

Date _____

Name _____ Sex _____

School _____ Grade _____ DOB _____

Address _____

Telephone _____

Natural Parents _____ **or Child resides with** _____ (check one)

Father's Name _____ Age _____ Education _____

Occupation _____ Business Phone _____

Mother's Name _____ Age _____ Education _____

Occupation _____ Business Phone _____

Names of guardians or other individuals with whom child resides_____

_____

Relationship _____ Relationship _____

Employment _____ Employment_____

Business Phone _____ Business Phone _____

Siblings

Names   Ages   School
_____   _____   _____
_____   _____   _____
_____   _____   _____

Others in Home

Name   Relationship   Age
_____   _____   _____
_____   _____   _____
_____   _____   _____

Presenting Problem (as perceived by respondent) _____

_____

3-16. Continued

Developmental History:

Birth and Infancy Periods—prenatal, birth, and postnatal facts. Include any unusual aspects in attainment of developmental milestones—critical stages, traumatic experiences, falls or injuries, hospital stays, previous testing, medical conditions, medication, etc. Include any medical facts that might have an implication in the outcome of this case.

_____

_____

_____

_____

Family History

_____

_____

_____

_____

Social History: Include indications of child's conduct in social skills, involvement in groups or organizations, relationship to peers, hobbies or interests, etc.

_____

_____

_____

_____

_____

3-16. Continued

School Adjustment: (Age and grade entrance to school, attendance, retention, change of schools, previous psychological evaluations or prior reviews by CSE in another district.)

_____

_____

_____

_____

_____

Behavioral Patterns: (Eating, sleeping, relationship with adults)

_____

_____

_____

_____

_____

Other Residences: (Hospitals, schools, with relatives, or foster homes, etc.)

_____

_____

_____

_____

_____

3-16. Continued

Recommendations

_____

_____

_____

_____

_____

Individual filling out form _____ **Title** _____

3-17. LEARNING PROFILE FOR CSE PACKET

There are times when an overall student profile can assist in the educational decision-making process faced by the CSE. This type of profile can be a quality-specific profile that addresses many of the student's qualities and along with professional evaluations and reports, can add to the overall understanding of the student. If such a profile is used, the responses should always be in behavioral and factual terms and never involve assumption, judgment, or interpretation. The following areas should be involved:

- Self-Concept
- Peer Relationships
- Adult Relationships
- Intellectual Characteristics
- Academic Characteristics
- Modality Strengths and Weaknesses
- Environmental Factors
- Classroom Structure
- Prior Evaluations
- Attention to Task
- Motivation
- Response to Pressure
- Response to Difficulty
- Organizational Ability
- Special Skills, Talents, Interests
- Home Environment
- Medical or Physical Problems

3-18. BASIC EDUCATIONAL LAW TERMINOLOGY

adaptive behavior—refers to the manner and effectiveness with which a child or adult deals with the social demands of the surrounding environment.

annual review—an annual review of a disabled child's classification and educational program by the CSE. The purpose of this review, which includes the parent and sometimes the student, is to recommend the continuation, modification, or termination of classification; placement; or IEP needs and related services for the upcoming year.

adaptive physical education—specially designed physical education program for disabled children who cannot, as a result of their disability, benefit from the normal school program. This program is an individually designed program of games, sports, and developmental activities that are individually suited to the needs, interests, capabilities, and limitations of each disabled child.

aging out—the date upon which the disabled child will no longer be eligible for tuition-free educational services.

approved private school—a private school that has met state and federal guidelines for providing appropriate services to disabled children and as a result appears on a state-approved list from which public schools may enter into contract for services.

change in program (with reference to a disabled child)—any change in any component of a child's IEP.

change in placement (with reference to a disabled child)—any change of educational setting from or to a public school, local special school, or state-approved school.

CSE (Committee on Special Education)—the multidisciplinary team that oversees the identification, monitoring, review, and status of all disabled children residing within the school district.

CPSE (Committee on Preschool Special Education)—the multidisciplinary team that oversees the identification, monitoring, review, and status of disabled preschool children under the age of 5.

impartial hearing officer—an independent individual assigned by the district's board of education or commissioner of education to hear an appeal and render a decision. These individuals can in no way be connected to the school district, may have to be certified (depending upon state regulations), are trained, and usually must update their skills.

independent evaluation—a full and comprehensive individual evaluation conducted by an outside professional or agency not involved in the education of the child.

individual psychological evaluation—a full and comprehensive evaluation by a state-certified school psychologist (if the child is evaluated within the school district) or a licensed psychologist for the purpose of educational planning.

occupational therapy—the evaluation and provision of services for disabled children to develop or maintain adaptive skills designed to achieve maximal physical and mental functioning of the individual in his or her daily life tasks.

3-18. Continued

paraprofessional—a teacher assistant or aide in a special education setting.

preschool program—a special education program for disabled children who are not of public school age.

physical therapy—treatment of students with motor disabilities by a specialist under the supervision of a physician.

pupil with a disability—any school-age child (any child who has not attained the age of 21 prior to September 1) who, for mental, physical, or emotional reasons has been identified as having a disability and is entitled to special education services.

related services—auxiliary services provided to disabled children including speech pathology, audiology, psychological services, physical therapy, occupational therapy, counseling services, and art therapy.

resource room program—part-time supplementary instruction for disabled children—on an individual or small-group basis outside the regular classroom.

special class—a class consisting of children with the same disability or different disabilities, who have been grouped together as a result of similar educational needs and levels for the purpose of being provided with special educational services.

surrogate parent—any person appointed to act on the parent's or guardian's behalf when a child's parents are not known or are unavailable, or when the child is the ward of the state.

transitional support services—temporary special education services, according to a child's IEP, provided to students who are no longer classified as disabled and may be transferring to a regular program, or to disabled children who may be moving to a program or service in a less restrictive environment.

triennial review—a full and comprehensive reexamination of a disabled child held every three years. This reexamination may include educational, psychological, medical, or other evaluation deemed necessary by the CSE to determine the child's continuing eligibility for special education.

121

3-19. DISABILITY CATEGORIES REQUIRING SPECIAL EDUCATIONAL SERVICES

- **Autistic**—Autism is characterized by a difficulty in the child's ability to respond to people, events, and objects. Responses to sensations of light, sound, and feeling may be exaggerated and delayed speech and language skills may be associated features. The onset of this condition is usually observed before age 2 1/2.

- **Blind**—The child who is classified as blind exhibits vision that requires special braille equipment and reading materials. The condition is so severe that the child does not have what is considered functional sight.

- **Deaf**—The individual classified as deaf has a loss of hearing so severe, usually above an 80-decibel loss, that it hinders effective use of the sense of hearing. This disability usually necessitates the use of specialized services or equipment in order for the child to communicate.

- **Emotionally disturbed**—Students classified with this disability have behavior disorders over a long period of time and to such a degree that they are unable to do well in school. These disturbances may interfere in developing meaningful relationships, result in physical symptoms or irrational fears, and limit the individual's overall production.

- **Hard of hearing**—A student in this category has a hearing loss that may or may not be permanent, and has some sense of hearing with or without an aid. This student, however, still requires specialized instruction and special education assistance.

- **Learning disabled**—These students have a disability in receiving, organizing, or expressing information. They are of average intelligence but have difficulty listening, thinking, speaking, reading, writing, or doing arithmetic and this results in a significant discrepancy between ability and school achievement. This is not the result of emotional, mental, physical, environmental, or cultural factors.

- **Mentally disabled**—These students have a developmental delay that causes them to learn at a slower pace. They also exhibit a significantly lower level of intelligence and marked impairment in social competency skills. This category includes Educable Mentally Disabled—IQ usually between 55 and approximately 80, and Trainable Mentally Disabled—IQ below 55.

- **Multiply handicapped**—This category is set aside for children who are disabled in more than one category, such as deafness and blindness.

- **Orthopedically impaired**—These students are physically disabled and their educational performance is directly affected by this condition. Conditions such as cerebral palsy and amputation fall into this category.

- **Other health impaired**—Students who are classified in this category range from limited strength, vitality, or alertness to chronic or acute health problems. Conditions that fall into this area include heart conditions, asthma, Tourette's syndrome, attention deficit hyperactive disorder, and diabetes.

3-19. Continued

■ **Partially sighted**—Children classified in this area have some functional sight, usually 20/70 or better with best correction. These students may be able to learn to read regular print with glasses or to read special books that are printed with large type.

■ **Speech impaired**—These students have a communication disorder. They are unable to correctly produce speech sounds, have difficulty in understanding or using words or sentences, or exhibit stuttering or some other voice impairment.

3-20. RESPONSIBILITIES OF THE COMMITTEE ON SPECIAL EDUCATION

1. Following appropriate procedures and taking appropriate action on any child referred as having a suspected disability.

2. Determining the suitable classification for a child with a suspected disability. The classifications from which the CSE chooses are defined as follows:

   a. Reviewing, at least annually, the status of each disabled child residing within the district.

   b. Evaluating the adequacy of programs, services, and facilities for the disabled children in the district.

   c. Reviewing and evaluating all relevant information on each disabled student.

   d. Maintaining ongoing communication in writing to parents with regard to planning, modifying, changing, reviewing, placing, or evaluating the program, classification, or educational plan for a disabled child.

   e. Advising the board of education as to the status and recommendations for all disabled children in the district.

   f. Determining the least restrictive educational setting for any child having been classified as having a disability.

3-21. THE CONCEPT OF PROCEDURAL DUE PROCESS

Due process, as it applies to special education, describes the legal procedures and requirements developed to protect the rights of children, parents, and school districts. In respect to children suspected of having a disability, due process guarantees a free and appropriate public education in the least restrictive educational setting. For parents, due process protects their rights to have input into the educational program and placement of their child, and to exercise options in cases of disagreement with the recommendations of the school district. For school districts, due process offers recourse in cases of parent resistance to a request for evaluation, challenges to an independent evaluation sought by parents at public expense, or unwillingness of parents to consent to the CSE recommendation.

The components of due process include such procedural safeguards as the following:

Appropriate written notice to parents is required in the following situations:

1. actions proposed by the CSE to evaluate the existence of a suspected disability

2. meetings by the CSE to discuss the results of the evaluation to determine a suspected disability

3. meetings to discuss the development of an individual educational plan

4. proposed actions to review an individual educational plan

5. proposed actions to reevaluate the child's classification or placement

6. aging out notification for disabled children no longer eligible for tuition-free educational services.

Written consent from parents is required in four specific situations:

1. consent for an initial evaluation on a child not previously classified as having a disability

2. consent allowing for the provisions recommended by the CSE with regard to classification and special education placement

3. notification prior to providing services for the first time for a disabled child in a 12-month program

4. prior to the disabled child's aging out of public education

Confidentiality of records is protected under due process. Confidentiality ensures that only educational institutions or agencies who have legitimate interest in the child's education will be permitted to see the records. Written consent from parents is required for the release of any information on their child other than the following:

3-21. Continued

1. to staff members or school officials within the school district in which the child is a resident—who must have a legitimate interest in the child's education.

2. to other school districts in which the disabled child may enroll. In this case the parents are notified of the transfer of information, may request copies of the information sent, and may contest through a hearing the content of the transferred information

A surrogate parent must be assigned: In most cases the child with a suspected disability is represented by his or her parents at CSE meetings; however, if the parents are unknown or unavailable, or the child is a ward of the state, the CSE must determine if there is a need for the assignment of a surrogate parent to represent the child. When this happens, the board of education chooses a surrogate from a list of eligible individuals.

An impartial hearing is a procedure used to resolve disagreements between parents and the school district. This procedure of due process can be utilized when:

1. a parent disagrees with a CSE recommendation

2. a parent disagrees with a board of education determination

3. the CSE fails to evaluate and recommend a program within 30 days of the signed consent by the parents

4. the CSE fails to implement its recommendations within the 30-day requirement period

5. there is failure on the part of the school district to administer a triennial evaluation

6. there is failure on the part of the school district to hold an annual review on a disabled child

7. parent or parents are unwilling to give consent for an evaluation

8. parents are unwilling to consent to the recommendations of the CSE concerning the classification or special education placement of a disabled child

Appeals to the Commissioner of Education provide another level of resolution for parents and school districts when an impartial hearing cannot resolve the disagreement. This is a legal process and the procedures are usually outlined in state manuals on the Commissioner's regulations.

3-22. CSE PRESENTATION BY THE SPECIAL EDUCATION TEACHER AS EDUCATIONAL EVALUATOR

If your role on the committee has resulted from your educational and perceptual evaluation of the child, you must keep the following in mind:

1. Prior to the meeting, you should meet with the parents and go over your results. Follow the procedures outlined in Part 2, "How to Report Test Results to Parents."

2. Make sure that you have your report complete and typed at least one week to ten days prior to the CSE meeting. In some districts, the CSE requires that the entire packet be forwarded a week in advance.

3. Prior to the meeting, outline the important points of your report. Do not go through the report at the CSE meeting, looking for the issues that you think need to be discussed. Preparation will make you look more professional.

4. Make sure you report strengths as well as weaknesses.

5. Even though everyone should have copies of your report, the length of the report may make it impossible for them to filter out the crucial sections in the time allotted for the meeting. Therefore you may want to develop a one-page summary sheet that clearly outlines what you will be presenting. Hand it out as you begin your presentation.

6. Remember that this is not a parent conference to review the entire report. You should have done that earlier, so keep it brief and highlight the important issues. Several individuals may need to report results or speak, and the CSE may have several meetings that day.

7. If you think the nature of the case may require more time than that normally set aside by the CSE for a review, call the chairperson and make a request for a longer meeting time. Crucial meetings should not have to be ended because of time constraints!

8. Be prepared to be questioned about your findings or some aspect of the report by a parent, a committee member, a lawyer (sometimes brought by the parent), or others. Carefully look over your report and *be prepared.*

127

3-23. CSE PRESENTATION BY THE SPECIAL EDUCATION TEACHER AS CLASSROOM TEACHER

There may be times when you will be asked as the child's classroom teacher to attend a CSE meeting—for review of classification, placement, annual review, change in an IEP, or a special meeting requested by the parent. When this occurs, keep the following in mind:

1. Find out the reason for the meeting. The material required may vary, but your preparation prior to the meeting is vital. If the meeting was called by the parents, you may want to have them in for a conference to discuss their concerns.

2. Once you know why the meeting will be held, organize yourself so that you will have information in front of you in the following areas:

- The child's present academic levels in reading, math, spelling, and writing. These may be available as a result of recent individual or group achievement tests, informal evaluations that you may have administered, observation (although try to be more objective), or class tests. Determine grade levels if possible, and where the child falls in comparison with others in the class.

- The child's present pattern of classroom behavior. Write this up in *behavioral terms* (factual, observable, and descriptive notes of behavior that do not include analysis or judgment).

- The child's present levels of social interaction and social skills.

- The child's interest areas and areas of strength.

- The child's present schedule.

- Samples of the child's work.

- Outline of parent conferences, phone conversations, or meetings and the purpose and outcome of each. These notes should be kept on an ongoing basis.

- Your opinion as to whether the child is benefiting from his or her present placement.

- Any physical limitations noted and their impact on the learning process.

- Your opinion of the child's self-esteem.

- Any pertinent comments made by the child that may have an impact on the present situation.

3. Be well prepared to answer any questions with the above information at hand. When it is your turn to present, do it in an organized manner. Here, too, you may want to provide the participants with an outline of the information you will be covering.

4. Try not to be defensive, even if the reason for the meeting is the parent's concern over the child's placement in your class or the work load. Try to listen carefully to what the parent is really asking for. Try to be solution oriented, even if the parent is blame oriented.

3-24. CSE PRESENTATION BY THE SPECIAL EDUCATION TEACHER AS MEMBER OF THE CSE

There are times when the special education teacher will be asked to sit on the CSE to review a case even though the teacher does not have or know the child and has not evaluated him or her. The participation of the special education teacher in this situation is for expertise in reviewing academic and perceptual material that may be presented. This material may come from other evaluators within the district or from an outside agency or professional. If your role involves this aspect, keep the following in mind:

1. Try to get a copy of the reports prior to the meeting. In some districts this is the procedure. If not, request it so that you can review the findings and make notes.

2. Your role here is to review and analyze the test results and offer concrete and practical suggestions to the CSE in the following ways:

- Indications of areas of strength and weakness.
- Level of severity of the problem—mild, moderate, or severe.
- Educational implications in determining least restrictive placement.
- Whether the recommendations coincide with the test result findings. For example, in some cases outside agencies or professionals will recommend resource room even though the child's scores do not reflect a disability.
- Whether the new findings support or disagree with past scores. For this you should do some research into the child's historical academic patterns by reviewing prior reports, achievement test scores, and report card grades.
- Whether the findings require modifications and which ones they should be (e.g., revised test format, flexible scheduling).

3. Be prepared. You will look more professional if you come with notes, questions, and suggestions.

3-25. EVALUATIONS THAT MAY BE REQUIRED FOR A CSE PRESENTATION

Psychological Evaluation

A full psychological evaluation including all identifying data, reason for referral, background and developmental history, prior testing results, observations, tests administered, test results (including a breakdown of scaled scores), conclusions, and recommendations is required. This evaluation must be conducted within one year of the CSE meeting. It may also be helpful to include any prior evaluations done over the years.

Educational Evaluation

A psychoeducational evaluation including identifying data, reason for referral, academic history, prior testing results, observations, tests administered, test results, conclusions, and recommendations is required. This report should identify achievement strengths and weaknesses and perceptual strengths and weaknesses.

Speech / Language Evaluation

A Speech/Language evaluation including identifying data, reason for referral, observations, tests administered, test results, conclusions, and recommendations should be included if applicable. A description of the severity of the language deficit should also be included and, if possible, the prognosis.

Reading Teacher's Report

If indicated, a full reading evaluation including identifying data, reason for referral, observations, prior standardized reading test percentiles, tests administered, test results, conclusions, and recommendations should be included. A description of the severity of the deficit, outlining the specific areas in need of remediation, should also be included.

Vocational Evaluation—Aptitude Test Results

A copy of the child's differential aptitude test results or other measures of vocational aptitude should be included where applicable—for middle school and high school students.

Outside Reports

From time to time, parents will have a variety of reports from outside agencies—medical, neurological, psychological, audiological, or visual training. These reports should be included only when they are relevant to the possible disability. If outside reports are to be used in lieu of the district's own evaluations, they should be fairly recent, that is, within the past six months to one year.

3-25. Continued

Assessments Related to the Suspected Disability as Required

These measures may include the following areas: communication skills, motor abilities, hearing, vision, gross motor abilities, fine motor abilities, physical therapist's evaluation, occupational therapist's evaluation, and adaptive physical education evaluation (e.g., Bruininks Oserestsky).

3-26. ACADEMIC DATA REQUIRED FOR A CSE PRESENTATION

Standardized Achievement Test Data from All Grades

This information should reflect standardized test score results, including percentiles, as far back as possible, and is included to allow the members to see patterns, strengths, and weaknesses in the child's group scores.

Report Cards

Elementary Level: Copies of all report cards, including teacher comments (Grades K-6).

Secondary Level: These copies should reflect quarter grades, final grades, and absences beginning with grade 7.

Classroom Teachers' Reports

This report should include a behavioral description of the child's academic, social, intellectual, behavioral, and physical status. Observations should be worded in behavioral terms, and any informal testing results should be included.

Attendance and Disciplinary Reports

Elementary and Secondary Levels: A listing of all disciplinary reports, including reason for referral and disposition should be included. An accurate attendance record should also be included.

Student Class Schedule

A copy of the child's present class schedule should be included, clearly outlining the level of classes enrolled (e.g., modified, regents, etc.) and teachers' names.

Classroom Observation Sheet

This form must be completed by the special education teacher, psychologist, administrator, social worker, or guidance counselor. This form must be included in the CSE packet for an initial referral.

© 1995 by The Center for Applied Research in Education

3-27. OTHER INFORMATION AND PROCEDURES REQUIRED FOR A CSE PRESENTATION

Written Consent for Evaluation

A copy of this form, signed by the parents/guardians of the child, should be included in the packet so that the Committee has a record of the consent as well as an indication of the 30-day time limit.

Draft of Recommended Objectives and Goals

Appropriate members of the PPT should develop a draft of initial goals and objectives. These goals and objectives will be used in the development of the Individual Educational Plan (IEP) at the time of the CSE meeting, and may be modified at the time of the meeting. The form, specific goals and objectives from which to choose, and other factors may differ from district to district.

Some districts may develop this form at the time of the meeting and not require a prior draft. If this is the case, prepare yourself anyway with your own recommended goals and objectives, so that you can contribute to the IEP at the time of the meeting.

Statement of Least Restrictive Environment

If a Pupil Personnel Team is recommending additional services under a classifying condition, state the reasons why additional services or less restrictive environment would be necessary. This statement is also very important if the PPT thinks that the child's needs may be better served in an out-of-district placement. While the final decision for placement is up to the CSE, the school must still substantiate its recommendation.

Parent Rights Booklet—Prior to CSE Meeting

A parent must be given a copy of the state booklet on parents' rights prior to the CSE meeting. This will give parents the opportunity to become familiar with the procedure and develop any questions they might have.

3-28. SPECIAL EDUCATION DOCUMENTATION FOR PHYSICAL AND OCCUPATIONAL THERAPISTS

Listed below are the various types of written documentation that a therapist is required to complete during the school year. Each type of report is discussed in greater detail in the handbooks for the physical and occupational therapies.

▦ Evaluation Report

An evaluation report is required for students new to the program or preschoolers advancing to kindergarten. The evaluation report should be submitted within two weeks of completing the evaluation.

A district-based therapist performs evaluations upon the request of the CSE. Evaluation reports should be completed in a timely fashion.

▦ Annual Review

The annual review should be written in the spring of each school year for all mandated students. The written report should be submitted to the CSE prior to the scheduled annual review.

▦ IEP—Goals and Objectives

Goals and objectives are written within the first 30 school days after a student starts in a special education program. For most students these goals and objectives are completed during the month of September.

▦ Notes—Weekly Treatment Note and Mid-Year Progress Note

A brief note should be written for each student treated weekly. Mid-year progress notes are written for all programs in January.

▦ Evaluation

When a physical and/or occupational therapist is evaluating or annually reviewing a student in regard to termination or continuance of the related service, he or she should evaluate the student totally within the school setting before suggesting a therapy-related recommendation.

The following are recommended steps that a therapist should follow when assessing the need for physical or occupational therapy services in the school setting:

—**Interview the classroom teacher** regarding the student's performance during the school day.

—**Perform an individual evaluation** with standardized and clinical observations.

—**Observe the student** in the classroom, gym, lunchroom or wherever appropriate to see the problems noted during the individual evaluation.

—**Discuss with the appropriate administrator** the program's educational philosophy to determine the most educationally supportive way to render the related service.

3-29. FACTS ABOUT INCLUSION

Inclusion Is

- All children learning in the same school environment with supportive services so that they can be successful in their adjustment and performance
- Having each student's specific needs addressed in the integrated environment of a regular school setting
- All children participating equally in all aspects and functions available within the school
- Educating and providing support for regular classroom teachers who will have disabled children in their classroom
- Educating children to be tolerant of and to respect the differences in one another
- Creating a comfortable environment within which students with and without disabilities can develop healthy social interactions and relationships
- Educating and supporting parents in their concerns
- Allowing parents to participate in the team process responsible for inclusion
- Arranging for appropriate work and educational experiences for disabled children within the community environments
- Using new delivery systems for special education programs that emphasize collaboration between special education staff and classroom teachers
- All children learning together in the same environment, even though their educational needs and prescribed goals may differ
- Making sure that each child has an appropriate individualized educational program

3-29. Continued

Inclusion Is Not

- Dumping children with challenging needs into regular classes without proper supports and services they need to be successful
- Trading the quality of a child's education or the intensive support services the child needs for integration
- Ignoring each child's unique needs
- Sacrificing the education of typical children so that children with challenging needs can be integrated
- All children having to learn the same thing, at the same time, in the same way
- Doing away with or cutting back special education services
- Expecting regular education teachers to teach children who have challenging needs without the support they need to teach all children effectively
- Locating special education classes in separate wings at regular schools
- Ignoring parents' needs
- Maintaining separate schedules for students in special and regular education
- Students with disabilities receiving their education and job training in facilities outside their community

3-30. CONDITIONS OF PUBLIC LAW 504

Coverage

Persons who have, have a record of having, or are regarded as having

- a physical or mental impairment substantially limiting one or more major life activity, but not severe enough to warrant classification under IDEA (Individual Disability Education Act)

Entitlement

- regular or special education and related services

Students covered under Section 504 but not covered under IDEA

- do not have one of the 13 disabilities under IDEA (Note: children with ADD may have a health impairment under IDEA)
- do not need special education but need related services or accommodations to benefit from an education

Students covered under IDEA but not covered under Section 504

- unilateral placements in private schools when the local educational agency has made available (not denied) to a child a free appropriate public education

Funding

- no federal funds available specifically for Section 504
- all agencies receiving any federal funds must comply with section 504

Procedural requirements similar to IDEA

- free education
- evaluation
- least restrictive environment
- procedural due process
- 504 Individual Educational Plan

3-30. Continued

Some equal educational opportunity issues pertinent solely to Section 504

- access to magnet schools
- program accessibility
- access to parents/community members with disabilities to school activities (e.g., parent conferences, board meetings, etc.)

Enforcement

- Office for Civil Rights, U.S. Department of Education

3-31. RIGHTS OF PARENTS OF CHILDREN WITH DISABILITIES

1. Your child is entitled to a free, appropriate public education that meets the unique educational needs of your child at no cost to you.

2. You will be notified whenever the school wishes to evaluate your child, wants to change your child's educational placement, or refuses your request for an evaluation or a change in placement.

3. You may request an evaluation if you think your child needs special education or related services.

4. You should be asked by your school to provide "parent consent," meaning that you understand and agree in writing to the evaluation and initial special education placement for your child. Your consent is voluntary and may be withdrawn at any time.

5. You may obtain an independent low cost evaluation if you disagree with the outcome of the school's evaluation. The school district will supply you with the names of such agencies.

6. You may request a reevaluation if you suspect your child's current educational placement is no longer appropriate. The school must reevaluate your child at least every three years, but your child's educational program must be reviewed at least once during each calendar year.

7. You may have your child tested in the language he or she knows best. For example, if your child's primary language is Spanish, he or she must be tested in Spanish. Also, students who are hearing impaired have the right to an interpreter during the testing.

8. The school must communicate with you in your primary language. The school is required to take whatever action is necessary to ensure that you understand its oral and written communication, including arranging for an interpreter if you are hearing impaired or if your primary language is not English.

9. You may review all of your child's records and obtain copies of these records, but the school may charge you a reasonable fee for making copies. Only you, as parents, and those persons directly involved in the education of your child will be given access to personal records. If you think any of the information in your child's records is inaccurate, misleading, or violates the privacy or other rights of your child, you may request that the information be changed. If the school refuses your request, you then have the right to request a hearing to challenge the questionable information in your child's records.

3-31. Continued

10. You must be fully informed by the school of all the rights provided to you and your child under the law. You may participate in the development of your child's Individualized Education Program (IEP) or, in the case of a child under school age, the development of an Individualized Family Service Plan (IFSP). The IEP and IFSP are written statements of the educational program designed to meet your child's unique needs. The school must make every possible effort to notify you of the IEP or IFSP meeting and arrange it at a time and place agreeable to you. As an important member of the team, you may attend the IEP or IFSP meeting and share your ideas about your child's special needs, the type of program appropriate to meeting those needs, and the related services the school will provide to help your child benefit from his or her educational program.

11. You may have your child educated in the least restrictive school setting possible. Every effort should be made to develop an educational program that will provide the greatest amount of contact with children who are not disabled.

12. You may request a due process hearing to resolve differences with the school that could not be resolved informally.

3-32. WHAT ARE A PARENT'S RESPONSIBILITIES IN THE SPECIAL EDUCATION PROCESS?

1. Develop a partnership with the school or agency. You are now an important member of the team. Share relevant information about your child's education and development. Your observations and suggestions can be a valuable resource to aid your child's progress.

2. Learn as much as you can about your rights and the rights of your child. Ask the school to explain these rights as well as the regulations in effect for your district and state before you agree to a special education program for your child. Contact disability organizations for their publications on special education rights.

3. Ask for clarification of any aspect of the program that is unclear to you. Educational and medical terms can be confusing, so do not hesitate to ask.

4. Make sure you understand the program specified on the IEP or IFSP before agreeing to it or signing it. Ask yourself if what is planned corresponds with your knowledge of your child's needs.

5. Consider how your child might be included in the regular school activities program. Do not forget areas such as lunch, recess, art, music, and physical education.

6. Monitor your child's progress. If your child is not progressing, discuss it with the teacher and determine whether the program should be modified. As a parent, you can initiate review of your child's educational program.

7. Discuss with the school or agency any problems that may occur with your child's assessment, placement, or educational program. It is best to try to resolve problems directly with the agency or school. In some situations, you may be uncertain as to how you should resolve a problem. All states have advocacy agencies that can usually provide you with the guidance you need to pursue your case.

8. Keep records. There may be many questions and comments about your child that you will want to discuss, as well as meetings and phone conversations you will want to remember. It is easy to forget information useful to your child's development and education if it is not written down.

9. Join a parent organization. In addition to the opportunity to share knowledge and support, a parent group can be an effective force on behalf of your child. Many times parents find that as a group they have the power to bring about needed changes that strengthen special services.

© 1995 by The Center for Applied Research in Education

141

3-33. PROCEDURES FOR CHANGING A STUDENT'S CLASSIFICATION OR PLACEMENT

On the Part of the Parent: There may be times when a parent thinks that his or her child's present classification or placement needs to be reviewed and possibly changed. When this occurs the parent should follow the following procedures:

1. While a request for a change of classification or placement can always be made by a parent, there should be some basis for such a request. These may include lack of growth on the part of the child, new diagnostic evaluations indicating another possible cause for the disability, distance from the house of an out-of-district placement, some danger to the child's safety either in transit or at the site, disagreements with the school's educational program, and lack of services.

2. Once parents decide that such a meeting is necessary, they should document their reasons carefully. The presentation to the committee is crucial; other professionals with a great deal of documentation will be present at the same meeting. Try to keep anecdotal records, papers, work samples, incident reports, calls to administration asking for assistance, and any other records that will present a basis for such a request.

3. Once you have developed a packet of information, call the director of the CSE and request a special meeting to discuss your concerns about your child's classification or placement.

4. The director may ask you some questions over the phone but if this occurs, ask for a preliminary meeting with him or her. Many times a compromise or solution may be obtained by such a meeting. If this does not happen, ask for a meeting of the full committee. Keep in mind that even if the chairperson agrees with you, any change in an IEP requires a full meeting of the CSE.

5. If the CSE does not agree with your request, you always have the option of asking for an impartial hearing, which is part of your due process rights. At this meeting an impartial officer—not an employee of the district—will hear both sides and offer a recommendation, usually within 10 days.

On the Part of the School: There may be times when the school thinks that a child's classification or placement needs to be changed. If this occurs, the school should follow certain procedures:

1. The reasons for such a request may include an improvement in a child's performance over a long period of time, possibly indicating declassification (no longer requiring supportive services to maintain adequate school performance); severe difficulties with the present placement and a need for a more restrictive setting; the development of a secondary disability, requiring a change to multiply disabled; or inability to provide appropriate supportive services within the present placement.

3-33. Continued

2. Once the school personnel decide that such a recommendation is necessary, they should contact the chairperson of the CSE and request a special meeting for the purposes of classification or placement review. This usually just requires filling out the necessary form.

3. The school should then call in the parent(s), discuss their concerns, and request a review by the CSE. If the parents have been involved along the way, such a request will not come as a total surprise.

4. The school should then put together a packet of information including but not limited to teachers' comments, work samples, grades, any testing updates, and outside evaluations. This packet should then be sent to the CSE with a cover letter indicating the request for such a meeting and the school's position.

5. The chairperson will then schedule a full meeting of the CSE, which is required for any possible change in an IEP.

6. At the meeting, school personnel should make a thorough presentation for any change in classification and placement; this kind of change constitutes a very serious modification, and the implications for the child are of the greatest concern.

7. If the school is recommending declassification, the child will still be able to receive transitional supportive services for one year. The school should be sure that such a recommendation is made on the basis of a historical pattern of success and not a short-term change. Declassifying and then having to reclassify a student can be traumatic.

8. If the review is based upon the school's perception that a more therapeutic setting is required, documentation should indicate what has been tried and why the school regards the present placement as unsuitable.

9. If the parent disagrees, the school also has the right to ask for an impartial hearing.

3-34. IEP GUIDELINES

There are seven general sections to any IEP.

General Identifying Data

Name:

Address:

Phone:

Date of Birth:

Parent(s)' Names:

Dominant Language of Child:

Dominant Language Spoken at Home:

Date Child Entered Program: (This is filled in only for previously classified students and informs the reader about when the child first started receiving special education services.)

Current Placement Data

Classification (filled in if the child has already been classified)

Grade: Current grade

Current Placement: Regular class for an initial review by the CSE, or special education setting if child has already been classified

Class Size Ratio (filled in only for previously classified students)

Length of Program: 10- or 12-month program

School: Current school

Teacher: Child's current teacher (or guidance counselor if a secondary level student)

Diploma (either a local diploma or an **IEP diploma**—given to classified students who may not meet the school requirements for graduation but have accomplished all the objectives on their IEP)

Transportation (filled in if the child is currently receiving special transportation arrangements)

Physical Education: Current class type—regular or adaptive

Annual Review Date: Usually April, May, or June of the school year

Triennial Review Date: Usually three years from the date of the last full evaluation

© 1995 by The Center for Applied Research in Education

3-34. Continued

Intelligence Test Results: must be within one year of review by CSE and indicates Verbal, Performance, or Full Scale IQ.

Recommendations by the CSE

Classification: The child must fit the criteria for one of the state-defined classification categories, and the disability must significantly impede his or her ability to learn.

Grade: Projected grade for the coming year.

Placement: This depends upon the child's least restrictive educational setting.

Class Size Ratio: Indicates the maximum student population allowed, the number of teachers required and the number of assistant teachers or aides required.

Length of Program: Some special education programs maintain a 10-month calendar. Programs for more seriously disabled students may be 12 months long.

School: Projected school for the coming year.

Teacher: Identifies the child's contact teacher for the coming year. When a child has several special education teachers, as in a departmentalized special education high school program, one teacher is assigned as the contact teacher. On the elementary and secondary levels it can also be the resource room teacher , if the child is assigned there, or the child's self-contained special education teacher if this more restrictive program is used.

Program Initiation Date: Indicates when the special education services will begin.

Transportation Needs: Indicates whether the child has special transportation needs; a severely physically handicapped child may require door-to-door service with a special bus to allow easy access and departure.

Physical Education: Indicates whether the child is being recommended for regular physical education or *adaptive physical education* (a specially designed program of developmental activities, games, sports, and rhythms suited to the interests, capacities, and limitations of pupils with disabilities who may not safely or successfully engage in unrestricted participation in the activities of the regular physical education program.)

Related Services: Defined in List 3-36.

Mainstreamed Courses: A listing must be included on the IEP if the child's disability allows for any mainstreamed class in which the student will participate.

Special Classes: Indicates the types of special education classes the child will have in the coming year, for example, math, social studies, or health.

Testing Information: This section reviews the academic test results, including the tests administered, date administered, percentile, and age or grade equivalents.

145

3-34. Continued

Comments: This section is used to indicate any questions, reminders, reviews, parent concerns, or identified areas of strengths and weakness and progress to date.

Goals and Objectives

Social Development: The degree and quality of the pupil's relationships with peers and adults, feelings about self, and social adjustment to school and community environments.

Physical Development: The degree or quality of the pupil's motor and sensory development, health, vitality, and physical skills or limitations that pertain to the learning process.

Academic Characteristics: The levels of knowledge and development in subject and skill areas, including activities of daily living, level of intellectual functioning, adaptive behavior, expected rate of progress in acquiring skills and information, and learning style.

Management Needs: The nature and degree to which environmental modifications and human material resources are required to enable the pupil to benefit from instruction.

The second part of this section deals with the specific academic goals and objectives that will be remediated. The basis for this area comes from the evaluation and the diagnosis of strengths and weaknesses. Also included in this section may be specific content area goals—science, social studies, math, or English, if the child is in a special education setting for these subjects.

Examples of goals and objective are included under "Mastery Levels."

Mastery Levels

When determining an objective, mastery levels must be considered. A *mastery level* is a predetermined level of competency indicating a clear understanding of a particular skill. This is the teacher's way of validating a child's movement to the next objective.

Setting the mastery levels too low will increase the possibilities that luck or chance will influence success, while setting them too high may set the child up for constant frustration and failure because of careless mistakes or minute errors. Mastery levels can be indicated according to the following standards:

- **ratio-based mastery level:** John will be able to _____ 8 out of every attempts
- **percent-based mastery level:** Mary will be able to _____ 75% of the time
- **time-based mastery level:** Ben will be able to _____ 12 responses within a 10-minute period

There may be times when one general statement of mastery level can apply to all the objectives: *All objectives will be completed with 80% accuracy.*

3-34. Continued

Evaluative Measures

- Student assignments and projects
- Informal conferences between student and teacher
- Student self-evaluation
- Textbook tests and quizzes
- Standardized tests
- Review of quarterly report cards
- Discussions with classroom teachers
- Parent-teacher conferences
- Record of attendance
- Stanford Diagnostic Test
- Teacher-made tests
- Teacher evaluation
- Homework assignments
- Criterion-referenced tests

Alternate Testing Modifications

- Requires flexible scheduling in testing
- Requires testing in a flexible setting
- Requires a revised test format
- Requires extended time for testing
- Requires revised test direction
- Requires the opportunity to record answers in any manner
- Requires the use of a calculator for testing
- Requires the use of a tape recorder for testing
- Requires the use of a typewriter or word processor
- Is in need of a Braille Writer
- Requires questions read; test may be read
- Will not be penalized for spelling errors on tests
- Will have use of computer/word processor for written work to compensate for handwriting/spelling deficits
- Requires enlarged print
- Requires enlarged answer sheets

3-35. SAMPLE IEP FORM

Individualized Educational Plan

STUDENT DATA

Student Name: _____

Date of Birth: _____

Parent(s) Names: _____

Address: _____

_____

Home Telephone: _____

Dominant Language—Home: _____

Dominant Language—Student: _____

RECOMMENDATIONS

Classification: _____

Grade: _____

Placement: _____

Class Size/Ratio: _____

Length of Program: _____

Program Initiation Date: _____

Diploma: _____

Transportation Required: _____

Annual Review Date: _____

Triennial Date: _____

IQ Test Information: Verbal IQ _____ Performance IQ _____ Full Scale IQ _____

Foreign Language Exempt: yes _____ no_____
Physical Education Recommendation: Regular _____ Adaptive _____

3-35. Continued

Related Services Recommended: (Check off those recommended and fill in suggested information)

SERVICE

	Sessions/WK	Minutes/Session
_____ Resource Room	_____	_____
_____ Speech/Language	_____	_____
_____ Physical Therapy	_____	_____
_____ Occupational Therapy	_____	_____
_____ Art Therapy	_____	_____
_____ In-School Counseling—Individual or Group (Circle)	_____	_____

149

3-36. RELATED SERVICES

Related services are other services the child will be receiving that support the academic special education process. Included in this section are the number of sessions per week, minutes per session, maximum group size, start date, and end date. Related services may include the following:

In-school individual counseling: When this service is recommended on an IEP, it usually means that the child would benefit from a more intimate therapeutic situation with emphasis on control, insight, cause-and-effect awareness, special attention, and developing a trusting relationship with an authority figure. While some children need only individual counseling, others might move from individual to group to try out the insights and experiences learned from the individual experience.

In-school group counseling: When this service is recommended on an IEP, it means that the child would benefit from a group situation that emphasizes interpersonal relations, social skills, cooperative play and interaction, interdependence, social delay of gratification, peer feedback, and social connections. The group usually meets once or twice a week and many times may be combined with individual in-school counseling.

Resource room: This service is recommended when the CSE thinks the child would benefit from extra academic assistance—depending on the diagnostic evaluation, IEP recommendation, and teacher observation. This assistance might involve remediation, compensation, or survival skills—depending on the age and grade of the child. Most children will be recommended for a minimum of three hours per week (divided as needed) to a maximum of 50% of the child's school day.

Speech/language therapy: This service is recommended when the CSE believes that the child's poor performance is directly related to disabilities in language or speech development. The emphasis with this service might include remediation in expressive or receptive language, articulation, voice disorders, or fluency disorders. These services may be administered in small-group or individual settings. This recommendation can also be made in conjunction with some other service such as resource room if indicated.

Physical therapy and occupational therapy: This recommendation is usually made by the CSE when the child is suffering from some physical or motor impairment. Physical therapists usually provide exercise therapy and special devices to improve the total physical functioning and strength of a disabled student. Generally, occupational therapists will focus more on fine motor skills such as hand control, using the mouth to chew, and any other factor involved in daily living skills.

Art therapy: This recommendation, while not as common as some other services, is usually recommended when the CSE thinks the production of art in its various forms would have benefits for exceptional students. Major factors involved in this recommendation include the opportunity for the disabled child to express creativity, to improve fine motor skills, and to develop appropriate leisure-time activities.

3-36. Continued

Adaptive physical education: This service is usually recommended when the CSE perceives that the disabled child's general physical development is impaired or delayed. When these programs are instituted, they tend to have a therapeutic orientation. The teachers performing this service must have special training in the use of specialized equipment to improve muscle development and coordination.

Music therapy: This recommendation may be made by the CSE when the committee decides that music can be used to prompt the development of various functional behaviors in disabled students. Examples are motivation, or improvement of speech, language, and communication skills through singing.

151

3-37. STUDENT ELIGIBILITY AND CRITERIA FOR TESTING MODIFICATIONS

Alternate testing techniques take into account the individual needs of a child having a disability, and as a result modify testing procedures or formats. The modifications attempt to provide these students with equal opportunity to participate in testing situations.

These techniques, which must appear on the student's IEP, offer a disabled student the opportunity to demonstrate mastery of skills without being unfairly restricted by the presence of that disability.

Student Eligibility for Use of Testing Techniques

Only students who have been identified as having a disability by the Committee on Special Education normally receive alternate testing techniques. There are, however, three other possible avenues that can be taken to provide alternate testing techniques even if a student is not classified.

1. The law usually allows the school principal the authority to approve a student's need for testing modifications that do not alter the intended purpose of a test for a student who may have a disability that is not severe enough to warrant identification by the CSE. An example of this may be a student who has **ADD** (attention deficit disorder), and as a result may have some mild problems, but they do not constitute a severe discrepancy in his or her functioning.

2. In cases of certain tests, for example, the college entrance SAT, two pieces of documentation from outside professionals (not working in the same agency) indicating the need for alternate testing techniques (e.g., untimed tests) may allow the student these privileges even though the student has not been identified by the CSE

3. Students who receive *transitional services* (services provided to students who have been declassified by the CSE) are entitled to receive services or modifications up to one year after declassification.

Criteria for Allowing Use of Testing Techniques

Alternate testing techniques are determined by the CSE for students identified as having a disability. The Committee takes into account several variables when making this determination:

1. The individual needs of the child as determined by evaluation, observation, background history, and other pertinent information presented at the CSE meeting

2. The necessity for modification in light of the student's past academic and test performance without modifications

3. The student's potential benefit from the modification

The CSE tries to keep in mind that all students could benefit from alternate testing techniques, and as a result a recommendation based just on potential to enhance performance may be inappropriate. The need for modifications must be substantiated in the evaluation results.

3-38. EXAMPLES OF TESTING MODIFICATIONS

Alternate Testing Techniques that Modify Manner of Presentation

Flexible Scheduling. This modification is usually applied for students who may have problems with the rate at which they process information—physical disabilities such as motor or visual impairments. Examples of modifications that fall in this category include:

- untimed tests
- administration of a test in several sessions during the course of the day
- administration of a test in several sessions over several days

Flexible Setting. This modification allows disabled students to take a test in a setting other than a regular classroom. This may become necessary in cases where a child has health impairments and may be unable to leave home or the hospital, or where a child's disability interferes with his or her remaining on task or causes the child to be easily distracted. In other cases a disabled student may require special lighting or acoustics or a specially equipped room. Examples include:

- individual administration of a test in a separate location
- small-group administration of a test in a separate location
- provisions for special lighting
- provisions for special acoustics
- provision for adaptive or special furniture
- administration of a test in a location with minimal distractions

Revised Test Format. This modification is used by students whose disability may interfere with their ability to take a test using the standard test format—students with visual or perceptual disabilities who may not be able to read regular-size print. Examples include:

- use of a large-print edition
- increased spacing between items
- reduction in the number of items per page
- use of a braille edition
- increases size of answer bubbles on test answer forms
- rearrangement of multiple-choice items with answer bubble right next to each choice

3-38. Continued

Revised Test Directions. This modification allows students with certain disabilities a greater chance of understanding directions and thereby successfully completing a test.

- reading directions to child
- rereading the directions for each page of questions
- simplifying the language in the directions
- providing additional examples

Use of Aids. Some disabled students require the use of aids to interpret test items (e.g., hearing-impaired children or those with visual impairment). These may include:

- auditory amplification devices
- visual magnification devices
- auditory tape of questions
- masks or markers to maintain the student's place on a page
- having questions read to the student
- having questions signed to the student

Alternate Testing Techniques that Modify Manner of Response

Use of Aids. These modifications allow a disabled student to record answers to examination questions other than in the conventional manner. These techniques may include:

- the use of a tape recorder
- the use of a typewriter
- the use of a communication device
- the use of a word processor
- the use of an amanuensis (secretary)

Revised Format. Some disabled students may be unable to record their responses to test questions on conventional answer forms and as a result require a change in the test format. These may include:

154

3-38. Continued

■ record answers directly in the test booklet
■ increase in the spacing between questions or problems
■ increase in the size of the answer blocks
■ provision of cues (stop sign, arrows) directly on the answer form

Alternate Testing Techniques that Modify Process Used to Derive Response

Use of Aids. Some students may possess the innate ability to process mathematical information, but have a disability that prohibits them from using paper and pencil to solve computations. Other disabled students may not be able to memorize arithmetic facts but can solve difficult word problems. When these problems occur with disabled students the following modifications are possible:

■ use of a calculator
■ use of an abacus
■ use of arithmetic tables

155

3-39. SPECIAL EDUCATION TEACHER'S ROLE AND RESPONSIBILITIES FOR IMPLEMENTATION OF ALTERNATE TESTING TECHNIQUES

The special education teacher plays a crucial role in the implementation of alternate testing techniques in the following ways:

1. A special education evaluator provides a clear understanding of a child's strengths and weaknesses, his or her learning style, and the effects of the child's disability upon academic performance. With this information in hand, the special education teacher can analyze the need for specific modifications; the need can be substantiated by the results of the evaluation.

2. A special education teacher in a self-contained special education classroom comes in direct contact with the student in classroom instruction. This experience provides a strong basis for recommending specific modifications on a student's IEP.

3. The special education teacher on the CSE provides background experience to assist the committee in recommending appropriate test modifications. They may become part of an initial referral IEP, constitute a change in an IEP during an annual review, or stem from a report from an outside agency.

4. The special education teacher can also assist the parent of a special education student in understanding alternate testing techniques and available options.

5. The special education teacher may serve as a consultant to teachers, parents, and administrators and offer advice on testing modifications to students.

6. The special education teacher may monitor the implementation of assigned modifications for a particular student to ensure that the student's rights are being honored.

3-40. ALTERNATIVE EDUCATIONAL DELIVERY SYSTEMS

Alternative delivery systems are management systems that provide support for students and maximize learning for them while they are being presented with the core curriculum. This approach uses success-oriented presentations and the elements of collaboration and school-based coordination in its implementation. The goal of alternative delivery systems is to develop many creative ways of working together for the benefit of all students.

The following are examples of how school specialists (e.g., the psychologist or special education teacher) can assist the classroom teacher in the delivery of information to students.

The impact of alternative delivery systems can be the following:

- more assistance provided to all students in general classrooms
- increased support for classroom teachers to expand the use of a range of instructional strategies for diverse student needs
- increased teacher effectiveness
- improved student academic performance and behavior
- increased classroom teacher understanding and skills, and confidence in intervening with students at risk
- increased coordination of individualized and classroom instruction

Collaborative Consultation

Collaborative consultation is a peer relationship, in which the partners recognize their own limits and their professional and personal biases in the effort to seek out information, materials, and strategies necessary to meet students' needs. It is an interactive process that enables teams of people from diverse areas of expertise to generate creative solutions to jointly defined problems. It is a one-to-one, indirect service delivery model.

After planning instruction through collaborative consultation, the classroom teacher has responsibility for monitoring the implementation plan. The special educator's role in this model is one of facilitator. It involves a variety of interpersonal skills including brainstorming, active listening, effective communication, and questioning.

Cooperative Teaching

Cooperative teaching is an educational approach in which general and special educators, as well as specialists from other categorical programs, are simultaneously present in the general education classroom, sharing responsibility for some specific classroom instruction. Cooperative teaching represents the implementation phases of program planning that evolve out of collaborative consultation.

3-40. Continued

Cooperative teaching can actively assist students currently receiving education programming in segregated or strictly pull-out programs with the transition back into the general education classroom. It makes integration successful, since the classroom teacher is teamed with the specialist. In the long term, collaborative teaching can be a preventive measure; for students with academic difficulties, the possibility of early intervention coupled with specific instruction in strategies to access the curriculum can greatly decrease the need for traditional services. Team teaching, complementary instruction, and supported learning activities are three examples of approaches to cooperative teaching.

Team Teaching

General and special educators jointly plan to teach academic subject content to all students. The general education teacher remains responsible for the entire class while the special educator is responsible for implementing the IEP for special education students.

Complementary Instruction

The general education teacher assumes primary responsibility for teaching specific subject matter, while the specialist has responsibility for teaching academic survival skills necessary for the student to access and master the core curriculum. The content may be delivered in the classroom and complemented when the special education student is pulled out of the classroom to another setting. The critical difference between complementary instruction and the traditional pull-out program is that two professionals prepare instruction together and it is delivered in the general classroom.

Supportive Learning Activities

The general educator introduces academic content and the specialist develops and implements learning activities designed to reinforce the specific content. The educators work together to develop and deliver the instructional content in the regular classroom even though each is responsible for a particular phase of development.

3-41. LEAST RESTRICTIVE EDUCATIONAL PLACEMENT

The concept of *least restrictive education* (LRE) applies to the placement of disabled students in the most advantageous educational setting for their needs. Contrary to the belief of many teachers and parents, LRE does not mean placing every disabled student in a regular classroom. The concept should be fully understood by special education teachers so that they can relieve the anxiety of teachers, parents, and students when it comes to appropriate educational placement.

The placement of disabled students is the responsibility of the Committee on Special Education with the input of staff and consent of parents. The CSE must analyze all the available information and determine the best "starting placement" for the child, to ensure success and provide the child with the highest level of stimulation and experience for his or her specific disability and profile of strengths and weaknesses.

To accomplish this task, the CSE has a variety of placements from which to choose. These placements range in levels of restriction—including class size, student-teacher ratio, length of program, and degree of mainstreaming.

Children should be placed in a more restrictive environment only if it is to their educational advantage; however, they should be moved to a less restrictive setting as soon as they are capable of being educated in that environment.

The placements below follow a path from least restrictive to most restrictive.

1. **Regular class placement.** This placement is the least restrictive placement for all nondisabled children; however, without some type of special education supportive services, it is not suitable for a disabled child and is usually not considered suitable by the CSE.

2. **Regular class placement with consulting teacher assistance.** A consultant teacher model is used when supportive special education services are required but the CSE determines that the child will be better served while remaining in the classroom rather than being pulled out for services.

3. **Regular class placement with some supportive services.** This placement may be used with mildly disabled students who require supportive services but can remain in the regular class for the majority of the day. The services that may be applied to this level include adaptive physical education, speech and language therapy, in-school individual or group counseling, physical therapy, and occupational therapy.

4. **Regular class placement with itinerant specialist assistance—itinerant services** (services subcontracted by the district and provided by outside agencies). These services are usually provided for students when the disability is such that the district wishes to maintain the child in the district but there are not a sufficient number of students with that disability to warrant hiring a teacher. An example of this is a hearing-impaired child who can maintain a regular class placement as long as supportive itinerant services are provided by a teacher specializing in hearing impairments.

159

3-41. Continued

5. **Regular class placement with resource room assistance.** This placement is usually provided for students who need supportive services but can successfully remain within the regular classroom for the majority of the day. This program is a "pull-out" program; the services are usually provided in a separate room. The student-teacher ratio with this type of service is usually 5:1 and the amount of time spent within the resource room cannot exceed 50% of the child's day.

6. **Part-time mainstreaming.** This placement is for students who need a more restrictive setting for learning, behavioral, or intellectual reasons. These students cannot be successful in a full-time regular class or with a "pull-out" supportive service, but they can be successfully mainstreamed for a part of the school day. The nature of the mainstream is determined by the special education teacher.

7. **Full-time special class in a regular school.** This placement is viewed as the LRE setting for students whose disability does not permit successful participation in any type of regular class setting, even for part of the day. These are students who usually require a very structured, closely monitored program on a daily basis, but not one so restrictive as to warrant an out-of-district placement. These students can handle the rules and structure of a regular school building, but not the freedom or style of a less restrictive setting within the school.

8. **Special day school outside the school district.** This type of restrictive educational setting is a desirable placement for students whose disability is so severe that they may require a more totally therapeutic environment and closer monitoring by specially trained special education teachers or staff members. The child is transported at district expense to the placement and most states try to limit travel time on the bus to less than one hour.

These programs may have student-teacher-aide ratios of 6:1:1, 6:1:2, 9:1:1, 9:1:2, 12:1:1, or 15:1:1 depending upon the severity of the child's disability. The more severe the disability the lower the number of the student-teacher ratio. These programs can run 10 or 12 months, again depending upon the severity of the disability and the individual needs of the child.

9. **Residential school.** In residential placements, the disabled student receives his or her education within this setting and usually resides there for the school term. The nature and length of home visits depend upon several factors that are usually determined by the residential school staff after evaluation and observation. For some students, home visits may not take place at all, while others may go home every weekend.

Some students are placed in residential schools by the court. In this case, the child's local school district is responsible only for the costs of the educational portion, including related services if needed.

10. **Homebound instruction.** This very restrictive setting is usually provided for students who are in transition between programs and have yet to be placed. It should never be used as a long-term placement because of the social restriction and limitations.

3-41. Continued

This option is also used when a child is restricted to his or her house because of an illness or injury, and it is the only realistic educational service until the child recovers. Homebound instruction requires an adult at home when the teacher arrives. Under certain circumstances, it may be held at a community center, library, or some other site deemed appropriate by the CSE.

11. **Hospital or institution.** The most restrictive setting used is a hospital or institutional setting. While this is the most restrictive setting, it may be the LRE setting for students in certain cases, for example, attempted suicide, pervasive clinical depression, severe or profound retardation.

3-42. OTHER SPECIALISTS AND THEIR ROLE IN HELPING CHILDREN

- **Audiologists** are trained to identify and measure types and degrees of hearing loss, assess how disabling the condition is, recommend rehabilitation, fit hearing aids, and counsel parents on how to help their child adjust to a hearing loss.

- **Occupational Therapists** are trained to build or rehabilitate the basic skills involved in everyday living by developing treatment activities and by adapting materials to suit the special needs of the child who is disabled. They focus on fine motor activities, especially the use of hands and fingers, coordination, and self-help skills.

- **Ophthalmologists** are physicians who specialize in the diagnosis of the eye and structures related to it.

- **Orthopedists** are surgeons who specialize in preserving and restoring the function of the skeletal system as well as muscles, joints, tendons, ligaments, nerves, and blood vessels.

- **Pediatricians** are physicians who specialize in the treatment of children, their development and care, and their diseases.

- **Physical Therapists** are skilled in the techniques of treatment to rehabilitate and restore fundamental body movements after illness or injury. PTs work under the supervision of a physician. Their focus is on large muscle and gross motor activities.

- **Psychiatrists** are physicians who specialize in the diagnosis and treatment of emotional problems and mental disorders. They are trained in psychotherapy.

- **Psychologists** are trained in the assessment and treatment of people with emotional, interpersonal, or behavioral problems. They work in a variety of settings—schools, clinics, mental health centers, and hospitals. School psychologists specialize in counseling school children and their families. They also work with families, teachers, and other school staff to improve the child's ability to function in a school setting. Psychological testing done in schools is done only by psychologists. A behavioral psychologist specializes in the objective observation and analysis of behavior, and in developing behavior management programs.

- **Speech Pathologists** are trained in the study of human communication—its normal development and its disorders. They evaluate the reception, integration, and expression of speech and language of children or adults, and assist in treating whatever problems exist.

PART 4

Specific Disabilities

4-1. PRINCIPLES OF NORMAL DEVELOPMENT

A child's developmental progression follows orderly step-by-step sequences where each achievement paves the way for the next one.

Individual differences among children also tend to remain apparent over time.

As a child's development progresses, small elements of behavior (e.g., finger movements) are combined and linked into larger, practical behaviors (e.g., grasping objects).

A child's developmental progress is often intermittent and the rate of change in one area of proficiency may vary while other skills are being learned.

Growth and development may vary in terms of rate among individual children and among different developmental areas within the same children.

Individual differences are evident in young children at a very early age.

Each child develops at his or her own pace and capability.

Motor development and voluntary movements progress from the head downward and from the trunk outward.

The continuity of development is basically the same for all children.

All areas of development (e.g., motor, conceptual, etc.) are interrelated.

Critical periods of learning are part of every child's developmental sequence. These are times during which children show that they are ready for new learning.

Preceding and following critical periods of learning, the child may exhibit periods where learning may prove to be more difficult.

Most children exhibit subtle behavioral mannerisms to their caregivers about their needs and readiness for new learning. A child's learning potential is best served when the stimulation provided matches the child's facility to learn a new task.

As children develop increasing capacities for learning and doing, they tend to use these capacities.

The outcome of development is governed by the nature/nurture principle which is influenced by many factors, including a child's genetic make-up, social environment, and family structure.

4-2. GROSS MOTOR DEVELOPMENTAL MILESTONES

Example of Activity	*Approximate Age*
▦ Able to raise chin while lying on stomach	1 month
▦ Raises chest while lying on stomach	2 months
▦ Able to reach for objects but misses	3 months
▦ Head set forward, steady, lumbar curvature	4 months
▦ Able to turn over	4–6 months
▦ Able to sit on lap and grasp object	5 months
▦ Can sit in high chair and grasp dangling object	6 months
▦ Sits with good posture	10 months
▦ Creeps and crawls	11 months
▦ Pulls to standing position	11 months
▦ Climbs stairs steps	13 months
▦ Walks alone unsupported, seldom falls	18 months
▦ Sits self in small chair	18 months
▦ Walks carrying large objects	20 months
▦ Raises self from sitting position with hips first	22 months
▦ Runs well without falling	2 years
▦ Kicks ball without overbalancing	2 years
▦ Jumps with both feet in place	2 1/2 years
▦ Picks up objects from floor without falling over	2 1/2 years
▦ Stands on one foot even momentarily	3 years
▦ Pedals tricycle	3 years

166

4-3. RECEPTIVE LANGUAGE MILESTONES

Receptive

Activity	*Approximate Age*
Understands few words	11 months
Points to one named body part on request	1 year
Stops activity to name	1 year
Stops activity in response to "no"	1 year
Points to familiar persons, animals, toys on request	15 months
Follows one-step simple commands	15 months
Points to three named body parts on request	17 months
Follows two-step command	20 months
Points to five or six pictures of common objects on request	21 month
Points to five body parts on self or doll	22 months
Follows three-step command given in one long utterance	2 years
Understands 200–400 words	2 years
Understands 800 words	3 years
Verbalizes past experiences	3 years
Points to *big, little, soft, loud*	3 years
Follows commands with two to three actions	4 years
Understands approximately 1,500 words	4 years

167

4-4. EXPRESSIVE LANGUAGE MILESTONES

Expressive

Activity	*Approximate Age*
Says first word	10 months
Shakes head and says "no-no"	11 months
Imitates the sounds of others (e.g., "mama")	1 year
Uses three words in speaking vocabulary	13 months
Use of verbs appears	14 months
Uses at least six words	17 months
Refers to self by name	21 months
Uses "me" and "you"	23 months
Says 50–200 words	2 years
Knows full name	2 years
Uses plurals	2 years
Asks questions	2 1/2 years
Uses negatives in speech	2 1/2 years
Enunciates vowel sounds	3 years
Enunciates consonant sounds	3 years
Speech is 75%–80% intelligible	3 years
Uses three- and four-syllable words	4 years
Says six- to eight-word sentences	4 years
Speech is about 90%–95% intelligible	4 years

4-5. MILESTONES FOR EATING SKILLS

Activity	Approximate Age
Sucks and swallows liquids	Birth
Gagging reflex	Birth
Sucks and swallows liquids supplied from spoons	2 months
Eats strained baby foods from spoon	3 months
Brings hand against bottle when eating	3 months
Sips from a cup that is held	4 months
Becomes excited when hearing sounds of food preparation	4 months
Holds spoon but needs assistance	5 months
Can feed self soft food	6 months
Begins to bite and chew food	6 months
Holds own bottle	7 months
Can chew small lumpy food	8 months
Can take bottle out of mouth and replace it	9 months
Can use fingers to feed himself or herself	10 months
Holds cup with two hands	1 year
Chews table food	13–15 months
Can grasp spoon and place in mouth with some spilling	15 months
Can manage spoon without assistance with little spilling	1 1/2 years
Requests food when hungry	23 months
Requests liquids when thirsty	23 months
Can hold a small glass with one hand unassisted	2 years
Can use a fork to grab food	3 years
Can spread butter on bread	3 years
Can help set table	4 years
Can use a fork to separate food	4 years
Can pour water from a pitcher into a glass	4 years
Can use a knife to cut food	5 years
Can set the table without assistance	6 years

4-6. MILESTONES FOR DRESSING SKILLS

Activity	Approximate Age
Can pull and tug at clothing	3–4 months
Cooperates in dressing by holding out limbs	1 year
Can remove shoes by self	14 months
Can place socks on feet by self	18 months
Can put on own hat	18 months
Can pull up pants	18 months
Can unzip	18–20 months
Attempts to put on own shoes	19 months
Can partially dress self	2 years
Pulls up pants	2 years
Undresses self	30 months
Can put on shirt and coat	30 months
Attempts to place shoes on feet	30 months
Can choose own outfit	3 years
Can unbutton clothes	3 years
Places clothing on in the correct direction	42 months
Can dress and undress with supervision (not including shoe laces)	48 months
Can button front buttons on clothing	52–56 months
Can zip up and down and can snap simple snaps	60 months
Can tie shoes with bows	66 months
Can unlace bows on shoes with no problem	66 months
Dresses self completely	66 months

4-7. MILESTONES FOR TOILETING AND GROOMING SKILLS

Activity	Approximate Age

Grooming

Activity	Approximate Age
Holds on to side of tub and cries when removed	5 months
Splashes water with hands and feet	6 months
Grimaces when face is washed with cloth	6 months
Exhibits resistance to washing face	8 months
Can open and pull out drawers	1 1/2 years
Can wash hands and face by self but not well	2 years
Can wash front of body while in bath	2 years
Can run a brush through hair	2 1/2 years
Can brush teeth with assistance	3 1/2 years
Can wash and dry face with towel by self	4 years
Can brush teeth with no assistance	4 years
Can put away own toys by self with supervision	4 years
Can hang up coat by self on hook	4 years
Brushes hair independently	5 years
Hangs up own clothes without supervision	5 years
Washes self alone	6 years

Toileting

Activity	Approximate Age
About four bowel movements a day associated with waking up	1 month
Two bowel movements a day either at waking or after being fed	2 months
Some delay shown between feeding and elimination	4 months
Stays dry for one- to two-hour intervals	7 months
May awaken at night and cry to be changed	1 1/2 years
May indicate wet pants	1 1/2 years

4-7. Continued

▦ Has only occasional accidents	22 months
▦ Uses same word for both functions of elimination	22 months
▦ Begins to differentiate between elimination functions	2 years
▦ Climbs on to toilet by self	2 1/2 years
▦ Can control bladder for up to five hours	2 1/2 years
▦ Begins to develop a routine for elimination	3 years
▦ Attempts to wipe self but not successful	3 1/2 years
▦ Stays dry at night	4 years
▦ Can toilet self without assistance	5 years
▦ Washes and dries own hands after toileting	5 years
▦ One bowel movement a day	5 years

4-8. COMMON DEVELOPMENTAL DISORDERS

1-Developmental Disorders

MENTAL DISABILITY

Description: This group of disorders is characterized by severe delayed development in the acquisition of cognitive, language, motor, or social skills. The general characteristics of this diagnostic category are

- consistent and significant subaverage intellectual performance

- significant deficits in the development of adaptive functioning

- onset prior to the age of 18

Types: There are several subtypes that are classified by educational or psychological terminology. They are:

Educational Category	DSM-IV-R Classification	IQ Range	DSM-IV-R Code
Educable Mentally Retarded	Mild	55–77.5 approx.	317.0
Trainable Mentally Retarded	Moderate	35–55 approx.	318.0
Severely Mentally Retarded	Severe	25–35 approx.	318.1
Profoundly Mentally Retarded	Profound	below 25	318.2

Educational Implications: The more severe the category, the greater the possibility of associated features being present, like seizures, or visual, auditory, or cardiovascular problems. Other educational implications involve poor social skills, severe academic deficits, and possible behavioral manifestations such as impulsivity, low frustration tolerance, aggressiveness, low self-esteem, and in some cases self-injurious behavior.

Possible Least Restrictive Educational Setting: Least restrictive educational settings for this type of student usually range anywhere from self-contained in a regular school with mainstreaming options for educable students to institutionalization for profoundly retarded individuals.

2-Pervasive Developmental Disorders

AUTISTIC DISORDER

Description: A very serious developmental disorder characterized by severe impairment in the development of verbal and nonverbal communication skills, marked impairment in reciprocal social interaction (a lack of responsiveness to, or interest in, people) and an almost nonexistent imaginative activity. Also known as *infantile autism* or *Kanner's syndrome.*

4-8. Continued

Educational Implications: Poor social skills, impaired cognitive functioning and language. The onset of puberty may increase oppositional or aggressive behavior. Other complications may include seizures and low intellectual development.

Possible Least Restrictive Educational Setting: Most children with this condition require the most restrictive educational setting possible. The student-teacher ratios are usually 6:1:2 or smaller because of the close supervision required. Those who are not capable of maintaining this type of setting may have to be institutionalized. In rare cases, the individual may improve to the point of completing formal education or advanced degrees.

3-Specific Developmental Disorders

DEVELOPMENTAL ARITHMETIC DISORDER

Description: A serious marked disability in the development of arithmetic skills. This condition, often called *dyscalculia,* cannot be explained by mental retardation, inadequate teaching, or primary visual or auditory defects, and may be consistent throughout school.

Educational Implications: Seriously impaired mathematical ability, which may require modifications like extended time, use of a calculator, flexible setting for tests, and revised test format. Other implications may involve poor self-esteem, social self-consciousness, and avoidance—which may increase secondary problems.

Possible Least Restrictive Educational Setting: Children with this disorder may receive assistance through special educational services like resource room or a consultant teacher, and are usually able to maintain placement within a normal class setting.

4-Developmental Expressive Writing Disorder

Description: This disorder is characterized by a serious impairment in the ability to develop expressive writing skills, and it significantly interferes with the child's academic achievement. This condition is not the result of mental retardation, inadequate educational experiences, visual or hearing defects, or neurological dysfunction.

Symptoms: The symptoms associated with this disorder include an inability to compose appropriate written text, coupled with serious and consistent spelling errors, grammatical or punctuation errors, and very poor organization of thought and text.

Educational Implications: Teachers should be aware that these children may exhibit a series of symptoms including avoidance, procrastination, denial, and possibly disruptive behaviors when written assignments are involved—as a means of covering up the seriousness of the disorder.

Possible Least Restrictive Educational Setting: Children with this disorder may receive assistance through special educational services like resource room or a consultant teacher, and are usually able to maintain placement within a normal class setting.

4-8. Continued

5-Developmental Reading Disorder

Description: The more common features of this disorder include a marked impairment in the development of the child's decoding and comprehension skills, which significantly interfere in the child's academic performance. As with most developmental disorders, this condition is not the result of mental retardation, inadequate educational experiences, visual or hearing defects, or neurological dysfunction. It is commonly referred to as *dyslexia*.

Symptoms: Typical symptoms of this disorder include a slow, halting reading pace, frequent omissions, loss of place on a page, skipping lines while reading without awareness, distortions, substitutions of words, and a serious inability to recall what has been read.

Educational Implications: Teachers should be aware that early diagnosis of this disorder is crucial to avoid serious secondary symptoms of poor self-esteem, behavior disorders, and educational failure. Teachers should focus on the possible symptoms exhibited by children with this disorder so that they can assist in early identification of this high-risk child. Teachers should also be aware of the various reading techniques used to assist children with this disorder.

Possible Least Restrictive Educational Setting: Children with this disorder may receive assistance through special educational services like resource room or a consultant teacher, and are usually able to maintain placement within a normal class setting.

6-Developmental Expressive Language Disorder

Description: This disorder is characterized by a serious impairment in the child's ability to develop expressive language. This condition is not the result of mental retardation, inadequate educational experiences, visual or hearing defects, or neurological dysfunction.

Educational Implications: Teachers should be aware that from 3% to 10% of school-aged children suffer from this disorder, which may greatly hamper a child's social interaction skills as well as academic performance.

Possible Least Restrictive Educational Setting: Children with this disorder may receive assistance through special educational services like resource room, a consultant teacher, or speech therapy, and are usually able to maintain placement within a normal class setting.

7-Developmental Articulation Disorder

Description: Children with this disorder have consistent problems using developmentally expected speech sounds, including but not limited to misarticulations, substitutions, or omissions—often sounding very similar to a more infantile form of speech. This condition is not the result of mental retardation; neurological, intellectual, or hearing disorders; or oral speech mechanism defects.

4-8. Continued

Educational Implications: The prognosis for complete recovery with this disorder is very positive, especially when speech therapy is part of the treatment plan. In some milder cases, the condition may run its course by age 8 without intervention.

Possible Least Restrictive Educational Setting: Children with this disorder may receive assistance through special educational services like resource room, a consultant teacher, or speech therapy, and are usually able to maintain placement within a normal class setting.

8-Developmental Receptive Language Disorder

Description: This disorder is characterized by a serious impairment in the child's ability to develop language comprehension. This condition is not the result of mental retardation, inadequate educational experiences, visual or hearing defects, or neurological dysfunction.

Educational Implications: Teachers should be aware that children with this disorder may have a difficult time communicating with gestures and actively participating in activities that require imaginary play.

Possible Least Restrictive Educational Setting: Children with this disorder may receive assistance through special educational services like resource room, a consultant teacher, or speech therapy, and are usually able to maintain placement within a normal class setting.

4-9. CHILDHOOD IMMUNIZATION CHECKLIST

Children need immunizations against polio, diphtheria, tetanus, pertussis (whooping cough), measles, rubella (German measles), and mumps in order to be protected against these diseases.

Please keep in mind that the charts give average ages:

2 months old	DTP (Diptheria-Tetanus-Pertussis) TOPV (Trivalent oral polio vaccine)
4 months old	DTP TOPV
6 months old*	DTP
15 months old	measles vaccine** rubella vaccine** mumps vaccine**
18 months old	DTP (booster) TOPV (booster)
4 to 6 years (school entry)	DTP (booster) TOPV (booster)

Thereafter, a Tetanus-diphtheria (Td) booster should be given every 10 years or following a dirty wound if a booster has not been given in the preceding five years.

*In some regions, doctors may give an optional dose of TOPV at this age.

**Some states recommend that these be given in a combined injection (MMR). A tuberculin skin test may also be administered.

For further information regarding immunization, contact a pediatrician.

4-10. CONTRIBUTING INDIVIDUALS IN THE FIELD OF CHILD DEVELOPMENT

Jerome Bruner. Bruner's major contributions centered around his concerns about cognitive development in children, including the presentation and sequencing of information to children in the manner most appropriate for the child's level of understanding. Bruner also stressed the impact of schools on the process of education and learning; he thought that school was one of the most important reasons that children exhibited differences in cognitive development.

J. McVicker Hunt. Hunt's contribution to child development centered around his belief that intelligence was not fixed and could be enhanced by preschool enrichment experiences. His theories and influence advanced the concept of preschool education.

Benjamin Bloom. Bloom was a firm believer in the need for a variety of experiences during child development and that these experiences had their greatest effect during the periods of rapid change associated with early development. Bloom also believed that 50% of an individual's intelligence is developed by the age of four.

Maria Montessori. Montessori's contributions to child development centered around the preschool years. She felt that the teacher played a crucial role in the development of cognition in early childhood and that the teacher should be a highly skilled observer. This skill would enable the teacher to formulate specific and individualized learning activities for children.

Alfred Binet. While Binet is best remembered for being the originator of the intelligence test, he never believed that intelligence was a fixed factor in development. His contributions to the field of retardation and attempts to raise intelligence have contributed greatly to the understanding of child development.

Jean Piaget. Piaget is best remembered for his work in the area of cognitive and moral development in children. Piaget theorized that all children move through the same cognitive stages of development, which are loosely tied to chronological ages, and are highly dependent upon the quality of the learning opportunities in the child's environment.

Arnold Gesell. Gesell's contributions to child development centered around his observations of children and descriptions of behaviors and the ages at which they appeared. He believed that the early years of development were crucial as the foundations of later development. As a result, Gesell placed great emphasis on critical stages of learning at specific chronological ages.

4-11. CRITERIA USED TO DIAGNOSE AUTISM

Kanner

■ The child shows an inability to relate to people, and extreme autistic aloneness.

■ The child fails to assume an anticipatory posture in preparation for being picked up.

■ The child exhibits speech problems such as delayed echolalia or repetition of personal pronouns; may be mute.

■ The child shows an anxious, obsessive desire for the maintenance of sameness.

■ The child shows a limitation in the variety of spontaneous activity.

■ The child may show behavioral awareness to such things as food, loud noises, and moving objects.

■ The child seems interested in objects and may not be able to distinguish between people and those objects. As a result, people and objects are treated as one.

■ The child may show excellent rote memory.

■ The child may appear to be physically normal.

■ The child may come from a highly intelligent family.

Rutter

■ The child exhibits profound and general failure to develop social relationships.

■ The child exhibits language retardation with impaired comprehension, echolalia, and pronominal reversal.

■ The child exhibits ritualistic or compulsive phenomena.

■ The child may show repetitive movements.

■ The child may exhibit a short attention span.

■ The child may resort to frequent self-injury.

■ The child may exhibit delayed bowel movements.

DSM IV-R

■ Marked lack of awareness of the existence or feelings of others

■ No or abnormal seeking of comfort at times of distress

■ No or impaired imitation

■ No or abnormal social play

■ Gross impairment in ability to make peer friendships

■ No mode of communication, such as communicative babbling, facial expression, gesture, mime, or spoken language

4-11. Continued

- Markedly abnormal nonverbal communication
- Absence of imaginative activity
- Marked abnormalities in the production of speech, including volume, pitch, stress, rate, rhythm, and intonation
- Marked abnormalities in the form of content of speech, including stereotyped and repetitive use of speech
- Marked impairment in the ability to initiate or sustain a conversation with others, despite adequate speech
- Stereotyped body movements
- Persistent preoccupation with parts of objects
- Marked distress over changes in trivial aspects of the environment
- Unreasonable insistence on following routines in precise detail
- Marked restricted range of interests and a preoccupation with one narrow interest

4-12. INTERDISCIPLINARY DIAGNOSIS OF AUTISM

Audiologist. The autistic child may be evaluated by an audiologist either as part of a multidisciplinary assessment or as a referral from a pediatrician who wants to rule out a hearing loss as a possible cause for the child's lack of responsiveness. Specialized procedures and equipment for eliciting responses to sounds have been developed for other groups of people who are difficult to test and they can be applied to autistic children. Two such methods are:

> **CORA** (Conditioned Orienting Reflex Audiometry)—a technique involving the pairing of an attractive visual object with a sound

> **TROCA** (Tangible Reinforcement Operant Conditioning Audiometry)—a technique using a machine that dispenses edible reinforcement (candy) when the child pushes a button in response to a sound)

Social Worker. The social worker contributes to the diagnostic process by providing the team with information on family dynamics, patterns of interaction among various family members, family members' perception of the autistic child, parenting responsibilities, and parent's use of behavior management techniques.

Pediatrician. When dealing with an autistic child, the physician first obtains the medical history from records and the parents without the child present. Second, the child is observed in the examination room with the parents present. The information gathered includes activity level, general state of physical health and development, and gross and fine motor coordination. Third, the general physical and neurological examinations are conducted with special attention directed toward looking for indicators of organic, not psychological, dysfunction. A diagnosis of autism is not made by the pediatrician, though it may be suggested in the conclusions.

Psychiatrist/Psychologist. The psychiatrist and the psychologist are responsible for the diagnosis of autism and the psychological evaluations involved in this process. When first approached by parents, psychiatrists and psychologists gather pertinent developmental history. This information—coupled with clinical interviews, evaluations, and parent intakes—assists in the diagnosis of autism.

Special Education Teacher. The special education teacher may be involved on two separate levels. He or she may first be involved in the diagnostic evaluation of the child suspected of a disability. Second, the special education teacher will be responsible for carrying out the services required for the education of the child.

Speech and Language Therapist. The parents of a potentially autistic child frequently begin their search for diagnostic answers at a speech and hearing clinic, since the child is unresponsive to speech and has either no language or unusual patterns of communication. The speech and language pathologist evaluates movement and behavior, cognitive skills, expressive language, deviant language patterns, and receptive language.

4-13. TEACHER'S CHECKLIST FOR ATTENTION DEFICIT DISORDER

Accurate and early diagnosis is crucial for the child with attention deficit disorder. This will facilitate a treatment plan and reduce the chances of secondary problems. Follow the checklist below if you think the child in your room may have attention deficit disorder. Compare the child's behavior with the following list of symptoms:

1. Inattention—At Least Three of the Following:

- The child often fails to finish things he or she starts.
- The child often doesn't seem to listen.
- The child is easily distracted.
- The child has difficulty concentrating on schoolwork or other tasks requiring sustained attention.
- The child has difficulty sticking to a play activity.

2. Impulsivity—At Least Three of the Following:

- The child often acts before thinking.
- The child shifts excessively from one activity to another.
- The child has difficulty organizing work.
- The child needs a lot of supervision.
- The child frequently calls out in class.
- The child has difficulty awaiting turn in games or group situations.

3. Hyperactivity—At Least Two of the Following:

- The child runs about or climbs on things excessively.
- The child has difficulty sitting still or fidgets excessively.
- The child has difficulty staying seated.
- The child moves about excessively during sleep.
- The child is always "on the go," or acts as if "driven by a motor."

4. Onset before the age of 7

5. Duration of at least 6 months

6. Not due to schizophrenia, affective disorders (disturbance of mood), or profound retardation

Procedures to Follow if Attention Deficit Disorder Is Suspected

1. See if the observed behaviors appear in the classroom as well as other school areas.

2. If they do, ask the school psychologist to observe the child.

4-13. Continued

3. If he or she agrees that such a possibility exists, have the psychologist notify the parent so that the family's doctor can examine the child. He or she may suggest a neurological examination to determine the presence of the disorder. Medication may or may not be suggested.

4. If the disorder is diagnosed, meet with the parent and psychologist to plan a management program at home and in school.

5. If the disorder is serious and affects the child's ability to learn, he or she may need to be reviewed by your district's Committee on Special Education so that a suitable program can be determined.

6. A full psychological and academic evaluation would also assist in determining a proper course of action.

In conclusion, early diagnosis and active treatment will greatly enhance the child's opportunity for a meaningful life both at home and in school.

4-14. TREATMENT PLANS FOR CHILDREN WITH ATTENTION DEFICIT DISORDER

Psychotherapy

- This process will help the child increase self-esteem, vent feelings and conflicts that may give rise to other symptoms, and gain some control over impulsive actions, and it will assist parents with their approach to behavior management.

- Some therapies may utilize a form of treatment called behavior modification, whereby children, assisted by parents and teachers, learn to modify unacceptable behavior through the use of a variety of management techniques including incentive systems, daily report cards, time out, and selective attention. Some treatment plans will include a combination of medication and psychotherapy.

Pharmacological Intervention (medication)

- The types of medication used may vary with age and severity.
- The most common psychostimulants include Ritalin, Cylert, and Dexedrine.
- Such stimulants tend to heighten the child's awareness of the world around him or her and allow for greater selectiveness of behavior. Approximately 50% of children with this disorder (ADHD) will exhibit a decrease in inappropriate symptoms. Approximately 10% respond so positively to this intervention that their behavior reaches the normative range.
- Other reports indicate improvements in attention span, classroom behavior, and ability to think more clearly during academic tasks.
- Keep in mind that such medication does not "cure" attention deficit hyperactivity disorder; it merely alleviates the primary symptoms.
- Other studies have indicated adverse side effects such as reduction of weight, nausea, and loss of appetite. Usually such symptoms can be relieved by regulating the dosage.

Family Therapy

This process assists parents in developing techniques that will reduce frustration at home in both the child and other family members.

School-Teacher Consultation

- Any treatment plan must include ongoing communication between the therapist or agency and the school and classroom teacher.
- Weekly updates and suggestions involving classroom management reduce frustration and feelings of helplessness on the part of the child and the teacher.

4-15. BEHAVIOR MANAGEMENT TECHNIQUES FOR CHILDREN WITH ATTENTION DEFICIT DISORDER

Classroom teachers of children with ADD can adjust certain factors to accommodate the individual needs of these children. Some examples include:

Social Interaction

- Identify appropriate social behavior for the child and reinforce it when exhibited.
- Sit with the child and set up a social contract which clearly outlines what goals he/she would like to accomplish. Also include the behaviors that may be required to attain these goals.
- Use verbal and written praise whenever possible. This type of praise gives the child the feedback necessary to understand his or her own behavior.
- Expose the child to small group interactions at first. Placing a child with ADD in large groups may be detrimental. Allow the group to be goal oriented and interdependent so that they can accomplish some simple task and feel success.
- Use peer interaction and cooperative learning for certain academic tasks which do not require sitting for long periods of time.
- Try to identify strengths in the child that can be publicly announced or praised. In this way, the other students will develop a more positive perception of the child.
- Role play social situations with the child emphasizing the use of specific skills. In this way the child can develop a "toolbox" of skills that can be applied at a later time.

Organizational Ability

- Prepare a copy of the homework assignments and hand it to the child at the end of the day. This will alleviate a great deal of stress on the part of the child, especially if he or she is disorganized and frequently forgets to copy the homework. The goal here is to create a comfortable and successful environment. In this case, having the child accomplish the homework is more important than the difficulty encountered in copying the assignment.
- Ask the parents to organize the child at night. Have them develop a checklist so that the child's clothes, books, assignments and so on are ready for the next morning. The stress and disorganization of the morning should be avoided at all costs. This will also make the child feel more secure when going to school.
- Avoid numerous directions or assignments. Allow the child to finish one assignment or direction at a time before going on to the next.
- Reinforce word processing and typing skills as well as spell checks on the computer. This device can be very motivating and the end product (i.e., typed report) will make the child feel very good about himself or herself.

4-15. Continued

■ Make weekly organization a part of the child's routine/contract. Children with organizational problems will usually maintain very disorganized notes, notebooks, desks, and lockers.

Inattentiveness

■ Have the child finish all assignments in school if necessary. There are times when the child may be so inattentive that sending homework home to be accomplished may result in more stress, especially in parental interaction.

■ Always allow extra time for completing assignments. Sometimes the time constraints set up by teachers are arbitrary and may not reflect the "real" time required by children with ADD.

■ Try to give shorter but more frequent assignments. Remember, confidence is repeated successful experiences and the ADD child will have a greater chance of success with shorter assignments.

■ Have a "buddy" take notes using a carbon paper if the child has problems listening and taking notes. A copy will then be available for the ADD child, and the stress of listening and writing will be reduced.

■ Stand in close proximity to the student while lecturing.

Impulsiveness

■ Be realistic about your expectations concerning the child's behavior. Choose your guidelines wisely. Try to ignore minor incidents and focus on the more intrusive or inappropriate ones.

■ Shape appropriate behavior by reinforcing positive responses or actions. Do not hesitate to set up specific consequences for inappropriate actions. In this way, the child will have to work at being more consciously aware of his or her behavior.

■ Build in periods of time when the child can leave his seat for some activity, i.e. collecting homework, getting some material for you from the closet, and so on.

■ Try to offer immediate gratification for appropriate behavior. Waiting too long for rewards may lose the desired effect.

■ Assign a monitoring "buddy" to offer the child feedback and hints about appropriate and inappropriate behaviors. This may be especially helpful during recess and lunch.

■ Try to preempt the child's behavior especially during changes in the schedule. Inform the child about five minutes before the change and offer him or her your expectations of what is appropriate behavior during this change.

4-15. Continued

Academic Skill Areas

© 1995 by The Center for Applied Research in Education

■ Allow the child to use graph paper while doing math. In this way the child will have a structured environment in which to place numbers. Use very large graph paper so that the child has little difficulty placing one number in each box. This will keep him or her organized and focused.

■ Allow him or her to use a calculator or basic math tables when doing assignments. The goal here is for successful accomplishment of the assignment. If the child becomes frustrated when trying to recall facts, he or she may give up. For older children, allow them to have a sheet with the formulas already printed.

■ Allow other forms of reporting information. A very thorough list can be found under Alternative Learning Activities in this book.

■ Do not use bubble sheets. Allow the child to answer directly in the booklet or on the paper. Reducing the amount of movement during academic tasks is more beneficial since ADD children have difficulty refocusing.

■ Use manipulative materials as often as possible.

■ Use books on tape as well as having the parent tape record a chapter so that the child can read and listen at the same time.

■ Window out single math problems so that the child only sees one at a time. This can be accomplished by cutting out a square on a piece of paper that the child can move from one problem to the next. When he or she does this all the other problems will be covered.

■ Determine what your goal is when presenting an assignment. Once you have done this pave all the roads for the child up to that point. For example, if your goal is to see if the child can find the circumference of a circle, provide him or her with the formulas, definitions, and examples. These materials will reduce frustration and confusion and will increase the chances of success.

■ Have the child do five problems, two questions, and other tasks at a time. Then offer immediate feedback. Numerous successful tasks can only add to his or her confidence levels. This will also prevent the child from progressing too far while making the same error.

■ Use unison reading when having the child read aloud. This means that both you and the child have the same book and read out loud together. The added sensory feedback and pacing will keep the child more focused.

■ Try to use interactive CD reading programs if possible. The multisensory stimulation will keep the child focused. However, make sure the program does not require the child to do too many tasks at one time, since this could overload him or her.

187

4-15. Continued

Emotional Expression

■ Be aware of the child's frustration "aura." Knowing when an ADD child is about to lose focus may prevent inappropriate behavior and feelings of failure. Do not be afraid to discuss this with the child so that both of you can identify the factors that lead to frustration.

■ Offer children an emotional vocabulary. Tension and frustration come out either verbally or behaviorally. While ADD children may not be able to control certain behaviors, the added tension resulting from stress should be reduced through venting. Having the proper labels enhances a child's ability to communicate feelings.

■ Teach students the concept of healthy anger. Offer them the rules of healthy anger; deal with the situation as close to when it happens as possible, deal directly with the person with whom the child is angry, and never use the word "you" when conveying feelings of anger. Using "I," "me," "we," and "us" is preferred.

■ Try to empower ADD children by focusing on all the parts of their life over which they have control. Children with ADD frequently feel out of control and helpless. This feeling can lead to feelings of depression and victimization. Empowering them with simple jobs, simple hobbies, and choices of food, clothing, room arrangement, and so on will offer some control over the environment and may help to balance their feelings of powerlessness.

4-16. EVALUATION PROCEDURES THAT CAN BE USED TO MEASURE GIFTEDNESS

■ **Intelligence Testing**

Slosson Intelligence Test

Otis-Lennon Mental Ability Test

Stanford-Binet Intelligence Test

Lorge-Thorndike Intelligence Test

Wechsler Intelligence Scales

Short Form of Academic Aptitude

California Test of Mental Maturity

Peabody Picture Vocabulary Test

■ **Achievement Testing**

Gates-MacGinitie Reading Tests: Reading Skills

Metropolitan Readiness Test

Stanford Achievement Test

California Achievement Test

■ **Aptitude Testing**

Differential Aptitude Test

■ **Tests of Creativity**

Torrance Test of Creative Thinking

Creativity Assessment Packet (CAP)

■ **Screening Assessment Measures**

Screening Assessment for Gifted Elementary Students–Primary (SAGES-P)

Screening Assessment for Gifted Elementary Students (SAGES)

Leadership Skills Inventory

Process Skills Rating Scales

■ **Parent Recommendation**

■ **Teacher Checklist and Recommendation**

■ **Behavioral Characteristics**

Renzuili-Hartman Scale for Rating Behavioral Characteristics of Superior Students

■ **Motor Development Tests**

4-16. Continued

- **Rating Scales**

- **Anecdotal Records**

- **Personality Tests**

- **Interest Inventories**

- **Pupil Products and Work Samples**

- **Observation of Actual Performance**

- **Parental Interviews**

- **Peer Nomination Rating Scales**

- **Autobiography**

4-17. EXAMPLES OF CLASSROOM ACTIVITIES TO ENHANCE THE DEVELOPMENT OF THOUGHT PROCESSES FOR THE GIFTED

Original Thinking

- Think of new ways to use a shoebox.
- Write a new ending to a famous play.
- Design a new type of clothing.
- Design a mechanism to allow cars to park in narrow spaces.
- Create a school room of the future.

Fluent Thinking

- How many ways can you prevent air pollution?
- What is the most useless expensive thing you can think of?
- Devise a list of products that are the universal name for all products of that type (e.g., Brillo, Jell-O).
- List all the things you can fit through a hole the size of a dime.
- Name all the things that can be held up with Scotch tape.

Flexible Thinking

- What different ways can you find to use a rubber band?
- How many items can you make from metal?
- List all the uses you can think of for a paper clip.
- Think of all the ways you can use items in your garbage can to reduce pollution.
- How would life be different if the wheel had not been discovered?

Elaborative Thinking

- Decorate your jeans jacket with some original idea.
- Draw a triangle and make as many objects as you can that include that shape.
- Expand on the safety items that have already been developed for cars.
- Add decorations to the outside of a house that will increase its beauty.
- Take a character from a famous story and give him or her new qualities.

4-17. Continued

Curiosity

- Devise an experiment that will cause the cork in a bottle to shoot up and hit the ceiling.
- How do the five senses make us aware of the world around us?
- What would happen if you suddenly became blind?
- What do you think the world would be like without trees?
- Did you ever wonder how thermometers work?

Risk Taking

- Predict how the world would look if we did nothing about pollution.
- Given an object in a box, determine how you would go about finding out what it is.
- Explain how you would defend Lee Harvey Oswald if you were his lawyer.
- Make a prediction on the laws governing abortion—will they change?
- What would happen if you put a thermometer in hot water?

Imagination

- What would happen if you could go to the center of the earth?
- How do you think your street will look ten years from now?
- Draw a picture of the first alien to visit the earth; his family; his spaceship.
- Pretend you are a cloud.
- Suppose Martians landed on the earth and all they found was a penny. How many things could they tell about our society from the penny?

Complexity

- Make a city out of blocks and objects around you.
- Take numerous pictures of all types of dogs and classify them with some new system.
- What would you do if you were able to teach?
- What solutions can be developed to stop car hijackers?
- What other ways of evaluation can be used in school besides numerical and letter grades?

4-18. APPROACHES TO EDUCATIONAL PROGRAMMING FOR GIFTED STUDENTS

Enrichment Programs

- Pull-out programs
- Special experiences within a regular classroom
- Tracking
- Special grouping within the regular classroom
- Resource rooms
- Mentor programs
- Guest speakers
- Internships
- Extraschool activities
- Special clubs
- Summer camps and programs
- Special regular classes
- Seminars
- Minicourses
- Team teaching
- Alternative schools
- Field trips and cultural programs

Acceleration Programs

- Honors classes
- Advanced placement classes for college credit
- Early admission to school
- Early admission to college
- Skipping a grade
- Advanced placement tests
- Seminars
- Programmed learning so that the student can accelerate at his or her own pace
- Ungraded classes
- Multi-age classes
- Tutoring
- Correspondence courses
- Extra classes for extra credit

4-18. Continued

- Credit by examination
- Independent study
- Continuous progress curriculum
- Year-round school
- Flexible scheduling

4-19. CLASSROOM APPLICATIONS OF BLOOM'S TAXONOMY OF THE COGNITIVE DOMAIN

Types of Learning	What Student Does	What Teacher Does
Mastery of subject matter	responds absorbs remembers rehearses covers recognizes examines	directs tells leads shows delineates enlarges
Comprehension (cognition)	explains extends demonstrates translates interprets contrasts examines	demonstrates listens reflects questions compares
Application (convergent and divergent production)	solves novel problems demonstrates use of knowledge constructs criticizes	shows facilitates observes
Analysis	discusses details uncovers lists dissects	probes guides observes acts as a resource
Synthesis	discusses generalizes relates compares contrasts abstracts	reflects evaluates extends analyzes
Evaluation	engages in commitment judges disputes	accepts lays bare establishes criteria

4-20. COMMON CHARACTERISTICS OF PROGRAM MANAGEMENT FOR THE GIFTED

Pull-out Programs

- Gifted students are removed from the classroom and placed in an out-of-classroom location for a portion of the school day or week.
- Grouping in the pull-out setting may be by grade or multi-age.

Cluster Grouping

- Identified gifted students from several classes are grouped or clustered into a regular class with other, nongifted students.
- Cluster groups of gifted students within classroom receive differentiated instruction based on their special needs.

Acceleration

- Gifted students are moved more rapidly through the usual sequence of instruction.
- Above-grade-level materials are used for instruction.
- Gifted students may be accelerated in one academic area, for example, mathematics, or the students may be moved to a higher grade.

Homogeneous Grouping

- Identified gifted students are placed together in a single class exclusively for gifted students.

Gifted Students in the Regular Classroom

- Identified gifted students remain in regular heterogeneous classes.
- Individualized instructional approaches are used to differentiate the program to meet the needs of gifted students.

Mentor Program

- Gifted students are matched to mentors or guides who work with them in individually selected areas.
- Programs frequently involve out-of-school experiences for students.
- Mentors are frequently community people in business and service areas or the arts.
- Mentors may assist gifted students in independent study projects, or acquaint gifted students with their particular area of expertise.

4-21. TERMINOLOGY FOR THE GIFTED

- **Analysis-** Breaking down a concept, problem or pattern into its components
- **Associating-** Relating objects or thoughts as they come to mind; may be free, controlled, or linked to preceding and following thoughts
- **Categorizing-** Placing objects, ideas, and phenomena into a given classification system
- **Classifying-** Establishing an arbitrary system of grouping and subgrouping on the basis of the common characteristics of elements
- **Comparing-** Determining similarities and differences on the basis of certain criteria
- **Convergent thinking-** Arriving at one pattern or one solution out of diverse elements, using some criterion
- **Creative thinking-** Developing or reorganizing ideas, objects, or words, and arriving at a product that is novel, original, unexpected, and imaginative in its new form
- **Critical thinking-** A complex process that involves analysis, a weighing of the components (either qualitatively or quantitatively), and making a selection or decision on the basis of the evaluation
- **Deduction-** Starting with generalizations or universal propositions and arriving at a specific conclusion
- **Divergent thinking-** Offering various patterns or solutions to the same problem
- **Induction-** Using specific situations, objects, and ideas and arriving at generalizations
- **Synthesis-** Putting together parts and pieces to form a whole; arranging, rearranging, and combining parts to establish a pattern or product not clearly present before.
- **Fluent thinking-** The ability to produce different and multiple ideas; thinking of many possibilities; flow of thought
- **Flexible thinking-** The ability to produce alternatives, different approaches, variety of ideas, acceptance of variations and modifications
- **Original thinking-** The ability to think of novel, unique, or universal possibilities—to be creative, inventive, and innovative
- **Elaborative thinking-** The ability to embellish upon an idea to produce a number of detailed steps, to express oneself in greater length or detail, to expand and develop thoroughly
- **Curiosity-** The willingness to examine things and ideas or the capacity to wonder about things; desire to know or learn, especially about something new or strange; inquisitiveness
- **Risk taking-** The courage to try out adventurous tasks or to venture a guess; commitment; ability to judge, dispute, question; perseverance

4-21. Continued

- **Complexity-** The ability to handle challenge and involved details, pursuit of intricate ideas
- **Imagination-** The power to form mental images that have not been actually experienced—building thought models about situations; ability to deal creatively with reality

4-22. CHARACTERISTICS OF THE GIFTED AND TALENTED

1. Keen power of observation
2. Sense of the significant
3. Willingness to examine the unusual
4. Power of abstraction
5. High-level conceptualization
6. Interest in inductive learning and problem solving
7. Interest in cause-and-effect relationships
8. Retentiveness
9. Verbal proficiency
10. Large vocabulary
11. Facility in expression
12. Interest in reading
13. Wide range of experiences and information
14. Questioning attitude
15. Intellectual curiosity
16. Inquisitive mind
17. Intrinsic motivation
18. Power of critical thinking
19. Creativeness and inventiveness
20. Power of concentration
21. Intense attention that excludes all else
22. Long attention span
23. Persistence
24. Goal directedness
25. High energy levels
26. Alertness
27. Eagerness
28. Independence in work and study
29. Preference for individualized work
30. Self-reliance
31. Need for freedom of movement and action
32. Versatility
33. Diversity of interests and abilities
34. Varied hobbies

4-23. TEACHER CHECKLIST OF CLASSROOM CHARACTERISTICS THAT MAY INDICATE GIFTEDNESS

1. _____ Reads earlier with greater comprehension of nuances in the language
2. _____ Learns basic skills faster than the other children
3. _____ Is able to make abstractions when other children his or her age cannot
4. _____ Has curiosity in interest areas beyond his or her age level
5. _____ Is able to comprehend implications with almost no verbal cues
6. _____ Takes independent direction earlier than peers
7. _____ Assumes responsibility more naturally than peers
8. _____ Can maintain longer periods of concentration when interested
9. _____ Is able to express thoughts readily
10. _____ Has a wide range of reading interests
11. _____ Seems to expend limitless energy
12. _____ Manifests creative and original verbal responses
13. _____ Demonstrates a more complex processing of information than his or her peers
14. _____ Responds and relates well to adult interaction in the higher level thinking processes
15. _____ Enjoys working on many projects at a time
16. _____ Assumes leadership roles
17. _____ Has an innate sense of justice
18. _____ Displays a great curiosity about objects, situations, or events
19. _____ Pursues individual interests and seeks own direction
20. _____ Offers unusual, clever, or unique responses or ideas
21. _____ Has unusual talent for expressing self in the arts—art, music, drama
22. _____ Generates many alternatives to problem-solving situations
23. _____ Seems to go at right angles to the mainstream of thought in the classroom
24. _____ Displays a willingness for complexity
25. _____ Thrives on problem-solving situations
26. _____ Seeks new associations among items of information
27. _____ Shows superior judgment in evaluating things
28. _____ Seeks logical answers
29. _____ Is able to elaborate with ease
30. _____ Loves to embellish materials and ideas

4-24. RESIDENTIAL ALTERNATIVES FOR INDIVIDUALS WITH MENTAL DISABILITIES

Institutions: These are large custodial institutions that offer severely and profoundly disabled persons 24-hour care and supervision. The concern about institutions involves the level of humane treatment and the concept of normalization.

Regional facilities: These programs offer total-care, 24-hour residential programs like large state institutions, but on a much smaller basis, serving only those persons in a given geographical area within the state. The reduced distance between this type of facility and the individual's family allows for more normalized and individualized treatment programs.

Group homes: These facilities usually consist of between 6 and 12 mentally disabled adolescents or adults living in a large, family-type dwelling in a residential neighborhood. Professional staff are responsible for supervision and overall programming for the residents. The residents often work at sheltered workshops and participate in social and recreational activities in the community.

Board and care homes: Board and care homes are less structured than group homes. Residents sleep and eat in the home, but the family or staff are not generally responsible for supervision of the residents. The responsibility for scheduling daytime activities and services falls on the resident or an outside case manager.

Apartment living: These alternatives include independent apartments with minimal supervision, apartment clusters, or coresidence arrangements (a disabled resident and a nondisabled roommate).

Sheltered workshops: These facilities provide supervised employment for many retarded teenagers and adults. Employees generally perform piecework labor and are paid on either an hourly or performance-output basis.

Special schools: These special schools offer an education and training curriculum specially designed for their students, usually moderately mentally disabled (trainable) children. The children in these programs usual live at home with their families.

Regular public schools: Traditionally, the mildly disabled child was educated in a self-contained classroom. The regular public schools are now leaning toward the concept of inclusion for such students. Inclusion involves the education of mildly disabled students within the normal classroom, supported by professionals and services.

4-25. INSTRUCTIONAL CONSIDERATIONS FOR THE MENTALLY DISABLED CHILD

Helping the Child Attain Functional Academics

GENERAL

- Design practice activities in any basic skill that may relate to the child's daily life problems.
- Provide materials that are commensurate with the child's skill levels.
- Provide activities that will reinforce independent work. If the activity is too hard the child may become too dependent on teacher supervision.

READING

- Provide activities that focus on reading for information and leisure.
- Provide activities that require the child to become more aware of his or her environment; having the child list the names of all food stores in the community, or all hospitals, and so on, will increase his or her familiarity with the surrounding environment.
- Have the child collect food labels and compare the differences.
- Allow the child to look up the names of children's families in the phone book. Use the smaller local guide for this activity.
- Develop activities that will allow the children to become familiar with menus, bus and train schedules, movie and television timetables, or job advertisements.

HANDWRITING/SPELLING

- Have the child make a list of things to do for the day.
- Have the child run a messenger service in the classroom so that he or she can write the messages and deliver them from one student to another.
- Provide activities for older children that incorporate daily writing skills necessary for independence, such as social security forms, driver's license applications, and bank account applications.

MATH

- Have the child buy something at the school store.
- Have the child make up a budget for spending his or her allowance.
- Encourage the child to cook in school or at home, to become more familiar with measurements.
- Have the child record the daily temperature.
- Involve the child in measuring the height of classmates.
- Have older children apply for a loan or credit card.

4-25. Continued

- Show the child how to use a daily planning book.
- Provide activities that teach the child how to comparison shop.
- Provide the child with a make-believe amount of money and a toy catalog and have him or her purchase items and fill out the forms.

Helping the Child Improve General work Habits

This particular area is composed of many skill areas needed to afford the child success in the regular classroom.

WORK COMPLETION

- Make reward activities contingent upon successful completion of work.
- Have the child maintain a performance chart on the number of tasks completed each day.
- Evaluate the length and level of an assignment to make sure it is within the ability level of the child.
- Give shorter but more frequent assignments.
- Build a foundation of success by providing a series of doable assignments. In this way the child can gain a sense of confidence.

ATTENDANCE AND PUNCTUALITY

- Communicate to the child the importance of being on time to class; let him or her know your expectations in clear terms concerning attendance and punctuality.
- Have the child maintain a record of attendance and on-time behavior.
- Develop a make-believe time clock that the child has to punch in on when he or she enters the classroom.
- Encourage punctuality by scheduling a favorite activity in the morning.
- Have the child sign a contract establishing the consequences and rewards of on-time behavior.

WORKING WITH OTHERS

- Provide the child with small group activities that are geared to his or her ability levels.
- Use peer tutors for the child so that relationships can be established.
- Have the child participate in many group activities that require sorting, pasting, addressing, folding or simple assembly.
- Provide the child with some simple job that requires the other students to go to him or her. For example, place the child in charge of attendance and have him or her check off the children when they report in.

4-25. Continued

- Help the child start a hobby, and then start a hobby club involving other students.
- Have the child be part of a team that takes care of the class pets or some other class activity. Calling it a team will make the child feel more connected.
- Speak with the school psychologist and see if he or she can run a group in your classroom.

4-26. ESSENTIAL SERVICES FOR THE MENTALLY DISABLED

Category	Description
Developmental Programs a. Day activity b. Education c. Training	Includes a variety of educational and care programs appropriate for an individual's age and severity of disability
Residential Services a. Domiciliary b. Special living arrangements	Include living quarters away from the primary home; 24-hour lodging and supervision, with less supervised living arrangements for less disabled persons
Employment Services a. Preparation for b. Sheltered c. Competitive	Include a continuum of vocational evaluation training and work opportunities in a supervised and independent environment
Identification Services a. Diagnosis b. Evaluation	Include efforts to identify the presence and the etiology of a disability, and to plan service needs of the individual
Facilitating Services	Include a variety of actions needed to ensure that disabled individuals are informed of current services that can assist them in their daily living; further awareness of rights and support services for individuals when required and reassurance of the constant review of these services
Treatment Services a. Medical b. Dental	Include appropriate and available medical care, prosthetic devices needed for maintaining environmental involvement, and dental care
Transportation	Transportation needs for training sites, work sites, and other daily activities
Leisure and Recreation	Definition and provision of structured and unstructured leisure opportunities, with transportation available if required

4-27. CHARACTERISTICS OF DOWN'S SYNDROME

The syndrome was initially categorized by Langdon Down as a type of mental retardation in 1886. The term *Mongolism* was used to describe this disorder for many years.

1. At birth, a large anterior fontanel and open sutures are present.

2. A flat broad head develops.

3. The skin is rough and dry.

4. The child develops almond-shaped eyes.

5. The tongue may be too large for the oral cavity.

6. The neck is short.

7. The features appear compressed.

8. Convolutions of the ear seem unusual.

9. The palms of the hand have one fissure.

10. There is a large gap between the first and second toes.

11. The palate is high.

12. The tongue is fissured.

13. Voice pitch is not normal.

14. Sex organs may be malformed.

15. The hair may be coarse.

16. The fingerprint patterns are distinctive.

17. The iris may be speckled.

18. Teeth are malformed.

19. Teeth are prone to decay.

20. Circulation is poor.

21. Respiration is fragile.

22. High concentrations of gamma globulin are found in the blood.

23. High incidence of spinal disorders exists.

24. There can be disorders of the pituitary, thyroid, and thymus.

25. Deviation of growth begins about the eighth week.

26. Main abnormality is the extra chromosome in the number 21 position.

27. Trisomy occurs; three normal chromosomes instead of two are formed, producing a total of 47 chromosomes per cell instead of 46.

28. There is a correlation of advanced maternal age and Down's syndrome.

4-28. CAUSES OF COMMUNICATION DISORDERS

Articulation Disorders

- These disorders are most prevalent among school-age children.
- Children may omit certain sounds.
- Children may substitute one sound for another.
- Children may distort certain speech sounds, while attempting to produce them accurately.
- Children may add extra sounds, making comprehension difficult.
- These problems may disappear as the child matures.
- Severe articulation disorders are present when a child pronounces many sounds so poorly that his or her speech is unintelligible most of the time.

Voice Disorders

- The quality, loudness, or pitch of the voice is inappropriate or abnormal.
- They are far less common in children than adults.
- Examples include hoarseness, breathiness, and nasality.
- Problems can have organic or functional causes.
- Problems include *hypernasality*—too many sounds come out through the air passages of the nose and *denasality*—not enough resonance of the nasal passages.

Fluency Disorders

- These disorders interrupt the natural, smooth flow of speech with inappropriate pauses, hesitations, or repetitions.
- One type of disorder is known as *cluttering*—a condition in which speech is very rapid and clipped to the point of unintelligibility.
- *Stuttering* is characterized by verbal blocks.
- Most children experience some dysfluency—repetitions and interruptions—at some time in their development.

Language Disorders

- Receptive language disorder interferes with the understanding of language.
- The child may be unable to comprehend spoken sentences or to follow a sequence of directions.
- Expressive language disorder interferes with the production of language.

4-28. Continued

- The child may have a limited vocabulary, use incorrect words and phrases, or communicate through gestures.
- Language disorders may be caused by environmental deprivation, emotional factors, structural abnormalities, or retardation.

4-29. SUMMARY OF NORMAL LANGUAGE DEVELOPMENT

Birth to 6 months

- First form of communication is crying.
- Babies also make sounds of comfort such as coos and gurgles.
- Babbling soon follows as a form of communication.
- Vowel sounds are produced.
- No meaning is attached to the words heard from others.

6 to 12 months

- Baby's voice begins to rise and fall while making sounds.
- Child begins to understands certain words.
- Child may respond appropriately to the word "no" or own name.
- Child may perform an action when asked.
- Child may repeat words said by others.

12 to 18 months

- Child has learned to say several words with appropriate meaning.
- Child is able to tell what he or she wants by pointing.
- Child responds to simple commands.

18 to 24 months

- A great spurt in the acquisition and use of speech occurs at this stage.
- Child begins to combine words.
- Child begins to forms words into short sentences.

2 to 3 years

- Child talks.
- Child asks questions.
- Child has vocabulary of about 900 words.
- Child participates in conversation.
- Child can identify colors.
- Child can use plurals.
- Child can tell simple stories.
- Child begins to use some consonant sounds.

4-29. Continued

3 to 4 years

- Child begins to speak more rapidly.
- Child begins to ask questions to obtain information.
- Sentences are longer and more varied.
- Child can complete simple analogies.

4 to 5 years

- Average vocabulary is over 1500 words.
- Sentences average 5 words in length.
- Child is able to modify speech.
- Child is able to define words.
- Child can use conjunctions.
- Child can recite poems and sing songs from memory.

4-30. TREATMENT AND REMEDIATION OF COMMUNICATION DISORDERS

Articulation Disorders

- Develop the child's ability to listen carefully and discriminate between similar sounds.
- Emphasize awareness and discrimination of sounds.
- Use a mirror so that the child can monitor his or her own speech production.
- Use a tape recorder to record his or her speech and listen carefully for errors.
- Provide good language models.
- Use positive reinforcement to encourage the child to talk

Voice Disorders

- Seek out a medical examination for possible organic causes.
- Recommend environmental modifications.
- Use vocal rehabilitation to help the child gradually learn to produce more acceptable and efficient speech.
- Use exercises and activities to increase breathing capacity.
- Use relaxation techniques to reduce tension.

Fluency Disorders

- Emphasize counseling or behavior modification.
- Teach child to manage his or her stuttering by prolonging certain sounds.
- Teach child to manage his or her stuttering by speaking more slowly.
- Increase confidence by having child speak in groups.
- Teach child to monitor his or her own speech.
- Teach child to speak to a rhythmic beat.
- Use tape recorders for drills.

Language Disorders

- Use precommunication activities that encourage the child to explore.
- Talk clearly to the child.
- Use correct inflections when speaking to the child.
- Provide a rich variety of words and sentences.
- Expose the child to group interaction.
- Emphasize the use of language through performing tasks.
- Use a variety of written and verbal labeling.

4-31. SEVERE LEARNING DISCREPANCY

Many state definitions of learning disabilities include a statement indicating that in order for a learning disability to exist, there must be a severe discrepancy between achievement and intellectual ability. This has been interpreted to mean achievement that falls at or below 50% of an individual's expected achievement level when intellectual ability, age, and previous educational experiences are considered.

Initially, a formula was derived that appeared in PL 94-142—the 1975 Federal guidelines for the education of the handicapped. The formula used was the following:

$$\frac{C.A. \, (IQ + .17)}{300} - 2.5 = \text{severe discrepancy level}$$

The following partial table was reproduced by using the above formula and feeding in different IQs and C.A.'s. The scores represent half of the child's potential when IQ and age are factored in. For example, a child with an IQ of 120 at age 10-0 (5th grade) has a *potential grade level* performance of 6.4. Half of that would be 3.2, which represents that child's severe discrepancy grade level. If he or she scored below this level on a standardized test in an achievement area, it would be considered severe enough to be classified as a learning disability.

Chronological Age (Years-Months)

		9-0	9-3	9-6	9-9	10-0	10-3	10-6	10-9
I N T E	135	3-1	3-2	3-4	3-6	3-7	3-9	4-0	4-2
	130	2-9	3-1	3-2	3-4	3-5	3-7	3-8	4-0
L	125	2-8	2-9	3-1	3-2	3-4	3-5	3-7	3-8
E C	120	2-6	2-8	2-9	3-1	3-2	3-3	3-5	3-6
T U A L									
Q U O	100	2-0	2-1	2-3	2-4	2-5	2-6	2-8	2-9
T I	80	1-4	1-5	1-7	1-8	1-9	2-0	2-1	2-2
E N	75	1-3	1-4	1-5	1-6	1-7	1-8	1-9	2-0
T	65	1-0	1-1	1-2	1-3	1-4	1-5	1-6	1-7

4-31. Continued

This formula was an attempt to quantify the definition of learning disabilities, since a word definition—interpreted differently by different Committees—may have caused greater numbers of identified students and resulted in more costs to state and federal governments. The formula was soon dropped, however, and did not appear in the state definitions, yet the concept of "severe discrepancy" did, and the interpretation was left up to the individual Committees on Special Education.

In conclusion, identification and diagnosis of a learning disabled child should include the following:

1. Average or above-average potential intelligence

2. A history of mild, moderate, or severe academic deficiencies

3. No indications of primary emotionality, mental retardation, poor teaching, or lack of motivation

4. A background history that supports a historical pattern of difficulties in development or achievement

5. Behavioral indications such as difficulties in attention, distractibility, coordination, or memory

6. A significant discrepancy between ability and achievement

4-32. CHARACTERISTICS OF CHILDREN WITH DYSLEXIA

Primary Characteristics for Early Detection

1. The child has poor ability to associate sounds with corresponding symbols.

2. The child ignores details of words and has difficulty retaining the words in his or her mind.

3. The child frequently guesses words—won't look at the word but will seek pictorial clues.

4. The child has confused spatial orientation. He or she reverses words, letters, and numbers. Mirror reading and writing are frequently encountered.

5. The child has poor auditory discrimination.

6. The child exhibits confusion of left and right (referred to as *mixed dominance*).

7. The child frequently loses his or her place on a page, and frequently skips lines.

8. The child has difficulty in working with jigsaw puzzles, holding a pencil, and walking a chalk line.

9. Newly learned words are forgotten from day to day. Reading rhythm is usually poor and labored.

Secondary Characteristics

1. There is no mental disability, and intelligence is measured as average to superior.

2. The child exhibits general confusion in orientation, confuses days, time, distance, size, and right and left directions.

3. The child displays poor motor coordination, a swaying gate, and awkwardness when playing games.

4. There are speech delays and the child has difficulty in pronunciation.

5. The child feels inadequate and has low self-esteem.

6. Special tutoring, with conventional reading methods, doesn't work.

7. The child displays general irritability, aggressiveness, avoidance reactions, defensiveness, withdrawal, and behavioral problems.

4-33. INSTRUCTIONAL CONSIDERATIONS FOR CHILDREN WITH LEARNING DISABILITIES IN THE CLASSROOM

Instructional Techniques

The teacher should be aware that not all techniques will work with all students, but try as many of them as possible. These techniques should create a better learning environment for children with learning disabilities.

How to make adjustments in the type, difficulty, amount, and sequence of materials

1. Shorten the length of the assignments to ensure a sense of success.

2. Give more frequent assignments.

3. Copy chapters of textbooks so that the child can use a highlighter for important facts.

4. Make sure that the child's desk is free from all unnecessary materials.

5. Correct the student's work as soon as possible to allow for immediate gratification and feedback.

6. Allow the student several alternatives in both obtaining and reporting information—tapes, interviews, and any other useful techniques.

7. Break assignments down to smaller units. Allow the child to do five problems at a time, or five sentences. This way, the child can feel success, or receive immediate feedback if he or she is doing the assignment incorrectly and turn to more manageable tasks.

8. Hold frequent, even if short, conferences with the child to allow for questions, sources of confusion, sense of connection, and avoidance of isolation—which often occurs if the work is too difficult.

How to adjust space, work time, and grouping

1. Permit the child to work in a quiet corner or a study carrel when requested or necessary, but not all the time since isolation may have negative consequences. This technique depends on the specific learning style of the child, who may be less distracted by working under these conditions.

2. At first, keep the child closer to you for more immediate feedback.

3. Try to separate him or her from students who may be distracting.

4. Alternate quiet and active time to maintain levels of interest and motivation.

5. Make up a work contract with specific times and assignments so that the child has a structured idea of his or her responsibilities.

4-33. Continued

6. Keep work periods short and gradually lengthen them as the student begins to cope.

7. Try to match the student with a peer helper for help with understanding assignments, reading important directions, drilling him or her orally, summarizing important textbook passages, and working on long-range assignments.

Consider adjusting presentation and evaluation modes

Some students learn better by seeing (visual learners), some by listening (auditory learners), some by feeling (tactile learners), and some by a combination of approaches. Adjustments should be made by the teacher to determine the best functional system of learning for children with learning disabilities. This will vary from child to child and is usually included in the child's evaluation.

If the child is primarily an *auditory learner,* offer adjustments in the mode of presentation by use of the following techniques:

1. Give verbal as well as written directions to assignments.

2. Place assignment directions on tape so that students can replay them when they need to.

3. Give students oral rather than written tests.

4. Have students drill on important information using a tape recorder, reciting information into the recorder and playing it back.

5. Have students drill aloud to themselves or to other students.

6. Have children close their eyes to try to hear words or information.

If the child is primarily a *visual learner,* offer adjustment in the mode of presentation by the following:

1. Have students use flashcards printed in bold bright colors.

2. Let students close their eyes and try to visualize words or information in their heads—see things in their minds.

3. Provide visual clues on chalkboard for all verbal directions.

4. Encourage students to write down notes and memos to themselves concerning important words, concepts, and ideas.

© 1995 by The Center for Applied Research in Education

4-34. CHARACTERISTICS OF CHILDREN WITH LEARNING DISABILITIES

A student with a learning disability is one who

1. Is not succeeding in school in one or more of the following areas:

- Basic reading skill (decoding)
- Reading comprehension
- Mathematics calculations
- Mathematics reasoning
- Written expression
- Oral expression
- Listening comprehension

2. Has had appropriate learning opportunities

3. Has at least average intellectual potential

4. Has a severe discrepancy between intellectual potential and achievement in one or several of the above areas of functioning

A student with a learning disability may also

1. Show performance variability across academic and nonacademic areas

2. Exhibit attention and behavior problems that appear related to school failure and frustration

Who Is Not a Student with a Learning Disability

A student with a learning disability is not a student whose learning problems are primarily due to

1. Other handicapping conditions such as

- Mental disability
- Emotional disturbance
- Visual or hearing loss
- Motor handicaps

2. Limited learning opportunities because of

- Prolonged absences from school
- Lack of consideration for language differences
- Inadequate instructional practices

217

4-34. Continued

3. Limited learning potential in all areas (i.e., a slow learner whose achievement is commensurate with his or her potential)

4. Sociological causes, including environmental, cultural, or economic disadvantages; limited proficiency in English language; or other such conditions that may result in, but are not the result of, a learning problem.

4-35. TECHNIQUES TO COMPENSATE FOR CERTAIN LEARNING PROBLEMS

High activity level (hyperactivity):

Shorten length of tasks.
Add more variety to tasks.
Reduce seatwork expectations.

Forgetfulness (memory problems):

Teach student to organize rather than memorize.
Allow the child to use multiplication tables.
Allow the child to use personal dictionaries.
Use a peer assistant.

Poor handwriting:

Encourage student to use graph paper for mathematical problems.
Use paper with raised lines.
Allow child to use pencil adaptations.
Fold paper into sections.
Decrease written work and increase response options.
Encourage use of word processor.

Distractibility:

Create a study area that is free from stimuli.

Focusing problems:

Stand close by student during lectures.

Organizational problems:

Allow extra time for responses.
Give credit for attempted responses.

Test inconsistency:

Allow student to take test in sections.

4-35. Continued

Allow for untimed testing.
Allow for flexible setting.
Give typed, not handwritten, tests.
Underline key words in test directions.

4-36. SCHOOL PROBLEMS REQUIRING OCCUPATIONAL THERAPY SERVICES

Sensory problems

- cannot tolerate touch or continuously touch others
- sensitive to sound
- sensitive to visual changes
- sensitive to odors

Gross motor problems

- trouble with balance
- problems with coordination
- difficulty with gross motor planning

Fine motor problems

- problems with coordination
- problems with handwriting
- problems using scissors

Perceptual problems

- problems in eye-hand coordination

Daily living activities

- cannot dress themselves
- cannot feed themselves
- cannot take care of their own personal hygiene

Attention span

- trouble focusing on task
- short attention span

Organizational skills

- difficulties with memory

4-37. CHARACTERISTICS OF WRITING, MATHEMATICAL, AND READING DISORDERS

Writing Disorders

CHILDREN WHO ARE PHONETICALLY ACCURATE SPELLERS

- make phonetically accurate errors
- spell words exactly as they sound—"lite" for "light"
- spell words with only a general similarity to the actual word—"word" for "work"
- have difficulty associating verbal labels with pictorial information
- have problems with advanced language expression such as vocabulary definitions

CHILDREN WHO ARE PHONETICALLY INACCURATE SPELLERS

- demonstrate significant weaknesses in basic auditory skills
- have difficulty breaking words into syllables
- have difficulty retaining auditory information
- do not process language effectively

CHILDREN WITH MECHANICAL WRITING DISORDERS

- find writing a slow and labored process
- usually have poorly developed fine motor coordination
- typically lack finger dexterity
- may have had earlier problems with buttoning and tying
- may have difficulty with the spatial aspects of writing
- may form letters of varying sizes
- may leave gaps between letters of a word
- may run words together
- may exhibit directional confusion by reversing letters

Mathematical Disabilities

CHILDREN WITH MATHEMATICAL DISORDERS

- may not fully comprehend the rules of arithmetic because of problems in applying language
- may not grasp language-based facts for arithmetic
- have difficulty remembering multiplication tables
- may have trouble understanding teacher's verbal explanations
- may have visual spatial problems

4-37. Continued

- have difficulty keeping track of numbers in the same column
- may switch from one column to another as they add or subtract
- have trouble with the concepts of borrowing and carrying

Reading Disabilities

CHILDREN WITH LANGUAGE-BASED DISORDERS

- are slower at naming objects and pictures
- have auditory receptive areas of the brain that react more slowly to auditory stimuli
- have difficulty comprehending complicated verbal directions
- have difficulty separating words into phonetic segments
- have poor memory for sequential information
- have difficulty decoding words

4-38. CHARACTERISTICS OF CHILDREN WITH EMOTIONAL DISABILITIES

Some common characteristics of emotional disorders that may be observed by the teacher over a period of time include

- academic underachievement
- social isolation or withdrawal
- excessive latenesses
- excessive absences
- frequent trips to the nurse
- negativism
- open defiance of authority or rules
- highly distractible
- poor social relationships
- feelings of hopelessness
- verbal aggression
- confrontational behavior
- inappropriate classroom behaviors
- impulsive behavior
- rigid behavior patterns
- anxiety and worry, excessive fears, and phobias
- frustration, even when confronted with a simple task
- resistance to change

Since the behavior of children with emotional disabilities can vary from withdrawal (in the case of depression) to aggressive tendencies (in the case of a conduct disorder) teachers must be aware of techniques that can be utilized in a variety of situations. Certain behaviors, however, should be targeted as priorities when dealing with emotionally disabled children in the classroom. These target behaviors include

- absence and tardiness
- challenges to authority
- inappropriate verbalizations and outbursts
- incomplete classwork
- difficulty remaining seated
- social relationships
- following directions and paying attention

4-39. INSTRUCTIONAL CONSIDERATIONS FOR THE EMOTIONALLY DISABLED CHILD

Dealing with problems of attendance and tardiness

- Reward the child for being on time. This reward can be extra free time, a token—if a token economy is being used, a note home, or a verbal compliment.
- Work with the parent on rewarding on-time behavior.
- Plan a special activity in the morning.
- Use a chart to visually project the pattern of punctuality and lateness for the child. This reduces the child's level of denial and may make him or her more aware of the behavior.
- Encourage and assist the child to join a club in his or her area of greatest interest and make participation contingent upon a positive pattern of attendance.
- Use a point system for on-time attendance. These points may be turned in later for class privileges.
- Set up a buddy system if the child walks to school, to encourage on-time behavior.
- Prepare a nightly contract for the child, listing all the things he or she needs to do to make the morning easier to manage. Have the parent sign it and reward the child when he or she brings it in.

Dealing with challenges to authority, inappropriate verbalizations, and outbursts

- Arrange a timeout area in the classroom. The time spent in the area is not as significant as your being able to begin the consequence and end it; therefore, make the timeout period something you can control.
- Structure a time where the child is allowed to speak to you freely without an audience around. In this way, the child will have an opportunity to talk about concerns rather than act them out. It will also allow you to deflect any confrontations to that specific time.
- Approach the child as often as possible and ask him or her if there is anything bothering him that he would like to speak about. Offering her the opportunity, even if she refuses, may reduce her need for "spotlight" behaviors in front of the class.
- Offer an emotional vocabulary so that the child is more able to label feelings. Tension is expressed either verbally or behaviorally. Providing the student with the proper labels may reduce frustration.
- Move the student away from those who might set her or him off.
- Preempt the behavior by waiting outside before class and telling him or her in private what you expect during class. Also make the child aware of the rewards and consequences of his or her actions.

4-39. Continued

- Offer other options and indicate that any inappropriateness is the child's decision. Making children aware that behavior is their responsibility allows them to realize that not doing something inappropriate is also in their control.
- Establish clear classroom rules stating rewards and consequences.
- Praise student for complying with rules and carrying out directions without verbal resistance.

Dealing with incomplete classwork

- Work out a contract with the child where he or she can determine the rewards for completion.
- Give shorter but more frequent assignments.
- Do not force the child to write if handwriting is beyond correction. Compensate with a word processor or typewriter.
- Correct assignments as soon as possible and hand them back for immediate gratification.
- Reward students for handing in neat, completed, and timely assignments.
- Help the student become organized by keeping very little in his or her desk, using a bound book for writing rather than a looseleaf where pages can fall out and add to disorganization, or using large folders for the child to keep work in.
- Have students mark their own work.
- Be *very* specific on what you mean by "neat," "organized," and other terms. Abstract labels have different meanings to different people. Instead say, "Please be neat and by neat I mean . . . ."

Dealing with the child's difficulty in remaining seated

- Try to determine a pattern when the child gets up out of his or her seat. Once this is determined, you can arrange to have them run an errand, come up to your desk, or move for some other purpose. In this way you are channeling the tension and remaining in control.
- Use an external control like an egg timer so that the child has an anchor to control behavior.
- Praise other students or hand out rewards for remaining in their seats and following the rules.
- Give the child a written copy of the rules that will result in reward or positive feedback. Also give him or her a list of the behaviors that will lead to consequences.
- Close proximity to the child will assist him or her in staying seated. Seat the child close to your desk or stand near him or her during a lesson.

4-39. Continued

Helping the child develop social relationships

- Have the child role play with another student during private time so that the child can get feedback from a peer.
- Provide the child with a "toolbox" of responses and options for typical social situations.
- Speak with the school psychologist about including him or her in a group.
- Arrange for a peer to guide the child through social situations. The child may be more willing to model peer behavior.
- Start the child in a small group activity with only one child. Slowly increase the size of the group as the child becomes more comfortable.
- Arrange for goal-oriented projects where students must work together to accomplish a task. At first, limit this to the student and one other child.
- Have the child and responsible peer organize team activities or group projects. Some children rise to the occasion when placed in a leadership role.
- Praise the student as often as is realistic when she or he is not exhibiting aggressive or inappropriate social behavior.

Helping the child follow directions and pay attention

- Use a cue before giving the child directions or important information.
- Give one direction at a time and make it as simple as possible.
- Have the child chart his or her own patterns of behavior in relation to attention and direction.
- Physical proximity may assist the child in focusing on your directions.
- Praise the student when he or she follows directions or pays attention. Be aware, however, that some emotionally disabled students have a hard time accepting praise, especially in front of a group. You can then do it privately.
- Provide optional work areas that may have less distraction.
- Randomly question the child and try to have him or her participate as often as possible to increase interest in the lesson.
- Make sure the materials being presented are compatible with the child's learning levels. In this way you can avoid frustration, which is also a cause of inattention.
- Use a variety of visual and auditory techniques, for example, overhead projector, tape recorder, or computer, to enhance the lesson and stimulate attention.

4-40. WARNING SIGNS OF A POTENTIAL SUICIDE RISK IN ADOLESCENTS

Behavioral Indications

1. Sudden changes in behavior—withdrawal, apathy, too much sleep or too little sleep, dramatic drop in academic grades or performance

2. Recent losses—divorce, separation from family members, loss of self-esteem, loss of a relationship (boyfriend, girlfriend), loss of status (exclusion from peer group, not making grades)

3. Moodiness or irritability—excessive fighting or abusive behavior, changes in behavior lasting more than two weeks, overnight feelings of happiness after long bouts of depression (frequently exhibited by teenagers who have decided to kill themselves and are now feeling the calm or peace of mind that follows the decision to die)

4. Giving away personal possessions

5. Preoccupation with dying—questions about dying, life after death, poetry with morbid themes, statements like, "Everyone would be better off without me," or more direct comments like, "I feel like killing myself"

Parents should also be aware of the criteria that determine the lethality of the suicidal threat.

Desire to Be Rescued: Teenagers who plan suicide attempts in areas with little or no chance of interruption have the greatest chance of success. When a teenager reports this to someone, the risk should be considered very serious. Many suicide attempts are made with the knowledge, because of routine, of someone coming home to ensure a rescue. Many deaths have occurred, however, when such a plan has not materialized, as when a parent stopped at a neighbor's house before coming home.

The Time of the Attempt: The chance of a suicide attempt increases dramatically whenever a teenager expresses the time he or she will "do it." According to statistics, most teenagers will attempt suicide in their homes between midafternoon and midnight.

Under the Influence of Alcohol or Drugs: Whenever a teenager is talking suicide and is under the influence of drugs or alcohol, the suicide risk is very high. Such factors greatly reduce controls and add to impulsivity.

Previous Attempts: Any teenager who has made previous attempts is a very high risk.

A Suicidal Note or Plan: Teenagers who write a note to parents, friends, or others indicating the possibility and manner of hurting themselves have a greater likelihood of attempting suicide.

Illness or Long-Standing Emotional Problems: When a chronic illness or long-term emotional stress is present, the teenager is more at risk for suicide.

4-40. Continued

Lack of Support Systems: The chances for suicide are greatest when teenagers have few peer support systems or little parental involvement or support.

Availability of Options: Teenagers who threaten to hurt themselves a certain way, and have the availability of that method are at a higher risk, for example, one who plans to use a parent's gun.

4-41. COMMON DISRUPTIVE BEHAVIOR DISORDERS

1-Attention Deficit Hyperactive Disorder

Description: Children with this disorder exhibit behaviors of inattention, hyperactivity and impulsiveness that are significantly inappropriate for their age levels. These behaviors may be severe and have an adverse affect on the child's academic achievement. (A more in-depth discussion of this condition appears earlier in this section.)

Educational Implications: Teachers should be aware of the academic as well as the social difficulties experienced by students with this disorder. Social rejection is common, and may contribute to low self-esteem, low frustration tolerance, and possibly aggressive or compulsive behavior patterns.

Possible Least Restrictive Educational Setting: Children with mild forms of this disorder may be able to maintain a normal class placement with the intervention of medication. More serious cases may require more restrictive settings, especially those children with associated oppositional or conduct problems. In such cases, special schools or residential settings may be the least restrictive setting.

2-Conduct Disorder

Description: This condition is characterized by a persistent pattern of behavior that intrudes and violates the basic rights of others without concern or fear of implications. This pattern is not selective and is exhibited in the home, at school, with peers, and in the child's community. Other behaviors present with this condition may include vandalism, stealing, physical aggression, cruelty to animals, and fire setting.

Categories:

Type	Description	DSM-IV-R Code
Solitary Aggressive Type	aggressive behavior towards peers and adults	312.0
Group Type	conduct problems mainly with peers as a group	312.2
Undifferentiated Type	for those not classified in either above group	312.9

4-41. Continued

Educational Implications: Children with this condition may be physically confrontational to teachers and peers, have poor attendance, have high levels of suspension thereby missing a great deal of academic work, and exhibit other forms of antisocial behavior.

Possible Least Restrictive Educational Setting: Children with this condition may be educated in a special class within a regular school if the condition is mild; however, the majority of students with this disorder are educated in a more restrictive program housed within special schools, residential schools, or institutions if the antisocial behavior is extreme.

3-Oppositional Defiant Disorder

Description: This disorder is usually characterized by patterns of negativistic, hostile, and defiant behaviors with peers as well as with adults. This disorder is considered less serious than a conduct disorder because of the absence of serious behaviors that violate the basic rights of others. Children with this disorder usually exhibit argumentative behaviors towards adults that may include swearing and frequent episodes of intense anger and annoyance. These symptoms are usually more serious and intense than those exhibited by other children of the same age.

Educational Implications: Teachers who have children with this disorder in their classes may observe low frustration tolerance, frequent temper outbursts, low sense of confidence, an unwillingness to take responsibility for their actions, consistent blaming of others for their own mistakes or problems, and frequent behaviors associated with attention deficit hyperactive disorder.

Possible Least Restrictive Educational Setting: Children with this condition may be educated in a special class within a regular school if the condition is mild; however, the majority of students with this disorder are educated in a more restrictive program housed within special schools, residential schools, or institutions if the antisocial behavior is extreme.

231

4-42. COMMON ANXIETY DISORDERS OF CHILDHOOD

1-Separation Anxiety Disorder

Description: This disorder is characterized by extreme anxiety associated with separation from someone whom the child views as a significant other. While this reaction may be common with very young children on their first day of school, continuation of the anxiety for more than two weeks indicates a problem that needs to be addressed. This separation anxiety is frequently exhibited at school and at home. It should be noted that if symptoms of separation anxiety occur in an adolescent, other factors such as social or academic pressure may be the contributing cause.

Educational Implications: Children with this disorder may require a great deal of the teacher's attention. The child may cling, be afraid to try new things, require a great deal of reassurance, and cry frequently. Panic attacks are common and the teacher may find that reason does not reduce the anxiety. Physical complaints are common and should never be ignored. In cases of separation anxiety, however, these "physical" symptoms are usually manifestations of the anxiety once medical causes are ruled out.

Possible Least Restrictive Educational Setting: Children with this disorder can usually be maintained in the regular class setting through the help of the school psychologist working with the child and parents. If the condition persists and the diagnosis changes, for example, to major depression, then outside professional help may be required and a more restrictive program, sometimes even homebound instruction if attendance at school is not possible, may have to be instituted.

2-Avoidant Disorder of Childhood or Adolescence

Description: This disorder results in the child's withdrawing from social contact or interaction with an unfamiliar peer or adult to the point of becoming a significant factor in social development.

Educational Implications: Children with this disorder can maintain regular class placement as long as achievement levels do not present problems—possibly signifying some other condition. Teachers with this type of student should be aware of social isolation, withdrawal from activity-based assignments, and a complete unwillingness to try new situations involving social interaction with unfamiliar peers. Trying to force the child into new social interaction situations may only result in further withdrawal socially as well as verbally. Work alone with the child or along with familiar peers only for a while. Once a trusting relationship is developed, your influence may be more rewarding. Referring the child to the school psychologist is also highly recommended. Individual outside counseling with a slow lead into small-group counseling should be explored. This transition, however, may result in a great deal of resistance on the part of the child.

4-42. Continued

Possible Least Restrictive Educational Setting: Children with this disorder can usually be maintained in the regular class setting through the help of the school psychologist working with the child and parents; however, children with other disabilities may also exhibit this disorder.

3-Overanxious Disorder

Description: The main feature of this disorder is an excessive level of anxiety or worry extending over a six-month or longer period of time.

Educational Implications: Teachers who have students with this disorder should be aware of the possibility of poor academic performance because of the child's preoccupation with worry. The teacher should also try to reassure and compliment the child as much as possible when he or she is not drawing negative attention to himself or herself.

Possible Least Restrictive Educational Setting: Most children with this disorder can be educated within a regular class placement unless the condition is coupled with more serious disabilities that require a more restrictive setting. Referral to the school psychologist is highly recommended.

4-43. COMMON EATING AND TIC DISORDERS

Eating Disorders

1-ANOREXIA NERVOSA

Description: Children with this condition show a marked disturbance and unwillingness to maintain a minimal body weight for their age and height. An extreme distorted sense of body image exists and intense fears and worries about gaining weight become obsessive. It is not uncommon for bulimia nervosa to be an associated feature. In more severe cases, death may occur.

Symptoms: Children with this disorder may also exhibit self-induced vomiting, use of laxatives, increased reduction of food intake, preoccupation with becoming fat, and noticeable increase in the frequency and intensity of exercise. In females, absence of menstrual cycles is common as the child's weight decreases and the body chemistry changes.

Educational Implications: Teachers should be aware of frequent absences because of medical complications. These children are usually high-achieving individuals but because of their medical conditions academic consistency may be difficult.

Possible Least Restrictive Educational Setting: Children with this type of disorder can be maintained in the regular school setting unless the condition becomes severe enough to warrant hospitalization. In some cases where the child is at home and unable to attend school, homebound instruction is used.

2-BULIMIA NERVOSA

Description: A condition characterized by recurrent episodes of uncontrolled consumption of large quantities of food (bingeing) followed by self-induced vomiting (purging), or use of laxatives or diuretics over a period of at least two months.

Symptoms: The individual with bulimia nervosa exhibits symptoms characterized by bingeing and purging, use of laxatives and diuretics, obsessive preoccupation with body shape and weight, and a feeling of lack of control over food consumption during binge episodes.

Educational Implications: Most teachers might not even know that a student is bulimic. Individuals hide this "secret" well and may not divulge the problem to anyone, not even a best friend. This is usually a private disorder until the person feels out of control enough to seek help and support. Consequently, teachers should be aware of frequent trips to the bathroom—especially in the morning after breakfast or after lunch. Changes in skin color and look may give some indications of problems. If you suspect anything, let the nurse investigate this further.

Possible Least Restrictive Educational Setting: Unlike those with anorexia nervosa, children with bulimia nervosa seldom suffer incapacitating symptoms except in rare cases when the eating and purging episodes run throughout the day. In most cases these children can be maintained in the regular school setting unless the condition becomes severe enough to warrant hospitalization.

4-43. Continued

Tic Disorders

3-TOURETTE'S DISORDER

Description: This disorder is characterized by motor and vocal ticing, which may be exhibited in the form of grunting, coughs, barks, touching, knee jerking, drastic head movements, head banging, and squatting.

Symptoms: The above symptoms may change as the child develops but the course of the disorder is usually lifelong. Associated features include obsessive compulsive disorders (OCD) and ADHD (attention deficit hyperactive disorder—discussed earlier). The condition is more common in males and family patterns are also common. *Coprolalia* (vocal tic involving the expression of obscenities) is an associated symptom in about 33% of the cases. See the section, "Tourette's Syndrome."

Educational Implications: Teachers of students with Tourette's disorder should be aware of and sensitive to the social difficulties and confusion exhibited by the student's peers. Social rejection, isolation and victimization may be common, and the teacher must step in to prevent these situations from occurring. In older students with this disorder, teachers should be aware of the child's use of a great deal of energy in an attempt to control the tics because of social pressure—at the cost of attention and consistent academic performance. If you have a student with this condition contact the local Tourette's Association in your area for further literature.

Possible Least Restrictive Educational Setting: Children with mild forms of this disorder can easily be maintained in a regular educational setting with supportive services. Since the condition does affect performance in many cases, children with this disorder are usually classified as disabled and do receive special education services including modifications. More severe cases that do not respond to medication may require a more restrictive setting. Medication, counseling and special education services provide a good treatment plan; however, the child may have to try many medications before finding one that relieves the ticing. Medications are also taken if OCD symptoms are associated.

4-44. OTHER DISORDERS OF CHILDHOOD AND ADOLESCENCE

Elimination Disorders

1-FUNCTIONAL ENCOPRESIS

Description: The major symptom of this disorder is repeated involuntary or intentional passage of feces into clothing or other places deemed inappropriate. The condition is not related to any physical condition, and must occur for a period of six months on a regular basis and be present in a child over the age of 4 for diagnosis to take place.

Educational Implications: Children with this disorder may experience social ridicule if the incidents take place in school. The teacher must be sensitive to the condition and involve the school psychologist and parents. Try to intervene as quickly as possible if a pattern exists to avoid further embarrassment for the child, and secondary complications such as avoidance.

Possible Least Restrictive Educational Setting: Children with this condition should have no problem maintaining a regular educational setting unless the condition is associated with other disabilities that require special education placement; however, this condition may create social pressures and isolation for the child.

2-FUNCTIONAL ENURESIS

Description: This disorder is characterized by repeated involuntary or intentional elimination of urine during the day or night into bed or clothes at an age at which bladder control is expected. A frequency of at least two times per month must be present for the condition to be diagnosed between the ages of five and six and at least once a month for older children.

Educational Implications: This condition may create social pressures and isolation for the child.

Possible Least Restrictive Educational Setting: Children with this condition should have no problem maintaining a regular educational setting unless the condition is associated with other disabilities that require special education placement.

3-ELECTIVE MUTISM

Description: This disorder is characterized by persistent refusal to talk in one or more major social situations, including school, despite the ability to comprehend spoken language and speak. The resistance to speech is not a symptom of any other major disorder.

Educational Implications: This condition may create a difficult situation for the classroom teacher. The teacher will not be able to measure certain language or social levels, will have to deal with social concerns and comments from classmates, and will have a difficult time encouraging the child to participate in necessary class activities or group projects. If a teacher has such a child in the classroom, he or she should contact the school psychologist as soon as possible. Individual and family counseling is highly suggested for such a disorder.

© 1995 by The Center for Applied Research in Education

4-44. Continued

Possible Least Restrictive Educational Setting: This type of child can usually be maintained in the regular educational setting as long as the child maintains sufficient performance levels. If the child's academic performance becomes discrepant, or social and intellectual factors interfere with performance, a more restrictive placement may have to be explored.

Anxiety Disorders

4-OBSESSIVE COMPULSIVE DISORDER

Description: The major characteristics associated with this disorder are persistent obsessions (persistent thoughts) or compulsions (repetitive acts) that significantly interfere with the individual's normal daily social, educational, occupational, or environmental routines.

Educational Implications: Children or adolescents with this disorder will have difficulty concentrating and maintaining consistent academic performance. These individuals may also experience depression as a result of their difficulties and medication may be instituted to relieve the anxiety associated with this disorder.

Possible Least Restrictive Educational Setting: This type of child can usually be maintained in the regular educational setting as long as the child maintains sufficient performance levels. If academic performance becomes discrepant, or social and intellectual factors interfere with performance, a more restrictive placement may have to be explored.

Mood Disorders

5-DYSTHYMIA

Description: The essential feature of this disorder is a chronic disturbance of the individual's moods involving chronic depression or irritable mood for a period of one year for children and adolescents.

Educational Implications: Teachers who experience this type of student need to work closely with the school psychologist or private therapist, if the child is in treatment. The teacher should also be aware that medication may be involved and an understanding of the side effects should be investigated.

Possible Least Restrictive Educational Setting: Students with this disorder can usually be maintained in a regular setting—or a more restrictive special education program, if the symptoms become more intense. The chronicity of this disorder rather than the severity usually accounts for a mild or moderate impairment. Consequently, hospitalization is rare unless suicide is attempted.

The above disorders represent only a cross-section of the conditions you may encounter in the classroom. While expertise is not suggested, an understanding and awareness of such disorders can only increase your effectiveness with these children. A more elaborate explanation—as well as further disorders associated with this developmental period—can be found in DSM-IV.

4-45. SPECIFIC PERSONALITY DISORDERS

1-Schizoid Personality Disorder

Description: The child with this disorder exhibits a restrictive range of emotional experiences and expression and indifference to social situations.

Educational Implications: In the classroom this type of child will be considered unapproachable. He or she will be resistant to group projects or group experiences. If the child is involved, he or she will remain on the outside and not participate in discussions. Other children will eventually ostracize the child. The teacher will also have a very difficult time establishing any meaningful relationship. Therapy and/or medication may be suggested by an outside professional or agency.

Least Restrictive Educational Setting: Children with this disorder eventually wind up in a special education setting; however, some remain in the mainstream because their academic performance is sufficient. They are viewed as "loners" by their classmates.

2-Antisocial Personality Disorder

Description: This disorder is characterized by a pattern of irresponsible and antisocial behavior. The condition is usually first seen in childhood or early adolescence and continues throughout the child's development. This diagnosis is usually made after the age of 18 and the individual must have had a history of symptoms indicative of a conduct disorder before the age of 15.

Educational Implications: The situation for the classroom teacher can be serious with this type of disorder. Since the individual has little or no regard for the personal rights of others, any antisocial act can occur, even acts that may place the teacher in danger. Medication may help reduce tension, while therapy may have limited success.

Possible Least Restrictive Educational Setting: Children or individuals with this disorder may have aged out and may no longer be part of the educational system. If they had already been classified as disabled, they would probably be placed in a very restrictive educational setting until the age of 21—if they had not been arrested by that time.

3-Borderline Personality Disorder

Description: The main features of this disorder include instability of self-image, inconsistent and unfulfilling interpersonal relationships, instability of mood, and persistent identity disturbance.

Educational Implications: In the classroom this individual will have a hard time maintaining any consistent academic performance. Frequent outbursts, truancy, hospitalization, legal problems, or school disciplinary actions may provide an inconsistent pattern of attendance and involvement.

4-45. Continued

Possible Least Restrictive Educational Setting: The individual with this condition will usually be placed in a more restrictive special education setting, hospital program, or institution.

4-Passive-Aggressive Personality Disorder

Description: Individuals with this disorder exhibit a pervasive pattern of passive resistance to the requests or requirements placed upon them in school, social, or occupational performance.

Educational Implications: Teachers will find that working with this type of student can be very frustrating. These students may become irritable, sulky, or argumentative, and often blame external causes for their lack of production. Assignments may have to be readjusted so that some sense of accomplishment can be obtained. Counseling is strongly suggested.

Possible Least Restrictive Educational Setting: Most students with this disorder can be educated within the normal setting; however, they exhibit a pattern of constant underachievement. In some cases where the discrepancy becomes significant, a referral for a more restrictive setting may be suggested. A history of severe academic discrepancy resulting from this disorder may result in the child's being classified as emotionally disabled.

4-46. DESCRIPTION OF TICS IN TOURETTE'S SYNDROME

Tourette's syndrome (TS) is a neurological disorder that appears to be genetically transmitted in most cases. Tourette's is one of a number of disorders classified as *tic disorders*. Tics are involuntary movements that present themselves through motion or sound.

The first tics or sympoms of Tourette's Syndrome are usually simple motor tics of the head, face, and neck area. *Simple motor tics* are usually rapid, apparently purposeless, and repetitive movements of one muscle group. Examples of simple motor tics include the following:

Motor

- eye blinking
- shoulder shrugs
- mouth opening
- arm extending
- facial grimaces
- lip licking
- rolling eyes
- squinting

Simple phonic (sound) tics are repetitive sounds that are not linguistically meaningful. They may include the following:

Sound (phonic)

- throat clearing
- grunting
- yelling or screaming
- sniffing
- barking
- snorting
- coughing
- spitting
- squeaking
- humming
- whistling

Complex motor tics are involuntary movements that involve the coordinated sequence or activation of two or more muscle groups. Examples include:

4-46. Continued

- pulling at clothes
- touching people
- touching objects
- smelling fingers
- jumping or skipping
- poking or jabbing
- punching
- kicking
- hopping
- kissing self or others
- flapping arms
- twirling around
- thrusting movements of groin or torso
- walking on toes
- copropraxia: sexually touching self or others, obscene gestures
- self-injurious behavior

Complex phonic tics represent involuntary linguistically meaningful utterances or expressions, such as repetitive use of phrases. Examples include:

- making animal-like sounds
- unusual changes in pitch or volume of voice
- stuttering
- coprolalia—socially taboo phrases or obscenities
- echoing one's own words or others'

4-47. DIAGNOSTIC CRITERIA FOR TIC DISORDERS

Transient Tic Disorders

- most common of the tic disorders
- onset during early school years
- affects 5% to 24% of all children
- single or multiple motor and/or vocal tics occurring daily for at least two weeks but for no longer than one year
- three to four times more common in males than females
- more common in the first-degree relatives of people who have transient tic disorders

Chronic Motor/Vocal Tic Disorder

- onset before age 21
- usually persist unchanged throughout a period of more than one year
- involves either motor or vocal tics
- generally related to Tourette's syndrome

Tourette's Syndrome

- Symptoms begin before age 21.
- Tics occur for more than one year.
- Tics are highly variable, changing over time in anatomic location, number, complexity, and frequency.
- Associated problems may include obsessive compulsive disorder.
- Associated behavioral difficulties may include problems in attention, hyperactivity, and emotional lability.
- Symptoms can be suppressed at school, then emerge abruptly upon arrival in the safety of the home.
- Fifty to sixty percent of children with TS have attention deficit hyperactive disorder.

4-48. PHARMACOTHERAPY AND TOURETTE'S SYNDROME

Pharmacotherapy has been reported to be the most widely used treatment for TS to date. The difficult with this treatment is the attempt to balance the alleviation of symptoms with the side effects of many medications. The following is a brief overview of medications currently know to alleviate symptoms of Tourette's:

Neuroleptics

- Symptoms of Tourette's are decreased in 70% to 80% of the patients.
- Side effects result in 50% of the patients discontinuing this medication.
- Side effects include Parkinsonian symptoms, sedation, weight gain, decreased concentration, impaired memory, depression, and personality changes.
- The medication is usually used in patients whose symptoms cause significant impairment.
- Examples include Haldol, Orap, and Prolixin.

Clonodine

- It is reported to be effective in 60% of Tourette's patients.
- Side effects are less disturbing.
- It may require up to a twelve-week trial to evaluate efficacy.
- Common side effects are sedation and dry mouth.

Antidepressants

- These are generally used to treat associated ADHD (attention deficit hyperactive disorder) and/or OCD (obsessive compulsive disorder) symptoms.
- Some patients report decrease in symptoms while others report increase.
- Side effects include dry mouth, sedation, low blood pressure, dizziness, and constipation.
- Examples include Tofranil, Clomipramine, and Prozac.

4-49. CLASSROOM STRATEGIES FOR CHILDREN WITH TOURETTE'S

Students with Tourette's will have to face many pressures in school associated with tics—social concerns, reactions, and associated learning difficulties. The teacher's response to these conditions can make a critical difference. Following are some classroom suggestions when working with a child who has Tourette's:

- Keep in mind that motor or vocal tics are occurring involuntarily.
- Try not to react with anger or annoyance.
- Try to be a role model for the students on how to react to the Tourette's symptoms.
- Provide the child with opportunities for short breaks out of the classroom.
- Try to find a private place somewhere in the school where the child can "let out" the tics, since the effort to suppress the tics causes a buildup of tension.
- Allow the student to take tests in a private room so that he or she does not waste energy suppressing the tics—interfering with the student's concentration.
- Work with the student's classmates to help them understand the tics and to reduce ridicule and teasing.
- Secure materials (e.g., audiovisuals or pamphlets to provide information for your pupils and colleagues.
- If the student's tics are particularly disruptive, avoid recitation in front of the class.
- Have the student tape-record oral reports.
- Keep in mind that students with Tourette's often have visual motor difficulties.
- Modify written assignments by reducing the number of problems presented or required to copy.
- Allow parents to copy down work so that the pupil can dictate his or her ideas to facilitate concept formation.
- Allow the student to write the answers directly on a test paper or booklet rather than use computerized scoring sheets.
- Allow the child untimed tests to reduce stress.
- Allow another child to take notes for the student so that she or he can listen to the lecture without the added stress of copying notes
- Try not to penalize for spelling errors.
- Try to use a multisensory approach whenever possible.
- Avoid multidirections.
- Use graph paper for math so that the student can place one number in each box.

4-50. CAUSES OF HEARING IMPAIRMENTS

Conductive Hearing Loss: Results from problems with the structures in the outer or middle ear, generally attributed to a blockage in the mechanical conduction of sound. To overcome this blockage, the sounds must be amplified. These conditions are usually temporary. The leading causes of this type of hearing loss are

- otitis media (middle ear infection)
- excessive earwax
- otosclerosis—formation of a spongy-bony growth around the stapes, which impedes its movement

Sensorineural Hearing Loss: Results from damage to the cochlea or the auditory nerve. This damage is caused by illness and disease and is not medically or surgically treatable. Causes of this hearing loss include

- viral diseases (rubella–German measles, meningitis)
- Rh incompatibility
- ototoxic medications (medicines that destroy or damage hair cells in the cochlea (e.g., streptomycin) taken by pregnant mothers or very young children.
- hereditary factors
- exposure to noise
- aging

Mixed Hearing Loss: A hearing loss caused by both sensorineural and conductive problems

Functional Hearing Loss: Problems that are not organic in origin. Examples include

- psychosomatic causes
- hysterical conversion
- malingering
- emotional or psychological problems

Central Auditory Disorders: These disorders produce no measurable peripheral hearing loss. Children with these disorders have trouble learning and are often considered learning disabled. Causes include

- auditory comprehension problems
- auditory discrimination problems
- auditory learning difficulties
- language development delays

4-51. AUDIOMETRIC EVALUATION MEASURES

Pure Tone Audiometric Screening

Pure tone screening is often referred to as sweep testing and is usually the child's first encounter with hearing testing. This type of testing, which is common in schools, presents the child with pure tones over a variety of frequency ranges. The child is then asked to respond if he or she hears a tone, usually by some gesture. A child who is unable to hear sounds at two or more frequencies is usually referred for further evaluation.

Speech Audiometry

This type of evaluation is used to determine a child's ability to hear and understand speech through the presentation of words in a variety of loudness levels.

Pure Tone Threshold Audiometry

In this procedure, the child is presented with a variety of frequencies through earphones, and is asked to make a gesture or push a button each time he or she hears a tone. This type of air conduction test reveals the presence of hearing loss.

Special Audiometric Tests

1. **Sound field audiometry:** This measure is used with very young children who cannot respond manually or are unable or unwilling to wear headphones. The child is evaluated by observing the intensity levels at which he or she responds to different levels of sounds broadcast through speakers.

2. **Evoked response audiometry:** This measure, which incorporates an electroencephalograph and a computer, measures changes in brain wave activity in response to a variety of sound levels. This measure can be used with infants who are suspected of being deaf.

3. **Impedance audiometry:** There are two major impedance audiometry tests. The first, *tympanometry,* measures the functioning level of the eardrum. The second, *stapedial reflex testing,* measures the reflex response of the stapedial muscle to pure tone signals. Since these tests do not require a response on the part of the child, they can be used with very young children.

4. **Behavioral play audiometry:** This technique involves placing the child in a series of activities that reward him or her for responding appropriately to tone or speech.

4-52. MODES OF COMMUNICATION FOR THE DEAF

Oral-Aural Approach

This approach stresses the primary reception of language through the auditory channel, with the use of individually prescribed amplification. Examples include the following:

Auditory training: The purpose of auditory training is to teach the hearing-impaired individual to use residual hearing to the greatest extent possible. It is

- usually provided by an audiologist or speech pathologist
- usually provided in individual or group therapy sessions
- reinforced in the classroom and at home
- used to reinforce environmental cues in conversations
- used to help sharpen the child's ability to discriminate among sounds and words

Cued speech: This is one method of supplementing oral communication and it

- is considered a visual-oral method of communication carrying no meaning without an accompanying speech signal
- uses cues that consist of hand signals used near the lips
- involves eight different hand shapes, used in four different positions

Manual Communication

Fingerspelling: A series of finger positions to represent the individual letters of the alphabet, and to spell out words

American sign language: a system of ideagraphic gestures representing words or concepts—used by most deaf people

Total Communication

This method combines the oral-aural and manual modes.

Technological Devices

Teletypewriter assistance for the deaf: Used to send and receive immediate written messages over telephone lines

Caption decoder: A device that allows deaf individuals to receive captions or subtitles on a television screen

4-53. THE MANUAL ALPHABET

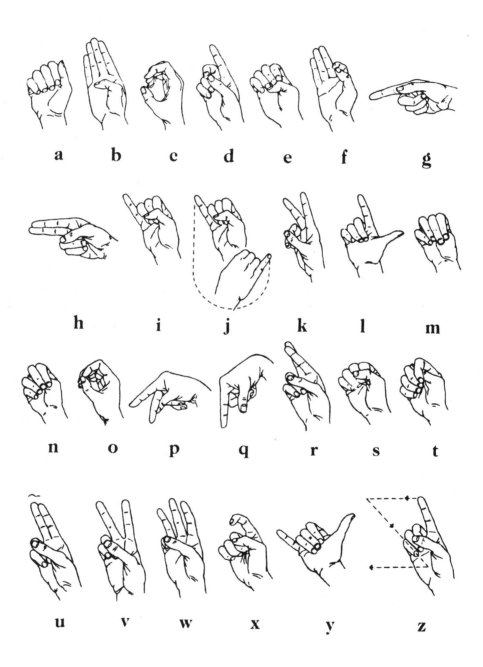

4-54. DEGREES OF HEARING IMPAIRMENT

Degree of Hearing Loss	Decibel loss	Resulting Impairment
Slight	27–40 dB	Difficulty hearing faint noises or distant conversation. The individual with a slight hearing loss will usually not have difficulties in the regular school setting.
Mild	41–55 dB	May miss as much as 50% of classroom conversations, and may also exhibit limited vocabulary and speech difficulties.
Moderate	56–70 dB	Able to hear only loud conversation, may exhibit defective speech, and vocabulary and language difficulties.
Severe	71–90 dB	Hearing may be limited to a radius of 1 foot. May be able to discriminate certain environmental sounds, shows defective speech and language ability, and has severe difficulty understanding consonant sounds.
Profound	91 dB or greater	Can sense, but is unable to understand, sounds and tones. Vision becomes the primary sense of communication and speech and language are likely to deteriorate.

4-55. EXAMPLES OF TYPICAL SOUND INTENSITIES

Intensity in Decibels (dB)	Examples
140	Jet plane taking off about 100 feet away
130	Industrial jackhammer
120	Discotheque, rock and roll concert
110	Industrial punch press
105	Bulldozer and construction equipment
100	Chain saw
90	Heavy street noises, factory noises
85	Person shouting from 5–10 feet away
80	The noise from cars on an expressway at 60 mph
75	Noise in a restaurant
70	Window air conditioner
40–65	Typical conversational level, typewriter, small office machines, washing machine
35	Typical house noise
30	Radio station studio
20	Whisper at 5 feet, windy day

250

CHART 1 CROSS SECTION OF THE EAR

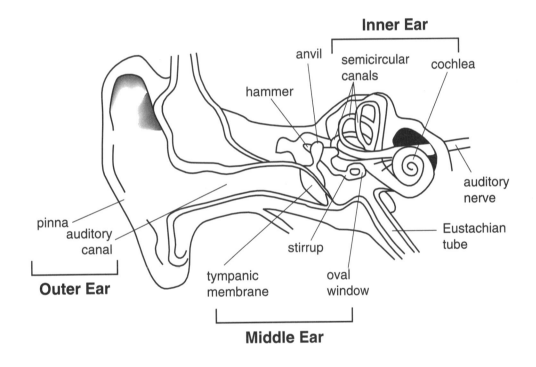

4-56. CAUSES OF VISUAL IMPAIRMENTS

Myopia. Referred to as *nearsightedness,* this condition occurs when the rays of light from distant objects are focused in front of the retina. The individual with this condition is able to see objects close up more clearly.

Hyperopia. Referred to as *farsightedness,* this condition occurs when the rays of light are focused behind the retina. The individual with this condition is able to see objects at a distance more clearly.

Astigmatism. Referred to as *blurred vision,* astigmatism is caused by uneven curvature of the cornea or lens. This curvature prevents light rays from focusing correctly on the retina. This condition can usually be improved by corrective lenses.

Cataracts. A cloudiness in the lens of the eye that blocks the light necessary for seeing clearly. Vision may be blurred, distorted, or incomplete.

Glaucoma. This condition is caused by the failure of the aqueous fluid to circulate properly, which results in an elevation of pressure in the eye that may gradually destroy the optic nerve.

Diabetic retinopathy. Children and adults with diabetes frequently have impaired vision due to hemorrhages and the growth of new blood vessels in the area of the retina. This results in a condition known as diabetic retinopathy, which may be helped with laser surgery.

Retinitis pigmentosa. An inherited disease, retinitis pigmentosa causes a gradual degeneration of the retina. This condition is not treatable.

Usher's syndrome. This syndrome results from a combination of congenital deafness and retinitis pigmentosa.

Macular degeneration. In macular degeneration—a fairly common disorder in which the central area of the retina gradually deteriorates—the individual usually retains peripheral vision but loses the ability to see clearly in the center of the visual field.

Retrolental fibroplasia. This condition results from the use of too much oxygen in the incubation of premature babies.

4-57. THE BRAILLE ALPHABET

4-58. WHAT IS MEANT BY *VISUAL IMPAIRMENTS?*

For legal and administrative purposes, the following definitions are used:

Legally blind: Central visual acuity of 20/200 or less in the better eye with correction, or, if greater than 20/200, a field of vision no greater than 20 degrees at the widest diameter.

Partially sighted: Central visual acuity between 20/70 and 20/200 in the better eye correction.

For functional educational purposes these definitions are used:

Visually handicapped: Requires special educational provisions because of visual problems.

Low vision: Has severe visual impairment after correction but visual function can be increased through the use of optical and environmental aids. Students with low vision learn using vision with other senses. Functional vision will depend on factors such as lighting, use of optical aids and devices, tasks, and personal characteristics. Modifications in lighting, size of print or objects, and distance may be required.

Blind: Has either no vision or, at most, light perception. (Students learn through the use of braille or related media.)

4-59. TYPICAL CHARACTERISTICS OF INDIVIDUALS WITH VISUAL IMPAIRMENTS

1. The lack of vision or reduced vision may result in delays or limitations in motor, cognitive, and social development.

2. Without visual input, an infant may not be motivated to reach and move toward interesting objects in the environment.

3. As soon as the infant with a visual impairment finds it exciting to hear sounds, he or she will begin to reach and move toward the objects in the environment that make sound. This does not occur until several months later, since hearing sounds does not motivate movement toward objects as soon as seeing objects does.

4. Cognitively, the child who has a visual impairment cannot perceive objects in the environment beyond his or her grasp, including those that are too large or too small, or that are moving.

5. While use of other senses enables the child to obtain information about the environment, a cognitive limitation does exist in the range and variety of experiences.

6. Socially, a child with a visual impairment is limited in interaction with the environment. The child cannot see the facial expressions of parents, teachers, and peers; cannot model social behaviors through imitation; and sometimes is unaware of the presence of others unless a sound is made.

7. While touch provides direct information, it is often socially unacceptable. The older child is limited in the ability to orient to environmental cues and to travel freely.

8. The unique curriculum for students who are blind includes reading and writing through the use of braille, listening skills, personal-social and daily living skills, orientation and mobility, career education, and instruction in the use of special aids and equipment.

9. In addition to these areas, students with low vision and visual limitations may need instruction in the efficient use of existing vision and in the use of optical aids and alternative learning materials.

10. A high proportion of students with visual impairments have additional disabilities and may require a curriculum that emphasizes functional living skills and communication skills.

11. Educational settings and services for children with visual impairments vary according to individual needs. Self-contained classrooms, residential schools, or regular classrooms with or without special assistance may be appropriate options for individual students.

CHART 2 CROSS SECTION OF THE EYE

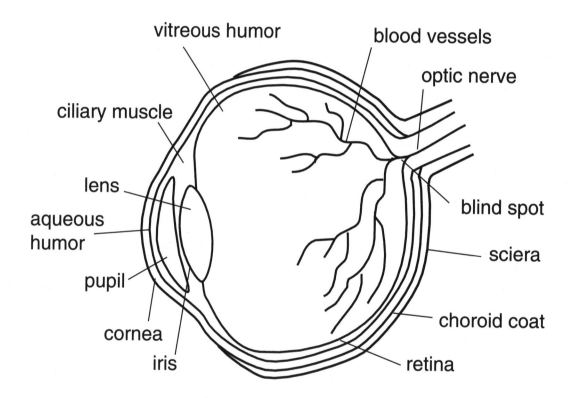

4-60. TERMINOLOGY ASSOCIATED WITH THE VISUALLY IMPAIRED

Albinism. A hereditary condition in which there is a lack of pigment throughout the body, including the eyes. Children with albinism are very sensitive to light and sometimes wear tinted glasses.

Astigmatism. Blurred vision caused by defective curvature of the refractive surface of the eye. As a result, light rays are not sharply focused on the retina.

Anterior Chamber. Space in front of the eye, bounded in front by the cornea and behind the iris; filled with aqueous.

Aqueous Humor. Clear, watery fluid which fills the anterior and posterior chambers within the front part of the eye.

Cataract. A condition in which the crystalline lens of the eye, or its capsule, or both, become opaque, with consequent loss of visual acuity.

Coloboma. Congenital cleft due to the failure of the eye to complete growth in the part affected.

Color Deficiency. Diminished ability to perceive differences in color, usually for red or green, rarely for blue or yellow.

Glaucoma. Increased pressure inside the eye; hardening of the eyeball caused by accumulation of aqueous fluid in the front portion.

Hemianopsia. Blindness of one-half the field of vision of one or both eyes.

Hyperopia. A condition in which the eyeball is too short from front to back, causing far-sightedness.

Isihara Color Plates. A test for defects in recognizing colors, based on the ability to trace patterns in a series of multi-colored charts.

Jaeger Test. A test for near vision; lines of reading matter printed in a series of various sizes of type.

Keratoconus. Cone-shaped deformity of the cornea.

Myopia. Nearsightedness. A refractive error in which, because the eyeball is too long in relation to its focusing power, the point of focus for rays of light from distant objects is in front of the retina.

Ophthalmologist. A physician who specializes in diagnosis and treatment of all defects and diseases of the eye by prescribing drugs and glasses, performing surgery, and other types of treatment.

Optometrist. A licensed, nonmedical practitioner, who measures refractive errors and eye muscle disturbances. The optometrist's treatment is limited to the prescribing and fitting of glasses.

4-60. Continued

Optician. A maker of glasses, the optician grinds lenses to prescriptions, fits them into frames, and adjusts frames to the wearer.

Retinitis Pigmentosa. A hereditary degeneration of the retina beginning with night blindness and producing a gradual loss of peripheral vision. Though some persons with this disease lose all their vision, many do retain some central vision.

Snellen Chart. Used for testing central visual acuity. It consists of lines of letters, numbers or symbols in graded sizes drawn to Snellen measurements. Each size is labeled with the distance at which it can be read by the normal eye.

Strabismus. Failure of the two eyes to simultaneously direct their gaze at the same object because of muscle imbalance.

Sclera. The white part of the eye.

Strephosymbolia. A disorder of perception in which objects seem reversed as in a mirror.

Tunnel Vision. Contraction of the visual field giving the affected individual the impression of looking through a tunnel.

4-61. VARIABLES THAT MAY INFLUENCE AN EXCEPTIONAL BILINGUAL CHILD'S PLACEMENT DECISION

Program placement should offer the best fit between the student's needs and the available resources. Placement decisions for the bilingual exceptional student should reflect the type and nature of instruction to be provided, the language of instruction, the conveyor of instruction, the duration of instruction, and the student's learning needs and style. The following special education variables and bilingual factors should be addressed in identifying placements:

1. Student's age

2. Type and degree of impairment or disability

3. Age at which disability occurred

4. Level of language involvement because of the disability

5. Level of academic achievement

6. Entry-level language skills (upon entering school)

7. Measured intellectual ability

8. Method and language used in measuring academic achievement and intellectual ability

9. Level of adaptive behavior

10. Time spent in United States

11. Current cultural home setting

12. Social maturity

13. Level of language proficiency in English and other language

14. Amount and type of language input received in the home environment

15. Speech and language capabilities in both languages

16. Presence of multiple handicaps

17. Ambulation or mobility

18. Success in past and present placements

19. Wishes of students and parents

4-62. BASIC ELEMENTS OF AN INDIVIDUALIZED EDUCATION PROGRAM (IEP) FOR EXCEPTIONAL BILINGUAL CHILDREN

IEPs for exceptional bilingual students should include the following elements:

1. The child's current educational status, including all service programs the child is receiving

2. Goals, including acculturation and growth in both the first and second languages

3. Realistic goals with regard to the time necessary—possibly years

4. The sequence of short-term instructional objectives leading up to each goal

5. A list of instructional and service requirements, including a balance between the first and second languages, as well as delineation of who will assist with acculturation needs

6. An indication of how much and what aspects of the program will be in the mainstream

7. The program's duration

8. IEPs realistic criteria and a schedule for evaluation of the IEP's effectiveness

9. A statement of the role of the parents

10. Specification of changes to be made in the physical, social, and instructional realms, including the first and second languages and cross-cultural adaptation

4-63. SELECTING AND ADAPTING MATERIALS FOR EXCEPTIONAL BILINGUAL CHILDREN

The following guidelines represent some of the many considerations teachers should bear in mind when evaluating, selecting, adapting, or developing materials:

1. Know the specific language abilities of each student.

2. Include appropriate cultural experiences in material adapted or developed.

3. Ensure that material progresses at a rate commensurate with student needs and abilities.

4. Document the success of selected materials.

5. Adapt only specific materials requiring modifications, and do not attempt to change too much at one time.

6. Try out different materials and adaptations until an appropriate education for each student is achieved.

7. Strategically implement materials adaptations to ensure smooth transitions into the new materials.

8. Follow some consistent format or guide when evaluating materials.

9. Be knowledgeable about particular cultures and heritages and their compatibility with selected materials.

10. Follow a well-developed process for evaluating the success of adapted or developed materials as the individual language and cultural needs of students are addressed.

Adapting Materials

The following list is not designed to be all-inclusive; variations may be required to meet individual needs.

1. Adjust the method of presentation or content.

2. Develop supplemental material.

3. Tape-record directions for the material.

4. Provide alternatives for responding to questions.

5. Rewrite brief sections to lower the reading level.

6. Outline the material for the student before reading a selection.

7. Reduce the number of pages or items on a page to be completed by the student.

8. Break tasks into smaller subtasks.

9. Provide additional practice to ensure mastery.

4-63. CONTINUED

10. Substitute a similar, less complex task for a particular assignment.

11. Develop simple study guides to complement required materials.

4-64. SUGGESTED IDENTIFICATION PROCEDURES FOR STUDENTS WITH LIMITED ENGLISH PROFICIENCY

The procedures for the identification of students with limited English proficiency (LEP) who are experiencing difficulty in the general educational setting may be divided into two areas.

LEP (Limited English Proficiency) Students with Formal School Experiences

Before you consider referring an LEP student with previous academic experiences for special education services, the following should be implemented and documented:

1. Provide instruction in the native language for content area development and extensive instruction in English as a second language (ESL).

2. Try to provide educationally related support services—speech and language services, and psychological, social work, and noncareer counseling services by qualified bilingual-bicultural professional personnel, as appropriate.

3. Document the extent to which these services have been provided in the regular education setting.

LEP Students with Little or No Formal School Experience

This area includes students who

- speak a language other than English
- have had limited schooling
- have nonequivalent academic instruction
- have no formal schooling in their native country
- perform poorly on standardized tests whose norms and content are based on experience and acculturation patterns of children raised in the United States
- experience some level of difficulty when enrolled, for perhaps the first time, in a formal educational setting

The following strategies and activities are suggested prior to a referral for special education services:

- school and community orientation by staff members
- native language development and enrichment
- reinforcement of self-identity
- reinforcement of self-concept
- reinforcement of interpersonal skill development across contexts

263

4-64. Continued

- use of specialized ESL methodology and strategies across all curriculum areas
- experience-based educational methodology and techniques
- hands-on enrichment activities and community-school participation
- instruction in literacy skills in the native language along with English
- strategies designed to develop proficiency in behaviors necessary in academic settings, for example, sitting in chair, raising hand
- planned parent orientation and involvement
- intensive English-as-a-second-language instruction
- educationally related support services
- speech and language improvement services in the native language of the student
- documented statements indicating the extent of activities and services provided

4-65. SPECIFIC REQUIREMENTS FOR REFERRAL OF BILINGUAL STUDENTS TO THE CSE

- Identify the reason for the referral and include any test results in both languages as appropriate.
- Include any records or reports on which the referral is based.
- Attach a home language survey indicating the home language(s).
- Specify the level of language proficiency.
- Describe the extent to which the LEP student has received native language instruction and/or ESL services prior to the referral.
- Describe experiential and/or enrichment services for students from diverse cultural and experiential backgrounds.
- Describe the school's efforts to involve parents prior to referral.
- Describe the amount of time and extent of services in an academic program for students who have had little or no formal schooling.
- Identify referred student's length of residency in the United States, prior school experience in the native country, and experience in an English-language school system.
- Describe all attempts to remediate the pupil's performance prior to referral, including any supplemental aids or support services provided for this purpose.

4-66. CAUSES OF PHYSICAL DISABILITIES

Cerebral palsy—a disorder of movement and posture due to damage to areas of the brain that control motor function. Important information about this condition includes the following:

- The condition becomes evident in infancy or early childhood.
- The incidence is around 3 per every 1000 live births
- The impairment may involve different parts of the body including:

   -hemiplegia—involves the arm, leg, and trunk on the same side

   -paraplegia—legs only

   -quadriplegia—both arms and both legs as well as the trunk and neck

   -diplegia—legs more involved than the arms

   -double hemiplegia—arms more involved than the legs, and one side more involved

Arthogyposis multiplex congenita—a condition of fixed stiffness and deformity of the limbs in any joint prior to birth. Important facts include the following:

- It is sometimes referred to as "fixed joint" disorder.
- Limb muscles are absent or much smaller and weaker than usual.
- Child has little or no joint motion.
- Curvature of the spine may also be present.

Hypertonia—a condition found in 60% of cerebral palsy victims involving increased stiffness.

Athetosis—a condition affecting the extrapyramidal tract of the central nervous system which results in involuntary movements. Facts about this condition include the following:

- The arms, hands, and facial muscles are typically more involved than the legs.
- Symptoms are exhibited by about 20% of individuals with cerebral palsy.
- The individual has little or no control over his or her movements.
- Attention deficit is exacerbated by a lack of head control.
- It results in severe dependence in activities of daily living and locomotion.

Ataxia—a rare condition of cerebral palsy characterized by an inability to achieve coordination in balancing and hand use.

Hemophilia—often called the "bleeders disease," characterized by poor blood clotting ability due to the absence of the clotting factor in the blood.

4-66. Continued

Juvenile diabetes—a metabolic disorder caused by the body's inability to burn sugars and starches to create energy. Adequate insulin is not produced by the pancreas.

Limb deficiency—characterized by the absence of a limb, may be congenital or acquired after birth. The acquisition of an artificial limb (prosthesis) can be important to the physical and psychological well-being of the individual.

Muscular dystrophy—characterized by increasing weakness of skeletal muscles. Progressive muscle weakness, awkwardness, and slowness in movement eventually force the child to become confined to a wheelchair. Further characteristics include the following:

- Progression is usually rapid, with death usually occurring in the teen years.
- Students fatigue more easily as the disease progresses.
- Initial symptoms may hamper a child while running or climbing stairs.

Osteogenesis imperfecta—characterized by "brittle bones." It results from the defective development of both quality and quantity of bone tissue. The condition is further characterized by abnormal growth of bones in length and thickness.

Spina bifida—a congenital disease, caused by a defect in development of the vertebral column, which results in spinal cord and nerve root damage. As a result related neurological problems develop.

- Myelomeningocele is the most severe form.
- Deficits in spina bifida range from minor sensory and ambulatory problems to paraplegia and lack of sensation.
- Orthopedic deformities may exist.
- Incontinence may occur in the severe form.
- Urinary tract infections are common
- Individual is more susceptible to the development of hydrocephalus, an abnormal buildup of cerebrospinal fluids in the cranial cavity.

Spinal cord injury—can result from automobile, bicycle, skiing, and other accidents causing traumatic injury to the spinal cord. The extent of the injury varies according to the level and type of lesion or injury to the spinal cord.

Traumatic brain injury—caused by an insult to the brain by an external physical force, resulting in an impairment of cognitive abilities or physical functioning.

Cystic fibrosis—a hereditary disorder characterized by chronic pulmonary involvement and pancreatic deficiency.

4-67. INFECTIOUS DISEASES—MODES OF TRANSMISSION

Infectious-Communicable Disease	Mode of Transmission
Chicken Pox	Respiratory secretions, such as sneezing
Cytomegalovirus	direct or indirect contact with respiratory secretions blood urine
Gonorrhea	sexual contact involving the exchange of body fluids, for example, blood or vaginal fluids
Hepatitis A	fecal oral transmission, direct contact
Hepatitis B	direct contact with blood
Herpes I (above waist) Herpes II (below waist)	direct contact with fluid vesicle
HIV Infection—AIDS	direct contact with blood, contaminated needles, sexual contact involving the exchange of bodily fluids
Measles	respiratory secretions
Mononucleosis	direct contact with respiratory secretions, saliva
Mumps	respiratory secretions, such as sneezing
Respiratory Syncytial Virus (RSV)	direct or indirect contact with respiratory secretions, for example, nasal discharge
Salmonella Bacteria	fecal-oral transmission

4-68. POTENTIAL CLASSROOM MODIFICATIONS AND TEACHER SKILLS REQUIRED FOR CERTAIN PHYSICAL DISABILITIES

Chronic condition	Modification	Skills required
Athsma	avoidance of allergans participation in physical activity administration of medication as needed	CPR recognition of signs of respiratory stress recognition of medication side effects
Congenital Heart Disease	participation in physical activity administration of medication as needed diet or fluids	CPR recognition of the signs and symptoms of heart failure recognition of medication side effects
Cystic Fibrosis	physical activity administration of medication as needed diet	recognition of signs and symptoms of respiratory stress recognition of medication side effects
Diabetes	diet, bathroom frequency, snacks balance of exercise and food	recognition of signs and intake of sugar recognition of symptoms of hypoglycemia (rapid onset)
Hemophilia	physical activity	recognition of signs and symptoms of bleeding management of bleeding (cuts and scrapes)
Juvenile Rheumatoid Arthritis	participation in physical activity environment (stairs) administration of medication as needed	recognition of signs and symptoms of increased inflamation frequency of movement recognition of broken bones
Kidney Disease	physical activity diet and fluids bathroom privilages medication administration	recognition of signs and symptoms of fluid retention
Leukemia	participation in physical activity exposure to communicative diseases	recognition of signs and symptoms of infection recognition of signs and symptoms of bleeding
Seizure Disorder	participation in physical activity environment administration of medication as needed	seizure management recognition of signs and symptoms of distress during and after seizures recognition of medication side effects

269

4-68. Continued

| Spina Bifida | participation in physical activity environment to accomodate mobility | recognition of signs and symptoms of shunt blockage |

Note: This chart contains general information; health care plans on an individual basis with a qualified physician are recommended.

4-69. PHYSICAL AND OCCUPATIONAL THERAPY MEASUREMENT AREAS

Evaluation by respective therapists may include, but is not limited to, the measurement of the following areas:

Physical Therapy

- endurance
- balance and equilibrium
- postural and joint deviation
- gait analysis
- personal independence
- wheelchair management
- checking of prosthetic and orthotic equipment/devices
- architectural barriers and transportation needs

Occupational Therapy

- oral-motor dysfunction and feeding problems
- sensory processing
- visual-perceptual-motor status
- neuromuscular function
- manual dexterity
- psychosocial behaviors
- play and leisure time abilities
- self-help skills
- physical facilities and environment on performance
- pre-vocational skills

Areas of Assessment Common to Both Services

- developmental assessment levels
- range of motion
- muscle testing functions
- sensory integration
- activities of daily living
- needs and uses of adaptive equipment

271

4-70. GUIDELINES FOR AN OCCUPATIONAL THERAPY EVALUATION

A formal occupational therapy evaluation is required only in the following situations:

NEW STUDENT TO PROGRAM—when the student is new to a program, whether it is home bound, preschool or school based, where therapy is mandated by the CSE. If a formal occupational therapy evaluation is available from the referring agency, school district or private occupational therapist, it may be used.

PRESCHOOLER ADVANCING TO KINDERGARTEN—when a preschool student is advancing to an elementary program, and the child has been receiving occupational therapy in a preschool program, a formal evaluation should be forwarded to the committee on special education upon the request of the appropriate building administrator or local school district. This can only be done with parental consent.

CONTENT OF EVALUATION—depending upon the program to which the therapist is assigned, the following formal test measurements and clinical observations may be addressed during the occupational therapy evaluation. Guidelines have been prepared for a diverse student population. The therapist is expected to evaluate only those areas appropriate to the assigned population such as:

- Background information—any pertinent medical or social history.
- Behavior—behaviors that interfere with program implementation and/or affect the student's compliance, e.g., level of alertness, concentration, and personality disorder.
- Vision—significant findings would include field deficits and tracking, focusing or visual acuity problems.
- Communication—significant findings would include alterations in muscle tone (hypotonicity, hypertonicity, rigidity), sensation and muscle strength. Consider reflex maturation. Report abnormal movement patterns or primitive reflexes that interfere with functional ability.
- Range of motion—significant findings would include any deviation from normal standardized joint range of motion. Document a finding in standardized goniometric measurements.
- Skeletal and joint condition—significant findings should include skeletal or joint conditions that limit function. Also report absence or asymmetry of extremity, joint disease or deformity, and surgical intervention (date and procedure).
- Skin and Soft Tissue—review the integrity of the skin and soft tissue. Significant findings would include decubiti, rash, discoloration, surgical scars, skin temperature, edema, and measurement of circumferential abnormality.
- Fine Motor—report upper extremity functioning such as graphomotor, prehension patterns, bilateral coordination, bilateral integration, hand dominance, functional application to age-appropriate task, e.g., cutting.
- Gross Motor—report the ability to perform functional age-appropriate tasks required in the school setting, e.g., ball-throwing, kicking, and catching.

4-70. Continued

- Perception—significant findings should include reporting of test results and clinical observations of visual-motor, body scheme position in space, right-left discrimination, crossing the mid-line, and so on.
- Sensory awareness—report clinical observations of vestibular, kinesthetic, tactile, auditory and visual senses.
- Balance and equilibrium—significant findings would include the inability to maintain independent static or dynamic balances during a functional activity including transfers.
- Activities of daily living—report the functional level or life skills, including personal hygiene, feeding, dressing, and so on.
- Equipment—note assistive devices, splints, orthosis and wheelchairs, etc., and need for, condition of, and fit of appliance.

4-71. GUIDELINES FOR A PHYSICAL THERAPY EVALUATION

A formal physical therapy evaluation is required only in the following situations:

- **New to program**—when a student is new to a program, whether it is home bound, preschool or school based, where therapy is mandated for the student by the CSE. If a formal physical therapy evaluation is available from the referring agency, school district or private physical therapist, it may be used.

- **Preschooler advancing to kindergarten**—when a preschool student is advancing to an elementary program and the child has been receiving physical therapy in a preschool program, a formal evaluation should be forwarded to the committee on special education upon the request of the appropriate building administrator or local school district. This can be done only with parental consent.

Content of Evaluation

Depending upon the program to which the therapist is assigned, the following general areas may be addressed during the physical therapy evaluation. Guidelines for these areas have been prepared for a diverse student population. The therapist is expected to evaluate only those areas appropriate to the assigned population.

- Background information—include any pertinent medical or social history.

- Behavior—behaviors that interfere with program implementation and/or affect the students compliance, e.g., level of alertness, concentration, personality disorder, etc., should be noted.

- Vision—significant findings would include field deficits and tracking, focusing, or visual acuity problems.

- Communication—significant findings would include receptive or expressive language deficits, augmentative devices, e.g., communication board, handivoice, etc.

- Neuromuscular—significant findings would include alterations in muscle tone (hypertonicity, hypotonicity, rigidity), sensation, coordination, motor planning and muscle strength. Muscle strength should be reported using standardized grades for consistency. Muscle strength grades are reported as follows: Normal, Good, Fair, Poor, Trace, (plus/minus) Zero. Note progression through a developmental sequence noting any deviations.

- Range of motion and muscle length—significant findings would include any deviation from normal standardized joint range of motion and muscle length. Document this finding in standardized goniometric measurements.

- Skeletal and joint condition—should include any skeletal or joint condition that limits function. Significant findings would include absence or asymmetry of extremity, joint disease or deformity, x-ray report of skeletal deviation (scoliosis, lordosis, kyphosis, subluxation or dislocation of hip) and surgical intervention (date and procedure).

4-71. Continued

- Skin and soft tissue—review the integrity of the skin and soft tissue. Significant findings would include decubiti, lesions, edema, discoloration, rash, scars, skin temperature, and measurement of circumferential abnormality.

- Pain and tenderness—note complaint of pain or tenderness—onset, location, and frequency.

- Developmental test—when utilizing a standardized developmental test for the birth-to-three population, report pertinent achievement of developmental milestones including gross motor, perceptual-fine motor, cognitive, social/emotional, and language. If a child is being followed by an occupational therapist and/or speech and language pathologist, defer reporting on the developmental areas that they would be addressing.

- Balance and equilibrium—significant findings would include the inability to maintain independent static and dynamic balance in sitting, standing, walking, unilateral stance, or tandem walking. Note the degree of assistance/guarding required. Note presence or absence of protective reactions.

- Posture—note deviations from normal segmental alignment: supine, sitting, or standing.

- Gait pattern—note all deviations from normal gait patterns: weight-bearing status, assistive devices, and guarding required.

- Functional mobility—note the student's functional ability in the school environment including wheelchair mobility, level of independence during transfers, ability to negotiate stairs and curbs, and getting on/off school bus and ramps.

- Endurance—significant findings include easy fatigability and limited distance, time, and speed.

- Equipment—includes assistive devices, orthosis, prosthesis and wheelchairs. Note need for, condition of, and fit of appliance.

4-72. INDIVIDUAL PHYSICAL AND OCCUPATIONAL THERAPY SESSIONS

The therapist must address the total management needs of a student who has been mandated for individual sessions. Depending upon the student's involvement and how it affects his or her performance, the therapist may utilize any or all of the following mechanisms.

1. DIRECT THERAPEUTIC TREATMENT

The therapist addresses specific dysfunction in order to achieve Phase II IEP goals and objectives. This treatment could be rendered in two ways:

- **treatment in a separate environment**—some students must be seen in a separate environment. This is particularly true with the moderate to severely physically handicapped and with students who are highly distractible or behaviorally disruptive.

- **treatment integrated into the school day**—some students benefit from individual therapy which is integrated into the normal routine of the school day. These students can learn faster through games and functional activities; motor-skill training is most effectively taught in the setting in which the skill will be used. This is particularly true with the learning disabled or mentally handicapped. Examples of individual therapy integrated into the student's day include situations such as a physical therapist working with the student during gym or playground activities or an occupational therapist working one-on-one with the student during art to improve fine-motor or manipulative skills.

2. EDUCATION AND COMMUNICATION

Therapists may need to coordinate various aspects of their management programs with others concerned with the education of the children including:

- **school personnel**—the therapist should discuss with appropriate individuals (administrator, teacher, classroom aide) how the student's dysfunction interferes with his or her ability to learn or perform activities in the normal school day which support the goals of the related service. They also suggest simple classroom modifications or daily activities which encourage or maintain the student's functional performance.

- **parents**—occasionally there are situations in which certain activities must be done daily to maintain or improve a physical ability. A student with muscular imbalance due to weakness or abnormal muscle tone is prone to progressive joint deformities that can hinder function. Instruction in range-of-motion exercises or strengthening exercises can be given to the parents, who then work daily with their child to prevent the progression of deformity. This is particularly important for students with muscular dystrophy, spina bifida, cerebral palsy, arthritis, or other conditions prone to progressive deformities.

4-72. Continued

3. ADAPTIVE EQUIPMENT OR ASSISTIVE DEVICES

When a student requires these, the therapist is actively involved in the recommendation, ordering, reevaluation of usefulness or fit, and modification of the device.

4. SMALL GROUP SESSIONS

Some students can be treated in small group sessions depending again on the individual student's specific needs, involvement, and the goals of the particular related service. The therapist may utilize any or all intervention strategies discussed under individual sessions to achieve goals established for a particular student.

5. MONITORING

Therapists can establish classroom programs or suggest the use of particular equipment. They would periodically (monthly, every other month, twice-a-year) review the effectiveness of the activities and the usefulness of the equipment.

6. CONSULTATION

Therapists and educators must establish a working relationship based on trust and respect for each other's expertise, working to find solutions to problems that the student encounters in his or her educational program.

For example, a minimally, physically handicapped child is semi-independent in school and does not require individual therapy; however, the physical and/or occupational therapist can suggest minor architectural modifications that will enable the child to become more independent.

4-73. AREAS OF DYSFUNCTION REQUIRING OCCUPATIONAL THERAPY AND THEIR IMPACT ON SCHOOL PERFORMANCE

Problem: Apraxia

1. difficulty learning any unfamiliar skilled activity (e.g., writing, crafts, sports)

2. poor tool usage

3. clumsiness, falling, especially when ascending or descending from equipment (gym, playground)

4. poor dressing skills, especially with gloves, belt, shoelaces, etc.

5. poor self-esteem

6. disorganized behavior

7. inordinate fear of failure

Problem: Bilateral Integration Deficit

1. poor development of hand dominance

2. inefficient use of hands

3. poor gross coordination (i.e., in sports such as baseball)

4. poor skilled manipulation

5. difficulty with arts and crafts, and playing an instrument

6. difficulty cutting, pasting, and writing

Problem: Deficient Balance

1. poor gym and playground skills

2. difficulty negotiating obstacles

3. clumsiness

4. fear of movement in space

Problem: Deficient Bilateral Coordination

1. poor gym and playground skills

2. difficulty with skilled manipulation

4-73. Continued

3. difficulty with arts and crafts, home activities, wood shop, and playing a musical instrument

4. difficulty pasting and cutting

5. difficulty with clothing closures, opening containers, wrapping and unwrapping objects (packages)

Problem: Difficulty Crossing

1. difficulty reading MIDLINE.

2. difficulty copying patterns requiring movement across midline

3. poor development of hand dominance

4. inefficient use of preferred hand for skilled manipulation

Problem: Deficient Response Speed

1. delayed reaction time

2. poor timed test performance, gym performance, and activities performance (e.g., baseball)

Problem: Deficient Running Speed and Agility

1. poor gym and playground skills

2. clumsiness

3. difficulty climbing stairs

4. difficulty getting on and off bus

Problem: Deficient Upper Limb Coordination

1. poor gym skills, especially with equipment such as a bat and ball.

2. difficulty doffing and donning garments

Problem: Deficient Upper Limb Speed and Dexterity

1. difficulty copying, writing, cutting, pasting

4-73. Continued

2. poor gym performance

3. poor skilled manipulation

4. difficulty manipulating classroom computer

5. poor performance in art and crafts, woodworking

6. difficulty playing musical instruments

Problem: Deficient Strength

1. fatigue results easily

2. difficulty opening heavy doors or lifting heavy objects

Problem: Immature, Bizarre, or Deficit Drawing

1. poor body image

2. poor spatial relations

3. poor motor planning

4. poor dressing skills

5. poor skilled manipulation

6. poor self-esteem

7. clumsiness

Problem: Impaired Figure Ground Perception

1. difficulty unwrapping packages

2. difficulty reading—cannot attack a word phonetically

3. poor organization

4. difficulty negotiating around crowded classroom and hallways

5. poor attention

6. difficulty reading maps

7. difficulty locating objects in room

8. scanning problems

9. careless in his or her work

4-73. Continued

Problem: Impaired Form Constancy

1. poor letter formation
2. difficulty learning beginning number skills
3. difficulty doing puzzles
4. difficulty reading maps
5. difficulty reading music

Problem: General Sensory-Motor Impairment

1. antisocial behaviors
2. poor self-esteem
3. poor peer relationships

Problem: Impaired Spatial Relations

1. difficulty reading and writing letters (reversals, etc.), spelling, arithmetic
2. difficulty copying letters or shapes from sample or from blackboard
3. poor arts and crafts skills (difficulty drawing and making three-dimensional crafts)
4. difficulty deciphering musical notes
5. difficulty reading maps
6. difficulty understanding graphs

Problem: Poor Fine-Motor Coordination

1. difficulty writing and cutting
2. difficulty with skilled manipulation
3. poor written test performance
4. sloppy manipulation
5. difficulty opening containers
6. difficulty with clothing closures

4-73. Continued

Problem: Position in Space

1. clumsiness and hesitant movement
2. inability to understand words designating spatial position
3. reversals on numbers, letters, or words: 42-24, b-d, saw-was, etc.

Problem: Tactile Deficits

1. poor attention span, distractibility, and hyperactivity
2. antisocial or acting-out behaviors
3. dislike of "messy" activities (arts and crafts)
4. sloppy eating, food fetishes
5. self-stimulatory behaviors
6. decreased awareness of pain

Problem: Visual Closure Deficits

1. difficulty with geometry
2. poor prewriting skills
3. poor craft performance
4. difficulty reading maps
5. difficulty completing puzzles

Problem: Visual Discrimination Deficits

1. poor reading and writing
2. difficulty completing puzzles
3. difficulty reading maps
4. difficulty using alternative communication system

Problem: Vertibular Dysfunction

1. fear of movement, especially on equipment or in playground
2. clumsiness and frequent falling

4-73. Continued

3. poor gym performance, especially on equipment

4. possible hyperactivity

Problem: Visual Form and Space Perception

1. difficulty with reading, writing, and math

2. difficulty negotiating obstacles (in hallway, around classroom)

3. poor visual attention

4. difficulty using classroom computers and visual screen equipment

5. difficulty wrapping, unwrapping packages, and opening containers

Problem: Visual Memory Deficits

1. difficulty with math and reading

2. poor test performance

3. poor arts and crafts skills

PART 5

Classroom Instruction Techniques for Various Exceptionalities

5-1. MAINSTREAMING CHECKLIST

1. ____ The child has become familiar with the rules and routines of the regular class in which he or she will be mainstreamed.

2. ____ The student's Individual Educational Plan objectives and modifications have been discussed with mainstream teacher.

3. ____ The child has indicated a positive desire to participate in a regular class environment.

4. ____ The child has been coached on dealing with possible reactions and situations presented by other students, both positive and negative.

5. ____ The child is capable of remaining focused for appropriate periods of time while in the regular classroom.

6. ____ The mainstream classroom teacher has been educated on the special needs of the disabled child.

7. ____ The mainstream teacher has been given the proper assistance on the use and purpose of any devices or apparatus used by the disabled student.

8. ____ The mainstream teacher has been apprised of the student's skill levels.

9. ____ The mainstream teacher has been apprised of the child's learning style.

10. ____ The mainstream teacher has been apprised of the child's strength areas and limitations.

11. ____ The mainstream teacher has been informed of the supportive services provided to the student.

12. ____ The mainstream teacher has prepared his or her class for the incoming student.

13. ____ The mainstream teacher has been assigned a specific special service staff member to contact in case of some difficulty.

14. ____ The mainstream teacher has been given the proper management skills that might be required in dealing with the child while in the mainstream class.

15. ____ The students in the mainstream class have been educated on handicapping conditions and the reasons for mainstreaming.

16. ____ The child's parents have met the mainstream teacher.

17. ____ The child's parents have been involved in the planning of their child's mainstreaming experience.

18. ____ The child's parents have been given assistance on parenting techniques that will encourage the child's progress and increase the chances of success of the mainstreaming experience.

5-1. Continued

19. ____ A member of the mainstreaming team has presented the concept of main-streaming, its purpose, and what is gained at a PTA meeting for parents of nonhandicapped children.

20. ____ The administrator has been informed of the mainstreaming procedure for this particular child.

5-2. ALTERNATE LEARNING ACTIVITIES

audiotape	large-group–small-group instruction
brainstorming	library research
bulletin board	listening
buzz groups	listing and diagramming
chalkboard	models
committees	oral recitation
community study	panel discussions
computer	problem solving
debates	programmed materials
demonstrations	projects
discovery	question and answer
discussion	reading out loud
displays	real objects
dramatizations	resource persons
drill and practice	review
exhibits	role-playing
field trips, research	simulation
film loops	slides
films	speaking panels
filmstrips	step-by-step procedure
flannel boards	supervised study
flip charts	team teaching
games	television
graphics	transparencies
homework assignments	verbal illustrations
illustrated talk	videotape
independent study	visual illustrations
information sheets	work-study
investigation, reporting	writing
laboratory work	

5-3. KEY CONCEPTS IN BEHAVIOR MODIFICATION

1. **Behavior modification:** Classroom management or consequence management

2. **Baseline data:** A starting point involving frequency and duration in determining a child's behavior change

3. **Continuous fixed-ratio schedule (CFR):** Reinforcement in which every response is reinforced

4. **Contracting:** A two-way agreement between the student and the teacher

5. **Differential reinforcement:** Involves two or more different responses; one is reinforced and the other is extinguished

6. **Discrimination training:** Involves a single behavior that is reinforced in the presence of one stimulus and is extinguished in the presence of other stimuli

7. **Extinction:** Occurs when a reinforcing event is withdrawn and the behavior that it followed decreases

8. **Fixed interval schedule (FI):** Reinforcement following the first behavior to occur after a fixed period of time has elapsed

9. **Fixed ratio schedule (FR):** Reinforcement following a fixed number of responses

10. **Fixed schedule:** Reinforcement occurring at a regular interval or after a set number of responses

11. **Generalization:** The occurrence of a response learned through discrimination training in the presence of a novel or unknown stimulus

12. **Interval schedule:** Delivers reinforcement after a specified amount of time has elapsed, rather than after a particular number of behaviors

13. **Modeling:** The use of verbal instructions or initiation to teach a child a new behavior

14. **Negative reinforcement:** A reinforcement procedure in which something aversive or negative is removed from the environment

15. **Positive reinforcement:** A reinforcement procedure in which something positive or pleasant is added to the environment

16. **Primary reinforcer:** Some tangible or physical object such as food or money

17. **Ratio schedule:** Reinforcement occurring after a particular number of behaviors

18. **Reinforcer:** Any event that follows a behavior and that increases the frequency or duration of the behavior or increases the chances that the behavior will reoccur

19. **Secondary reinforcer:** Some social reinforcer that often gains power from being associated with a primary reinforcer such as receiving an *A* or verbal praise

5-3. Continued

20. **Shaping:** The differential reinforcement of successive approximations of a behavior

21. **Target behavior:** The behavior identified as needing change

22. **Token Economies:** Settings where the children receive tokens with which they can later buy tangible items or privileges

23. **Variable ratio schedule (VR):** Reinforcement following an average number of responses

24. **Variable schedules:** Reinforcement occurring at irregular intervals or after varying numbers of responses

5-4. CURRICULAR MATERIALS FOR CHILDREN WITH SPEECH/LANGUAGE DISORDERS

- *Articulation Modification Programs.* Collins & Cunningham
- *Basic Vocabulary Study Cards.* McCarr
- *Contrasts.* Elbert, Rockman & Saltzman
- *Countless Categories.* Gustafson
- *Directions.* Schuldt
- *Game Playing Kit*
- *Gameway Articulation Cards*
- *Handbook for Speech Therapy.* Medlin
- *Idiom Workbook Series.* Austin
- *Imaginative Adjectives.* McCarr
- *IZIT Cards.* Anderson, Spearman & Redwine
- *Language Making Action Cards.* Lippke
- *Language Making Action Stickers*
- *Library of Vocabulary Photographs*
- *Multiple Meanings.* Dedrick & Lattyak
- *My Speech Workbooks.* Parker
- *My Words.* McCarr
- *Oral Motor Assessment and Treatment.* Riley & Riley
- *Patterns Articulation Modification Program.* Bakke
- *Phonological Fun.* Jacobson & Watkins
- *Phonological Remediation Targets.* Buteau & Hodson
- *Photo Resourse Kit*
- *Play and Say.* Warkomski
- *Plurals.* Collins & Cunningham
- *PLUSS—Putting Language into Social Situations.* Zirkelbach
- *Pragmatic Activities in Language and Speech.* Davis
- *Read the Pictures Stories*
- *Remediation of Common Phonological Processes.* Broudy
- *Speech Class Goes Home.* Tayzel
- *Speech Language Development Chart.* Gard, Gilman & Gorman
- *Speech Lingo*
- *Stuttering Intervention Program.* Pindzola
- *Symptomatic Voice Therapy.* Polow & Kaplan
- *Syntax Flip Book.* Terasaki & Gunn

5-4. Continued

- *Systematic Fluency Training for Young Children.* Shine
- *The Big Book of Hidden Pictures.* Sanders
- *The Big Book of Language Through Sounds.* Flowers
- *The Big Book of Sounds.* Flowers
- *The Boone Voice Program for Adults.* Boone
- *The Boone Voice Program for Children.* Boone
- *Vee's Verbs, Sets 1 & 2.* Medlin
- *Vocabulary Building Exercises for the Young Adult.* McCarr
- *Vocabulary in Context.* Dedrick & Lattyak
- *Vocal Abuse Reduction Program.* Johnson
- *Vocal Rehabilitation Practice Book.* Agnello & Garcia
- *Word Making Cards.* Medlin
- *Word Making Stickers*

293

5-5. CURRICULAR MATERIALS FOR CHILDREN WITH LEARNING DISABILITIES

- *Apple Tree Language Program.* Anderson, Boren, Kilgore, Howard & Krohn
- *BOLD-2—Behavioral Objectives for Learning Disabilities.* Wallace, DeWolfe & Herman
- *By Myself Books.* Hooper & Reidlinger
- *Capture the Meaning—Strategies for Reading Comprehension.* Schmitt
- *Classroom Visual Activities.* Richards
- *Counting Money.* Foster
- *Dormac Easy English Dictionary.* Baker & Bettino
- *Dysgraphia—Why Johnny Can't Write.* Cavey
- *I Can Write.* McCarr
- *Jordan Prescriptive/Tutorial Reading Program—for Moderate and Severe Dyslexia.* Jordan
- *One-to One—A Tutorial Program in Core Subjects for Grades K–6.* Lundell & Lundell
- *Perceptual Activities Packets.* Ann Arbor Perceptual Activities
- *Phonological Awareness Training for Reading.* Torgesen & Bryant
- *Real-Life Math.* Schwartz
- *Right Line Paper*
- *Sequence.* Collins & Cunningham
- *Speed Spelling 1 & 2.* Witt
- *Stetson Spelling Program.* Stetson
- *Stop-Go Right Line Paper*
- *Teaching Competence in Written Language.* Terasaki & Gunn
- *The Time Is Now.* Foster
- *Time Concepts Series.* Lattyak & Dedrick
- *Understanding Math Story Problems.* McGlothlin

5-6. CURRICULAR MATERIALS FOR CHILDREN WITH EMOTIONAL, BEHAVIORAL, AND DEVELOPMENTAL DISABILITIES

- *A Special Picture Cookbook.* Steed
- *Activities for Developing Pre-Skill Concepts in Children with Autism.* Flowers
- *Being Me—A Social/Sexual Training Program.* Edwards & Wapnick
- *Daily Living Skills Program*
- *Developing the Functional Use of a Telephone Book.* Jorgensen & Bernhard
- *Developmental Art Therapy.* Williams & Wood
- *Doing Home Laundry*
- *Functional Living Skills for Moderately and Severely Handicapped Individuals.* Wehman, Renzaglia & Bates
- *How to Hold Your Job.* Fudell
- *Job Finder's Workbook.* Muklewicz & Bender
- *Name Writing.* Brackman
- *Personal Care Skills*
- *Social Skills for Daily Living.* Schumaker, Hazel & Pederson
- *Social Skills Intervention Guide.* Elliot & Gresham
- *Social Skills on the Job.* Marco Systems
- *Taking Care of Simple Injuries*
- *Teaching Activities for Autistic Children.* Schopler, Lansing & Waters
- *Teaching Developmentally Disabled Children—The Me Book.* Lovaas
- *Teaching Functional Academics.* Bender & Valletutti
- *Teaching Spontaneous Communication to Autistic and Developmentally Handicapped Children.* Watson, Lord, Schaffer & Schopler
- *Teaching Strategies for Parents and Professionals (Autistic).* Schopler, Lansing & Reichler
- *Teaching the Moderately and Severely Handicapped.* Bender, Valletutti & Bender
- *Teaching the Young Child with Motor Delays.* Hanson & Harris
- *Telling Time.* Tringo & Roit
- *The Good Life Video Series—Social Skills.* Gadbury
- *The Picture File and Mini Decks—Peabody Picture Collection.* Dunn, Dunn, Smith, Smith & Horton
- *TMR Pre-Vocational Training Kit*
- *TMR Survival Skills*
- *TMR Training Fun*
- *Using a Telephone*
- *Vocational Curriculum for Developmentally Disabled Persons.* Wehman & McLaughlin

5-7. CURRICULAR MATERIALS FOR GIFTED CHILDREN

- *Creative Expression.* Milliken Pub. Co.
- *Creative Writing Skills.* T.S. Denison & Co.
- *Critical Reading.* Ann Arbor Publishers
- *For Those Who Wonder—Ginn & Co. Super Center Activity Cards.* Media for Education
- *Gifted and Talented Information Handouts.* Karnes
- *Independent Study Program.* Johnson & Johnson
- *Reading to Discover Activity Cards.* Prentice Hall Learning Systems
- *Recipes for Creative Writing.* Creative Teaching Press
- *Story Starters.* Creative Teaching Press
- *Creative Learning Centers.* Creative Learning Press
- *Creative Activities for Language Arts.* Hayes Publishing
- *Creative Language Projects.* Milliken Publishing Co.
- *Creative Expression Books.* Scholastic Book Services
- *Read-Study-Think.* Xerox Education Publications
- *The Stop, Look and Write Series.* Bantam Books
- *Geoboard Activity Cards.* Creative Publications
- *100 Geometric Games.* Cuisenaire Co. of America
- *A Cloudburst of Math Lab Experiments.* Midwest Publications
- *Aftermath.* Creative Publications
- *Fun and Games with Mathematics.* Prentice Hall Learning Systems
- *Superior Mathematical Puzzles.* Simon and Schuster
- *Hot-Cold Shoebox.* Fisher Scientific Company
- *Baker Nature Study Packet.* Baker Science Packets
- *Pollution Test Kit.* Edmund Scientific Company
- *The Planet Management Game.* Houghton Mifflin
- *Bacteria Study Kit.* Macmillan Science Company
- *Space Puzzles.* Simon and Schuster
- *Elaborate Thinking Kit.* Curriculum Associates
- *New Dimensions in Creativity.* Harper & Row, Publishers

© 1995 by The Center for Applied Research in Education

5-8. CURRICULAR MATERIALS FOR DEAF CHILDREN

- *Auditory Discrimination Training Program.* Ehlert
- *Auditory Memory for Language.* Stefanakos & Prater
- *Auditory Rehabilitation—Memory-Language-Comprehension.* Prater & Stefanakos
- *CLUES—Speech Reading for Adults.* Feehan, Samuelsen & Seymour
- *Communication Training for Hearing-Impaired Children and Teenagers— Speechreading, Listening and Using Repair Strategies.* Murry
- *Teaching Sign Language—The First Vocabulary.* Rittenhouse & Meyers

5-9. SELECTED READINGS ON INSTRUCTION AND MANAGEMENT FOR SPECIAL EDUCATION TEACHERS

- *A Survival Kit for the Special Education Teacher.* Pierangelo
- *Adaptive Play for Special Needs Children—Strategies to Enhance Communication and Learning.* Musselwhite
- *At Risk Youth in Crisis—A Team Approach in the Schools.* Morgan
- *Beyond Behavior Modification—Behavior Management in the School.* Kaplan & Drainville
- *Bilingual Education and Bilingual Special Education.* Fradd & Tikunoff
- *Bilingualism and Special Education.* Cummins
- *Can't Your Child See?—A Guide for Parents of Visually Impaired Children.* Scott, Jan & Freeman
- *Career Ladders for Challenged Youths in Transition from School to Adult Life.* Siegel, Robert, Greener, Meyer, Halloran & Ross
- *Children at Risk—An Interdisciplinary Approach to Child Abuse and Neglect*
- *Children on Medication.* Gadow
- *Children's Arithmetic—How They Learn It and How You Teach It.* Ginsburg
- *Complete Learning*
- *Computers and Exceptional Children.* Lindsey
- *Conferencing Parents of Exceptional Children.* Simpson
- *Coping with Noncompliance in the Classroom.* Walker & Walker
- *Counseling Persons on Physical Disabilities.* Marshak & Seligman
- *Curriculum Development for the Gifted.* Maker
- *Effective Discipline.* Smith & Rivera
- *Effective Instruction for Special Education.* Mastropieri & Scruggs
- *Families of Handicapped Children.* Fenwell & Vadasy
- *How to Create a Curriculum for Autistic and Other Handicapped Children.* Romanczyk & Lockshin
- *How to Integrate Autistic and Other Severely Handicapped Children into a Classroom.* Koegel
- *How to Reduce Autistic and Severely Maladaptive Behaviors.* Luce & Christian
- *How to Teach Autistic and Other Severely Handicapped Children.* Koegel & Schreibman
- *How to Teach Prevocational Skills to Severely Handicapped Persons.* Mithaug
- *How to Teach Sign Language to Developmentally Disabled Children.* Carr
- *How to Treat Self-Injurious Behavior.* Favell & Greene
- *How to Use Sensory Extinction.* Rincover

5-9. Continued

- *Interventions for Students with Emotional Disorders*. Morgon & Reinhart
- *Language Arts—Teaching Exceptional Children*. Wallace, Cohen & Polloway
- *Language Interaction in Curriculum and Instruction*. Gruenewald & Pollak
- *Life Skills Instruction for all Students with Special Needs*. Cronin & Patton
- *Limiting Bias in the Assessment of Bilingual Students*. Hamayan & Damico
- *Management of Autistic Behavior*. Simpson & Regan
- *Medical Problems in the Classroom—The Teacher's Role in Diagnosis and Management*. Haslam & Valletutti
- *Meeting the Needs of Culturally and Linguistically Different Students*. Fradd & Weismantel
- *Models of Curriculum-Based Assessment*. Idol, Nevin & Whitcomb
- *PEEK—Peabody Early Experiences Kit*. Dunn, Chun, Crowell, Dunn, Halevi & Yacket
- *PLDK—Peabody Language Development Kits*. Dunn, Smith, Dunn, Horton & Smith
- *Preventing School Dropouts—Tactics for At-Risk, Remedial and Mildly Handicapped Adolescents*. Lovitt
- *Remedial Techniques in Basic School Subjects*. Fernald & Idol
- *Teaching Behavioral Self-Control to Students*. Workman
- *Teaching Mathematics to the Learning Disabled*. Bley & Thornton
- *Teaching Models in Education of the Gifted*
- *Teaching Secondary Students with Mild Learning and Behavior Problems*. Masters, Mori & Mori
- *The Challenge of Complex School Problems*. Norby, Thurlow, Christenson & Ysseldyke
- *The Resource Room—Organization and Implementation*. Wiederholt, Hammill & Brown
- *The Resource Teacher—A Guide to Effective Practices*. Wiederholt, Hammill & Brown
- *Tools for Transition: Preparing Students with Learning Disabilities for Postsecondary Education*. Aune & Ness
- *Transition Goals for Adolescents with Learning Disabilities*. Trapani
- *Visual Handicaps and Learning*. Barraga & Erin

5-10. SELECTED READINGS ON ASSESSMENT AND TESTING FOR SPECIAL EDUCATION TEACHERS

- *A Consumer's Guide to Tests in Print.* Hammill, Brown & Bryant
- *A Guide to Vocational Assessment.* Power
- *A Psychoeducational Assessment of Students Who Are Visually Impaired or Blind.* Johnson
- *Assessing the Abilities and Instructional Needs of Students.* Hammill
- *Auditory Processes.* Gillet
- *Educational Assessment of Learning Problems.* Wallace, Larsen & Elksnin
- *85 Tests for Special Educators.* Compton
- *Handbook on the Assessment of Learning Disabilities.* Swanson
- *How to Write an I.E.P.* Arena
- *Infant-Toddler Assessment.* Rossetti
- *Learning Process Skills.* Riley
- *Limiting Bias in the Assessment of Bilingual Students.* Hamayan & Damico
- *Models of Curriculum-Based Assessment.* Idol, Nevin & Whitcomb
- *Prescriptive Teaching from the DTLA-2.* Banas
- *Psychoeducational Assessment of Hearing-Impaired Students.* Johnson & Evans
- *Test Critiques—Volumes I–X.* Keyser & Sweetland
- *Testing Children.* Weaver
- *Testing Young Children.* Culbertson & Willis
- *Tests—A Comprehensive Reference for Assessment in Psychology, Education and Business.* Sweetland & Keyser
- *The I.E.P. Primer.* School & Cooper
- *The WISC-III Companion.* Truch
- *Understanding Children's Testing.* Aylward
- *WAIS-R Tutorial Workbook.* Swiercinsky

5-11. SELECTED MISCELLANEOUS READINGS FOR SPECIAL EDUCATION TEACHERS

Brain Injury

- *Cognitive Rehabilitation of Closed Head Injured Patients.* Adamovich, Henderson & Auerbach
- *Community Re-entry for Head Injury Adults.* Ylvisaker & Gobble
- *Educational Dimensions of Acquired Brain Injury.* Savage & Wolcott
- *Head Injury Rehabilitation.* Ylvisaker
- *Psychopathology and Education of the Brain-Injured Child.* Strauss, Lehtinen & Kephart
- *Traumatic Brain Injury in Children and Adolescents.* Mira, Tucker & Tyler
- *Traumatic Brain Injury.* Bigler

Early Intervention

- *Atypical Infant Development.* Hanson
- *Early Intervention.* Hanson & Lynch
- *High-Risk Infants.* Rossetti
- *Infant-Toddler Assessment.* Rossetti
- *The Medically Fragile Child.* Krajicek & Tompkins

Speech / Language Disorders

- *Alaryngeal Speech Rehabilitation.* Salmon & Mount
- *Children's Phonetic Disorders.* Hoffman, Schuckers & Daniloff
- *Cleft Palate.* Karlind, Moller & Starr
- *Clinical Management of Childhood Stuttering.* Wall & Meyers
- *Clinical Management of Voice Disorders.* Case
- *Clinical Methods on Communication Disorders.* Leith
- *Clinical Research in Communicative Disorders.* Hegde
- *Communication Disorders Following Traumatic Brain Injury.* Beukelman & Yorkston
- *Counseling the Communicatively Disordered and Their Families.* Luterman
- *Developmental Apraxia of Speech.* Hall, Jordan & Robin
- *Evaluation and Treatment of Swallowing Disorders.* Logemann
- *Genetic Syndromes in Communication Disorders.* Jung
- *Handbook of Clinical Phonology.* Elbert & Gierut

5-11. CONTINUED

- *Introduction to Communicative Disorders.* Hegde
- *Keep Your Voice Healthy.* Brodnitz
- *Language Intervention and Academic Success.* Wallach & Miller
- *Laryngectomee Rehabilitation.* Keith & Darley
- *Later Language Development.* Nippold
- *Manual of Voice Therapy.* Prater & Swift
- *Nature of Communication Disorders in Culturally and Linguistically Diverse Populations.* Taylor
- *Neural Bases of Speech, Hearing, and Language.* Kuehn, Lemme & Baumgartner
- *Practical Procedures for Children with Language Disorders.* Nesson
- *Reference Manual for Communicative Sciences and Disorders.* Kent
- *Research on Child Language Disorders.* Miller
- *Research Strategies in Human Communication Disorders.* Doehring
- *Targeting Intelligible Speech.* Hodson & Paden
- *Teaching Aphasic Children.* Myers
- *Treating Disordered Speech Motor Control.* Vogel & Cannito
- *Treatment of Communication Disorders in Culturally and Linguistically Diverse Populations.* Taylor
- *Treatment Procedures in Communicative Disorders.* Hegde

Hearing Impairment

- *Assessment and Management of Mainstreamed Hearing-Impaired Children.* Ross, Brackett & Maxon
- *Auditory Evoked Potentials.* Hood & Berlin
- *Can't Your Child Hear?* Freeman, Carbin & Boese
- *Facilitating Classroom Listening.* Berg
- *Hearing Disorders.* Green
- *Language Learning Practices with Deaf Children.* McAnally, Rose & Quigley
- *Manual Communication.* Christopher
- *Our Forgotten Children: Hard of Hearing Pupils in the School.* Davis
- *Reading and Deafness.* King & Quigley
- *Speech Acoustics and Perception.* Boothroyd
- *They Grow in Silence.* Mindel & Vernon

5-11. Continued

Visual Impairment

- *Supporting Visually Impaired Students in the Mainstream.* Martin & Hoben
- *Visual Handicaps and Learning.* Barraga

Physical Disabilities

- *Individuals with Physical Disabilities: An Introduction for Educators.* Best
- *Physical and Multiple Handicaps.* Bigge & Sirvis
- *Teaching Individuals with Physical and Multiple Handicaps.* Bigge

Learning Disabilities

- *A Cognitive Approach to Learning Disabilities.* Reid, Hresko & Swanson
- *Attention Deficit Disorder Comes of Age.* Shaywitz & Shaywitz
- *Collective Perspectives on Issues Affecting Learning Disabilities.* National Joint Committee on Learning Disabilities
- *Directory of Facilities and Services for the Learning Disabled*
- *Handbook of Learning Disabilities—Volume I—Dimensions and Diagnosis.* Kavale & Bender
- *Handbook of Learning Disabilities—Volume II—Methods and Interventions.* Kavale & Bender
- *Handbook of Learning Disabilities—Volume III—Programs and Practices.* Kavale & Bender
- *Handbook on the Assessment of Learning Disabilities.* Swanson
- *Helping Children Overcome Learning Difficulties.* Rosner
- *Higher Order Thinking—Designing Curriculum for Mainstreamed Students.* Carnine & Kameenui
- *Learning Disabilities—Educational Principles and Practices.* Johnson & Myklebust
- *Learning Disabilities.* Myers & Hammill
- *Learning Disabilities—The Challenges of Adulthood.* Patton & Palloway
- *Overcoming Dyslexia in Children, Adolescents, and Adults.* Jordon
- *Promoting Postsecondary Education for Students with Learning Disabilities.* Brinckerhoff, Shaw & McGuire
- *Reading, Writing, and Speech Problems in Children.* Orton
- *Resource Book for the Special Education Teacher.* Lucas & Barbe
- *School Survival Guide for Kids with LD.* Cummings & Fisher

5-11. Continued

- *Strategy Assessment and Instruction for Students with Learning Disabilities.* Meltzer
- *Teaching Students with Learning and Behavior Problems.* Hammill & Bartel
- *Teaching the Dyslexic Child.* Griffiths
- *The Assessment of Learning Disabilities.* Silver
- *The Learning Disabled Child: Ways that Parents Can Help.* Stevens
- *The Tuned-In, Turned-On Book About Learning Problems.* Hayes
- *Written Language Disorders.* Bain, Bailet & Moats

Emotional Disabilities

- *Applications of Human Behavior in School and Home.* Hall
- *Basic Principles of Human Behavior.* Hall
- *Childhood Behavior Disorders.* Algozzine, Schmid & Mercer
- *Depression and Suicide in Children and Adolescents.* Muse
- *Helping the Child Who Doesn't Fit In.* Nowicki & Duke
- *Life Space Intervention—Talking with Children and Youth in Crisis.* Wood & Long
- *Readings in Emotional Disturbance.* Newcomer
- *Teaching Disturbed and Disturbing Students.* Zionts
- *The How To Book of Teen Self-Discovery.* Childre
- *The Measurement of Behavior.* Hall & Van Houten
- *Understanding and Teaching Emotionally Disturbed Children and Adolescents.* Newcomer
- *Understanding and Treating Conduct Disorders.* Toth
- *Understanding Children and Youth with Emotional and Behavioral Problems.* Zionts & Simpson

Autism

- *Autism—Information and Resources for Parents, Families, and Professionals.* Simpson & Zionts
- *Emergence-Labeled Autistic.* Grandin & Scariano
- *Preschool Education Programs for Children with Autism.* Harris & Handleman
- *The Ultimate Stranger—The Autistic Child.* Delacato

© 1995 by The Center for Applied Research in Education

304

5-11. Continued

Attention Deficit Disorder

- *ADHD Adolescence: The Next Step.* Robin
- *ADHD in Adults.* Barkley
- *ADHD in the Classroom: Strategies in the Classroom.* Barkley
- *Attention Deficit Disorder and Learning Disabilities: Realities, Myths, and Controversial Treatments.* Ingersoll & Goldstein
- *Dr. Larry Silver's Advice to Parents on Attention Deficit Disorder.* Silver
- *Identification and Treatment of Attention Deficit Disorder.* Nussbaum & Bigler
- *Jumping Johnny Get Back to Work.* Gordon
- *The ADD Hyperactivity Handbook for Schools.* Parker
- *Advice to Parents on ADHD.* Silver
- *ADD and the College Student.* Quinn
- *ADD Hyperactivity Workbook.* Parker
- *Helping Your Hyperactive Child.* Parker
- *Why Can't I Eat That?* Taylor
- *CHADD Educators Manual.* CHADD
- *Driven to Distraction.* Hallowell
- *Attention Deficit and the Law.* Latham

Mental Disabilities

- *Advances in Down Syndrome.* Dmitriev & Oelwein
- *Cognitive Skills for Community Living.* McClennen
- *Developmental Disabilities.* Baroff
- *Encyclopedia of Mental and Physical Handicaps.* Tver & Tver
- *Individuals with Profound Disabilities.* Sternberg
- *Music Therapy for the Developmentally Disabled.* Boxill
- *Speakeasy—People with Mental Handicaps Talk About Their Lives in Institutions and in the Community.* Schwier
- *The Conquest of Mental Retardation.* Blatt

Gifted

- *Critical Issues in Gifted Education—Volume I—Defensible Programs for the Gifted.* Maker

5-11. Continued

- *Critical Issues in Gifted Education—Volume II—Defensible Programs for Cultural and Ethnic Minorities.* Maker
- *Critical Issues in Gifted Education—Volume III—Programs for the Gifted in Regular Classrooms.* Maker
- *Gifted and Talented Children.* Pendarvis
- *Gifted Children: Psychological and Educational Perspectives.* Tannenbaum
- *Growing Up Gifted.* Clark
- *Teaching the Gifted Child.* Gallagher
- *The Gifted and Talented: Their Education and Development.* Passow

Tourette's Syndrome

- "Adult Tics in Gilles de la Tourette's Syndrome: Description and Risk Factors," Goetz, C., et al. *Neurology* 42 (1992): 784–788.
- *Advances in Neurology: Tourette Syndrome: Genetics, Neurobiology, and Treatment.* Chase, T., A. Friedhoff, and D. Cohen.
- "Development of Behavioral and Emotional Problems in Tourette Syndrome," Singer, H. S., and L. A. Rosenberg. *Pediatric Neurology* 5 (1989): 41–44.
- "Developmental Perspective of the Gilles de la Tourette Syndrome," Incagnoli, T., and R. Kane. *Perceptual Motor Skills* 57 (1983): 1271–1281.
- *Gilles de la Tourette Syndrome.* Shapiro, E., J. G. Young, and T. Feinberg.
- *Guide to the Diagnosis and Treatment of Tourette Syndrome.* Bruun, R. D. , D. J. Cohen, and J. F. Leckman.
- "Neuropsychological Performance in Children with Tourette Syndrome," Bornstein, R. *Psychiatry Resources* 33 (1990): 73–81.
- *New England Journal of Medicine* 332:1694 (letter). Leckman, J. F. , and L. Schahill.
- "Sensory Tics in Tourette's Syndrome," Kurlan, R., D. Lichter, and D. Hewitt. *Neurology* 39 (1989): 731–733.
- "Tourette Syndrome and Other Tic Disorders: Diagnosis, Pathophysiology, and Treatment," Singer, H. S., and J. T. Walkup. *Medicine* 70 (1991): 15–32.
- Tourette Syndrome Association, 42-40 Bell Blvd., Bayside, NY 11361 (718) 224-2999.
- *Tourette's Syndrome and Tic Disorders: Clinical Understanding and Treatment.* Cohen, D. J., R. D. Bruun, and J. F. Leckman.
- "Tourette's Syndrome: Current Concepts," Kurlan, R. *Neurology* 39 (1989): 1625–1630.

5-12. SELECTED SOURCES OF COMMERCIALLY PRODUCED INSTRUCTIONAL SOFTWARE

- American Educational Corporation
- Apple Computer
- Automated Simulations
- Avant-Garde Publishing Corporation
- Computer Courseware
- Cross Educational Software
- Davidson and Associates
- Dorsett Educational Systems
- Educational Activities
- Educational Micro Systems
- Educational Teaching Aids
- Edu-Ware Services
- EMC Publishing
- Encyclopedia Britannica Educational Corporation
- Follett Software Company
- J.L. Hammett Company
- Harcourt Brace Jovanovich
- The Learning Company
- McGraw-Hill School Division
- Media Materials
- Milliken Publishing Company
- Milton Bradley Educational Division
- Pendulum Press
- Psychological Corporation
- Quicksoft
- Random House School Division
- Reader's Digest Services
- Reston Publishing
- Science Research Associates
- Scott, Foresman and Company
- Society for Visual Education
- Southeastern Educational Software
- Sunburst Communications, Inc.

5-13. PSYCHOSTIMULANTS AND SEDATIVES

Psychostimulants

Medication	*Generic Name*
1. Amphedroxyn	methamphetamine
2. Benzedrine	amphetamine
3. Biphetamine	amphetamine plus dextroamphetamine
4. Cylert	pemoline
5. Deaner	deanol
6. Desoxyn	methamphetamine
7. Dexedrine	dextroamphetamine
8. Pondimin	fenfluramine
9. Ritalin	methylphenidate

Sedatives / Hypnotics

1. Alurate	aprobarbital
2. Amytal	amobarbital
3. Dalmane	flurazepam
4. Doral	quazepam
5. Doriden	gluthimide
6. Halcion	triazolam
7. Mebaral	mephobarbital
8. Nembutal	pentobarbital
9. Noludar	methyprylon
10. Nortec	chloralhydrate
11. Paral	paraldehyde
12. Placidyl	ethchlorvynol
13. ProSom	estazolam
14. Quaalude	methaqualone
15. Restoril	temazepam
16. Seconal	secobarbital
17. Solfoton	phenobarbital
18. Tuinal	secobarbital + amobarbital

5-14. ANTIPSYCHOTIC MEDICATIONS

These medications work by blocking one of the chemical messengers of the central nervous system—dopamine. These drugs are sometimes referred to as *neuroleptic drugs* because they block the dopamine receptors in the brain and correct the imbalance of nerve transmissions associated with psychotic behaviors.

Neuroleptic drugs should be considered very powerful, and as a result they pose potential risks. Careful monitoring is required and withdrawal symptoms such as headaches, nausea, dizziness, and increased heart rate may occur if abruptly stopped. It should also be noted that alcohol consumption during the time the individual is on these medications may enhance the effects of the drug and increase the risk of depression.

Medication	Generic Name
1. Clozaril	clozapine
2. Compazine	prochlorperazine
3. Daxoline	loxapine
4. Etrafon	perphenazine + amitriptyline
5. Haldol	haloperidol
6. Inapsine	droperidol
7. Loxitane	loxapine
8. Mellaril	thioridazine
9. Moban	molindone
10. Navane	thiothixene
11. Orap	pimozide
12. Orazine	chlorpromazine
13. Permitil	fluphenazine
14. Prolixin	fluphenazine
15. Serentil	mesoridazine
16. Serpasil	reserpine
17. Sparine	promazine
18. Stelazine	trifluoperazine
19. Thorazine	chlorpromazine
20. Tindal	acetophenazine
21. Triavil	perphenazine + amitriptyline
22. Trilafon	perphenazine
23. Vesprin	triflupromazine

5-15. ANTIDEPRESSANT MEDICATIONS

Sometimes referred to as *tricyclic drugs,* these drugs affect the symptoms associated with depression by adjusting the levels of neurotransmitters in the brain such as dopamine, serotonin, and epinephrine. These medications are usually prescribed when the treatment of the condition is considered long term. Doctors do not usually like to use such powerful tricyclic antidepressants for short-term or transitory depression.

These medications tend to elevate the individual's mood, improve sleep patterns, increase energy levels and physical activity, and restore perception to a more positive level.

In the case of some antidepressants, once the doctor feels comfortable with the levels of medication attained, he or she may prescribe a single dose at night, a practice called *night-loading.*

Medication	*Generic Name*
1. Adapin	doxepin
2. Anafranil	clomipramine
3. Asendin	amoxapine
4. Aventyl	nortriptyine
5. Desyrel	trazadone
6. Elavil	amitriptyline hydrochloride
7. Endep	amitriptyline
8. Etrafon	perphenazine + amitriptyline
9. Janimine	imipramine
10. Limbitrol	chlordiazepoxide and amitriptyline
11. Ludiomil	maprotiline
12. Marplan	isocarboxazid
13. Nardil	phenelzine
14. Norpramin	desipramine
15. Pamelor	nortriptyline
16. Pertofrane	desipramine
17. Parnate	tranylcypromine
18. Prozac	fluoxetine
19. Sinequan	doxepin
20. Surmontil	trimipramine
21. Tofranil	imipramine
22. Vivactil	protriptyline
23. Wellbutrin	buproprion
24. Zoloft	sertraline

5-16. ANTI-ANXIETY MEDICATIONS

These medications work by diminishing the activity of certain parts of the brain, called the *limbic system.* The symptoms associated with anxiety may include tension, agitation, irritability, panic attacks, and feelings of dying or going crazy. Physical symptoms include excessive sweating, heart palpitations, chills, fainting, racing pulse, and flushes. Anxiety may be a disorder by itself or a component of other psychiatric disorders.

Medication	*Generic Name*
1. Atarax	hydroxyzine
2. Ativan	lozazepam
3. BuSpar	buspirone
4. Catapres	clonidine
5. Centrax	prazepam
6. Corgard	nadolol
7. Dalmane	flurazepam
8. Deprol	meprobamate + benactyzine
9. Doral	quezepam
10. Equanil	meprobamate
11. Halcion	triazolam
12. Klonopin	clonazepam
13. Inderal	propranolol
14. Librium	chlordiazepoxide
15. Libritabs	chlordiazepoxide
16. Lopressor	metoprolol
17. Miltown	meprobamate
18. Paxipam	halazepam
19. Restoril	temazepam
20. Serax	oxazepam
21. Tenormin	atenolol
22. Tranxene	chlorazepate
23. Transcopal	chlormezanone
24. Valium	diazepam
25. Valrelease	diazepam
26. Vistaril	hydroxyzine
27. Xanax	alprazolam

5-17. ANTICONVULSANT MEDICATIONS

Medication	Generic Name
1. Amytal	amobarbitol
2. Anxanil	amobarbitol
3. Celontin	methsuximide
4. Depakene	valproic acid
5. Depakote	divalproex
6. Diamox	acetazolamide
7. Dilantin	phenytoin
8. Gemonil	methobarbital
9. Klonopin	clonazepam
10. Mebaral	mephobarbital
11. Mesantoin	mephenytoin
12. Milontin	phensuximide
13. Myidol	primidone
14. Mysoline	primidone
15. Nebutal	pentobarbital
16. Peganone	ethosuximide
17. Phenurone	phenacemide
18. Seconal	secobarbital
19. Tegretol	carbamazepine
20. Tridione	trimethadione
21. Tranxene	chlorazepate
22. Valium	diazepam
23. Zarontin	ethosuximide

PART 6

Parent Education

6-1. HOW TO IMPROVE A CHILD'S SELF-ESTEEM

1. **Be solution oriented.**

An important step in building self-esteem is to teach solutions rather than blame. Teaching children solutions to problems or frustrating situations begins with statements like, "Who's at fault is not important. The more important question is what can we do so that it doesn't happen again?"

2. **Allow children the right to make decisions.**

Allowing children the right to make decisions that affect their daily life can only enhance their self-esteem. Decisions about clothing, room arrangement, friends to invite to a party, and menu for dinner can make children feel some sense of control in what happens to them.

3. **Offer alternate ways of handling a situation.**

Conditioning children to see many alternate ways of handling a situation or obstacle can also enhance a sense of power and self-esteem. Asking children what they have tried and offering other possible solutions enlarges their "tool box."

4. **Teach children the proper labels when communicating feelings.**

When children are unable to label an internal feeling they become frustrated more quickly. When such feelings go unlabeled, they may become manifested in some negative behavior that will reduce self-esteem. Parents can offer children the correct labels: "While the feeling you are expressing sounds like anger, it is really frustration and frustration is . . . . Now that you know this, is there anything that is causing you frustration?"

5. **Allow children the opportunity to repeat successful experiences.**

A foundation of positive experiences is necessary for self-esteem. Once the child has mastered skills required for the job, any opportunity to repeat success can only be an ego-inflating experience.

6. **Allow avenues for disagreement.**

Children with high self-esteem feel they have an avenue by which to communicate their concerns. Even though the result may not go in their favor, the knowledge that a situation or disagreement can be discussed with their parents allows them to feel a sense of power over their destiny rather than feeling like victims.

7. **Help your child set realistic goals.**

Some children will set unrealistic goals, fall short, and feel like failures. If this is repeated over a period of time, a child begins to develop a sense of urgency for success, and this in turn may lead to more unrealistic goals. Parents can help children by assisting them in defining their objectives and determining the steps necessary to accomplish them. Children should not see one final goal, but a series of smaller goals leading to a final point.

6-1. Continued

8. Use a reward system to shape positive behavior.

Punishment tells a child what not to do, while reward informs a child of what is acceptable behavior. Rewarding positive behavior increases self-esteem. Rewards can be in the form of special trips, extra time before bed, special dinners with one parent, a hug, a kiss, or a note in the lunchbox.

9. Don't pave every road for children.

Some parents or teachers make the mistake of reducing frustration for children to the point where they receive a distorted view of the world. Children with high self-esteem get frustrated; however, they tend to be more resilient since they have previous success in handling frustrating situations themselves. Teaching children alternate solutions, proper labels for their feelings, ways to set realistic goals, solution orientation, and techniques to verbalize their disagreements are more productive than bailing them out when they are confronted with frustration.

6-2. POSSIBLE CAUSES OF LEARNING PROBLEMS

Intellectual Reasons

Limited intelligence—slow learner
Retardation

Emotional Reasons

Consistent school failure
Traumatic emotional development
Separation or divorce
High parental expectations
Sibling performance
Health-related problems
Change in environment—moving

Social Reasons

Peer pressure
Peer rejection

Academic Reasons

Learning disabilities
Poor academic skills—math, reading
Style of teacher vs. style of student
Language difficulties

BE AWARE OF AVOIDANCE SYMPTOMS INDICATING POSSIBLE LEARNING PROBLEMS.

Child selectively forgets.
Child takes hours to complete homework.
Child can't seem to get started with homework.
Child frequently brings home unfinished classwork.
Child complains of headaches, stomachaches, etc.
Child forgets to write down assignments day after day.

BE AWARE OF OTHER SYMPTOMS REFLECTIVE OF TENSION, STRESS, OR DIFFICULTIES WITH LEARNING.

At School

Child may exhibit:

-inability to focus on task
-disorganization
-inflexibility
-irresponsibility
-poor judgment
-denial

Social Interaction

Child may exhibit:

-social withdrawal
-finding fault with other children
-low peer status
-unwillingness to try new relationships

At Home

Child may exhibit:

-oversensitivity
-forgetfulness
-daydreaming
-unwillingness to venture out
-unwillingness to reason
-denial

Sleep

Child may exhibit:

-trouble falling asleep
-restless sleep
-resistance to rising
-frequent nightmares

6-2. Continued

While many of these symptoms may not by themselves indicate a major problem, several guidelines should be used in determining the severity of the problem:

1. **Frequency of Symptoms.** Consider how often the symptoms occur. The greater the frequency, the greater chance of a serious problem.

2. **Duration of Symptoms.** Consider how long the symptoms last. The longer the duration, the more serious the problem.

3. **Intensity of Symptoms.** Consider how serious the reactions are at the time of occurrence. The more intense the symptom, the more serious the problem.

If you suspect serious problems, contact the school psychologist, special education teacher, or a private mental health clinic for an evaluation or at least a consultation. The more immediate the response to such symptoms, the greater the chance of success with the child.

6-3. HOW PARENTS CAN HELP THEIR CHILDREN WITH HOMEWORK

1. Set up a homework schedule.

For some children, the responsibility of deciding when to sit down and do homework may be too difficult. Children may decide to do their homework after school or after dinner. This is a personal choice and has to do with learning style; however, once the time is determined, the schedule should be adhered to as closely as possible.

2. Rank assignments.

For some children, the decision as to what to do first becomes a major chore. They may dwell over this choice for a long period of time because everything takes on the same level of importance. Ranking assignments means that the parent determines the order in which the assignments are completed.

3. Do not sit next to your child while he or she does homework.

Employing this technique may create learned helplessness because the same "assistance" is not imitated in the classroom. Parents serve their children better by acting as resource persons to whom the child may come with a problem. After the problem is solved or the question answered, the child should return to his or her work area without the parent.

4. Check correct problems first.

When your child brings you a paper to check, mention to him or her how well he or she did on the correct problems, spelling words, or other work. For those that are incorrect say, "I bet if you go back and check these over you may get a different answer."

5. Never let homework drag on all evening.

The only thing accomplished by allowing a child to linger on homework hour after hour with very little performance is increased feelings of inadequacy. If this occurs, end the work period after a reasonable period of time, and write the teacher a note explaining the circumstances.

6. Discuss homework questions before your child reads the chapter.

Discuss the questions to be answered before the child reads the chapter. In this way he or she will know what important information to look for while reading.

7. Check small groups of problems at a time.

Many children can benefit from immediate gratification. Have your child do five problems and then come to you to check them. Additionally, if the child is doing the assignment incorrectly, the error can be detected and explained, preventing the child from doing the entire assignment incorrectly.

8. Place textbook chapters on tape.

Research indicates that the more sensory input children receive, the greater the chance the information will be retained. For instance, parents can place science or social studies chapters on tape so that the child can listen while reading along.

6-3. Continued

9. Be aware of negative nonverbal messages during homework.

Many messages, especially negative ones, can be communicated easily without your awareness. If children are sensitive, they will pick up these messages (raised eyebrows, inattentiveness) which can only add to their tension

10. Avoid finishing assignments for your child.

Children tend to feel inadequate when a parent finishes their homework. If children cannot complete an assignment, and they have honestly tried, write the teacher a note explaining the circumstances.

11. Be aware of possible signs of more serious learning problems.

Parents should always be aware of symptoms indicating the possibility of more serious learning problems. Many of these symptoms may show up during homework. If these symptoms present a pattern, contact the psychologist or resource room teacher for further assistance. Such symptoms may include constant avoidance of homework, forgetting to bring home assignments, taking hours to do homework, procrastination of classwork, low frustration tolerance, labored writing, or poor spelling.

12. Check homework assignments at the end of the evening.

This will reduce the child's concerns over the thought of bringing incorrect homework to school. It also offers children a feeling of accomplishment, a source of positive attention, and a sense of security that the work is completed.

6-4. HOW TO COMMUNICATE WITH YOUR CHILDREN

1. Communication is a two-way street.

Many people feel they are communicating, but they never listen. Use the technique "I'll talk and you listen and then you talk and I'll listen" as a first step in developing communication with your child.

2. Don't attack when communicating your feelings.

When communicating feelings, try using the words "I," "we," or "me" as often as possible and stay away from the word "you." Even if someone has done something to hurt you, focus on your feelings rather than the other's behavior. Tell your child how the behavior affected you.

3. Teach children to label feelings properly.

Children may have a very difficult time communicating because they lack the experience in labeling their feelings. Therefore it is crucial for parents to assist their children in correctly labeling a feeling or emotion. You may want to say, for example, "While the feeling you are expressing sounds like anger, it is really frustration and frustration is . . . ."

4. Use connective discussion whenever possible.

When faced with a direct question concerning a feeling or a reason for some behavior, most children will shrug their shoulders in confusion or immediately respond, "I don't know." Instead of this direct communication, try connective discussion. This technique assumes that the parent may be aware of the trigger and connects the feeling and resulting behavior for the child. For example, parents may say, "It seems to me that you are feeling jealous over the attention your new baby brother is getting and that may be the reason for your behavior." At this point, a child may have an easier time responding since the foundation and labels have been presented.

5. Remember that all behavior has a trigger.

If parents can trace back children's responses to the source or trigger, they will have a very good chance of identifying the real problem. Remember that all behavior is a message, and for many children their behavior is the only means of communicating their frustrations or feelings. The problem is that such behavior is frequently misunderstood and misinterpreted—resulting in more problems.

6. Be aware of nonverbal misinterpretations.

Children are very prone to nonverbal misinterpretations. They frequently misread a look on a parent's face and personalize it into something negative. If you are upset, angry, or frustrated with something other than your children, let them know that fact in a verbal way. Try, "I am very upset right now about something, but I wanted to tell you that it has nothing to do with you and after I think for awhile we will get together."

321

6-4. Continued

7. Use written communication whenever possible.

The use of writing to communicate feelings is an excellent tool in that it allows parents and children to phrase thoughts as desired. Notes thanking a child for some positive behavior or telling him or her how proud you are of her or him are just two examples. Notes can also be used to register a complaint without nose-to-nose confrontation.

8. Try to use direct love as often as possible.

The need to feel loved and cared for is a primary need for any individual at any age. Direct messages of love require no interpretation or assumptions on the part of the child and should be viewed on the same level of importance as gasoline to a car. Examples of direct love include hugging, kissing, cuddling, holding, and stroking.

9. Make yourself as approachable as possible.

The higher the approachability factor on the part of parents, the easier it will be for children to express and show direct love. Parents may want to evaluate just how easy their children feel in approaching them with feelings or problems and make adjustments if necessary. In later life, these children may have an easier time using direct forms of love in relationships.

6-5. HOW PARENTS CAN USE EFFECTIVE DISCIPLINE

1. **Limits and guidelines are very necessary for a child's emotional development.**

For children, realistic, fair, and well-defined limits and guidelines represent a "safety net" within which they can behave. Children will know that any act showing poor judgment will be brought to their attention if limits are well defined. Consequently they will be brought back to the safety net. Parenting cannot be a popularity contest.

2. **All behavior should have a consequence.**

This means appropriate behavior is rewarded and negative behavior punished. Consistency of consequence, whether reward or punishment, will assist the child in developing a frame of reference for how to behave.

3. **Punishment by itself will not work.**

Punishment tells children what not to do, but rewards tell children what behavior is acceptable. If long-term changes in behavior are desired, then reward must be included. Rewards need not be monetary. They can include verbal praise, written notes of thanks, extended playtime or TV time, or a special trip or dinner with a parent.

4. **Punishment should be limited to something that you can control.**

Quantity or severity of punishment is not always important. The most important thing to remember with discipline is that a parent begins it and the parent ends it. Maintaining both boundaries is crucial. In too many situations, the parent begins the discipline but due to its harshness, unrealistic expectations of time, manipulation by children, or inability of parent to follow through, there is no closure. For young children with no concept of time, 2 minutes in a "timeout" chair (controllable) rather than 30 minutes (uncontrollable) is just as productive.

5. **Never trade a punishment for a reward.**

If children do something inappropriate and then something appropriate, the two incidents should be treated separately. If you begin to trade off, children become confused and may be forced to become manipulative.

6. **Focus on inappropriate behavior, not the personality.**

Remember, children know that their inappropriate behavior is unacceptable. You may want to use such phrases as "poor judgment," "inappropriate behavior," "lapse of judgment," and "acting before thinking" when confronting the act. Focusing on the act allows children to save face. Children who grow up in homes where personalities are attacked tend to model that behavior in their social relationships.

7. **Choose your battlegrounds wisely.**

Try to view energy like money. In this way you will be deciding whether an issue is worth $2.00 worth of energy or $200.00. Investing too much energy in situations may lead to early parent burnout; however, it is very important that both parents agree on the priority of issues so that the child is not confused.

6-5. Continued

8. **Try to project a united front.**

If one parent should disagree with the other's tactics or reasoning, try to discuss it at a private moment. Open disagreement concerning a disciplinary action can sometimes confuse children and place them in the uncomfortable position of having to choose between parents.

9. **Try to use a forced choice technique whenever possible.**

Choose two options, solutions, or alternatives that are acceptable to you. Then say to the child, "You may do . . . or . . . . Which do you prefer?" Using a forced choice technique allows children to feel that they are making the decision and creates less problems than an open-ended question such as, "What would you like?"

10. **Delay a consequence when you are angry.**

The use of delay allows for a different perspective from that which is held at the height of anger. Say, "I am so angry now that I don't want to deal with this situation. Go to your room and I'll deal with you in 15 minutes." The use of delay will reduce impractical consequences.

6-6. HOW PARENTS CAN SPOT POSSIBLE LEARNING DISABILITIES IN THEIR CHILDREN

1. **Intellectual requirements.** Children with learning disabilities usually exhibit intellectual potential within the average range and above. This usually translates into a score of 90 or better. Such potential should only be measured by an individual intelligence test like the Wechsler Intelligence Scale for Children–Revised.

2. **Academic requirements.** Children with learning disabilities usually exhibit mild academic deficits (6 months–1 year below grade level), moderate academic deficits (1–2 years below grade level) or severe academic deficits (more than 2 years below grade level). These deficits may exhibit themselves in any one of the following areas:

- Decoding (word attack skills)
- Reading comprehension
- Mathematical computation
- Mathematical reasoning
- Written expression
- Oral expression
- Listening comprehension

3. **Exclusion requirements.** Children with learning disabilities are not retarded, primarily emotionally disturbed, hearing impaired, visually impaired, slow learners, or the result of inadequate instructional practices or cultural or economic disadvantages.

4. **Background requirements.** Children with learning disabilities usually exhibit a history of learning, social, and developmental difficulties dating back to early grades.

5. **Behavioral requirements.** Children with learning disabilities usually exhibit several of the following:

- Variability in performance across subject areas
- Attention problems, such as distractibility or poor concentration
- Organizational problems with information, space, or time
- Poor motivation and attitude, due to repeated academic failure
- Memory problems
- Language deficits in listening, speaking, or writing
- Poor motor abilities, fine motor (small muscle) or gross motor (large muscles)
- Inappropriate social behavior—difficulty making friends or poor reactions to social situations

6-6. Continued

6. **Processing requirements.** Children with learning disabilities usually exhibit deficits in the learning process. The strengths or weaknesses in this process are usually measured by process (perceptual) tests such as the Slingerland, Woodcock Johnson, Detroit Tests of Learning Aptitudes, or the ITPA. The following list indicates some difficulties exhibited by children with processing problems:

Visual Motor Disability

- poor motor coordination
- poor perception of time and space
- gets lost easily
- poor handwriting, artwork, drawing
- restless, short attention span, perseveration
- awkward, frequent tripping, skipping

Auditory-Vocal Disability

- appears not to listen or comprehend
- responds with one-word answers
- may emphasize wrong syllables in words
- offers little in group discussions
- follows directions better after he is shown
- trouble with rote memory, for example, math facts

Auditory Association Disability

- fails to enjoy being read to
- has difficulty comprehending questions
- slow to respond, takes a long time to answer
- relies heavily on picture clues

Visual Association Disability

- unable to tell a story from pictures
- unable to understand what he or she reads
- fails to handle primary workbook
- needs auditory cues and clues

Manual Expressive Disability

- poor handwriting and drawing
- poor at game playing, can't imitate others
- clumsy, uncoordinated
- poor at acting out ideas or feelings

Verbal Expression Disability

- mispronounces common words
- uses incorrect word endings
- difficulty in sound blending
- omits correct verbal endings

Auditory Memory Disabilities

- fails to remember instructions
- can't memorize nursery rhymes, poem
- doesn't know alphabet
- unable to count

Visual Memory Disabilities

- misspells own name frequently
- inconsistent word identification
- frequent misspellings, even after practice
- can't write alphabet, numbers

6-7. FREQUENTLY ASKED QUESTIONS CONCERNING LEARNING DISABILITIES

1-**Q- What is a learning disability?**

A-In general, a learning disability is a problem in acquiring and using skills required for listening, speaking, reading, writing, reasoning, and mathematical ability. Such problems in the acquisition of skills cannot be traced to inadequate intelligence, school environment, emotional problems, visual or hearing defects, cultural deprivation, or lack of motivation.

2-**Q- How many children have learning disabilities?**

A-This is somewhat difficult, depending upon the definition used. The U.S. Department of Education reports approximately 5% of a school's population may be learning disabled. According to their statistics taken in 1984, this represented 1,811,451 students throughout the country.

3-**Q- What causes learning disabilities?**

A-Several theories have been proposed concerning the cause of learning disabilities. Some of the more widely held theories center around heredity, complications of pregnancy, lag in nervous system development (sometimes referred to as a maturational lag), or some subtle neurological impairment—sort of like crossed wires in a telephone line.

4-**Q- Can a true learning disability show up in later grades with no earlier indications?**

A-This is a widely held misconception. In most cases a true learning disability has a historical pattern, with symptoms appearing as early as a child's first school experience or sooner. A fifth-grade child who is referred by a teacher for suspected learning disabilities and has *no* prior educational difficulties should be considered a low-risk LD youngster.

5-**Q- Are dyslexia and learning disabilities the same?**

A-No. Dyslexia is a specific and severe form of a learning disability. Dyslexia refers to a severe problem in learning how to read. All learning-disabled children are not dyslexic; however, all dyslexic children are learning disabled.

6-**Q- Are reversals an indication of a learning disability?**

A-This symptom has been greatly inflated by the media. Parents should keep in mind that reversals of letters and numbers may be very common in children up to grade 3 and may not by themselves indicate any learning disability. However, if a child frequently reverses letters and numbers along with other symptoms or continues after age 8, you should discuss this with a professional as soon as possible.

7-**Q- Can a child be learning disabled in only one area?**

A-Yes. Some children may have a learning disability in the area of short-term memory, or mathematical computations, or spelling, or reading comprehension. Of course, the more areas affected, the more serious the disability.

6-7. Continued

8-Q- What kinds of symptoms signal a possible learning disability?

A-There are a variety of symptoms that may signal the presence of such a problem. Some of the more common include disorganization, poor muscle coordination, impulsivity, distractibility, short attention span, trouble in completing assignments, poor spelling, poor handwriting, poor social skills, low reading level, difficulty in following directions, discrepancy between ability and performance, and language difficulties.

9-Q- What is the first thing to do if I suspect that my child may have a learning disability?

A-The school should have identified this possibility before you. If this is not the case, immediately contact the school psychologist, or head of the school's child study team, and make that person aware of your concerns. If you do not wish to go through the school, then contact a qualified professional in the field, or a clinic that specializes in learning disabilities. They will be happy to evaluate your child. Keep in mind, however, that such an evaluation can be very expensive, while it is free through the school.

10-Q- Must my child be referred to the committee on special education if he or she has a learning disability?

A-The answer in most cases will be yes. It is the legal and moral responsibility of every school district to refer such a child for a review before the CSE (Committee on Special Education). A review does not mean immediate classification; it just means that enough evidence exists to warrant a "look" by the district. If the child has a learning disability and is encountering frustration in school, then the services he or she will receive should greatly reduce such problems.

6-8. WHAT PARENTS NEED TO KNOW ABOUT RETENTION

Retention of a student's grade placement is a very difficult decision for both parents and educators. When parents are first presented with this suggestion by the school, they may become overwhelmed and confused. If parents are presented with this option, great care should be taken in examining all the variables that will affect the outcome.

Present research seems somewhat divided about the use of such an educational alternative. Some studies have shown that the greatest success for such an action occurs prior to grade 1. The chances for success dramatically decrease as children grow older. Other studies indicate that if retention is exercised as an option in kindergarten and first grade, boys seem to benefit most. This result seems to support the developmental pattern of a more advanced social and academic maturity in girls.

Since parents should be involved in the decision of retention, it is important that they become educated in this area. The following factors should be taken into consideration prior to the final action.

1. Present Grade Placement

The greatest chance for retention to work is in kindergarten or first grade. By the time children are in fourth or fifth grade, the chances for success decrease dramatically.

2. Immature Behavior Patterns

The level of interpersonal relations exhibited by children is also a factor to consider. If they tend to play with children much younger than themselves, retention will have fewer consequences; however, if children choose playmates who are equal or older in age, retention may have more negative results.

3. Age of the Child

Children who are younger than their classmates will experience fewer problems with retention. Children who are one or two years above their classmates may have more serious adjustments to this action.

4. Brothers and Sisters

Children without siblings seem to make a better adjustment when repeating a grade. Others with brothers or sisters in the same grade or one year below find retention much more difficult. Children in this category find the experience ego deflating; they feel a loss of familial status.

5. Attendance

The more times a child is out of school, the greater the reason for retention. Children who are ill and miss over 25 days of school are prime candidates. This is especially important in the early grades where the foundations of reading and basic skills are taught. Some children with excellent attendance are less suitable candidates.

6-8. Continued

6. Intellectual Ability

Children with average intelligence have the better chance of success with retention. Those with below-average (lower 2%–10%) or superior ability (upper 2%–10%) tend to have more difficulty. Children who fall into these categories may be having difficulties in school for other reasons (emotional problems, retardation), which would not be addressed by retention.

7. Physical Size

Children who are smaller in stature make better candidates. Those who are physically larger than their present classmates will have more problems when retained.

8. Gender

Boys in kindergarten and first grade make the best candidates. After fourth grade, both boys and girls will have little chance of success when it comes to retention.

9. Present Classroom Performance

Students who are performing one year behind in most academic subjects may find retention a help. Those who are more than two years behind may need an alternate program, such as special education class or resource room.

10. Present Emotional State

Children who do not exhibit any signs of serious emotional difficulties (impulsivity, nervous habits, distractibility, unwillingness to reason, and tantrums) have a better chance when retained. Children who exhibit serious emotional concerns should not be considered for retention; however, other educational options should be explored.

11. Parent's Attitude About Retention

This factor is crucial. Children will have the best chance of adjusting to retention when their parents see it as a positive step. Frustrated, angry, and disappointed parents will negate any chance of success.

12. Number of Schools Attended

Children who have attended several schools within their first two years of school will have less success with retention.

13. Attitude

Children who see retention as an opportunity to "catch up" will have a better chance of success. Children who become very upset, exhibit denial about poor performance, or show indifference may have greater difficulty.

6-8. Continued

14. Evidence of Learning Disabilities

Children with intact learning skills and processes have a greater chance for success when it comes to retention. Children who have been diagnosed as having learning disabilities should receive alternate educational support. In such cases, retention should not be considered as an option.

The above factors are offered as a general guide for parents to follow. There may be other factors that should be considered as well. Regardless, parent input into this decision is crucial.

6-9. SELECTED ORGANIZATIONS FOR EXCEPTIONAL CHILDREN

1. Alexander Graham Bell Association for the Deaf, Inc., 3417 Volta Place, NW, Washington, DC 20007

2. American Academy for Cerebral Palsy, University Hospital School, Iowa City, IA 52240

3. American Association for Rehabilitation Therapy, P.O. Box 93, North Little Rock, AR 72116

4. American Association for the Advancement of Behavior Therapy, 420 Lexington Avenue, New York, NY 10017

5. American Association for the Education of Severely and Profoundly Handicapped, 1600 West Armory Way, Garden View Suite, Seattle, WA 98119

6. American Association on Mental Deficiency, 5201 Connecticut Avenue NW, Washington, DC 20015

7. American Diabetes Association, 18 E. 48th Street, New York, NY 10017

8. American Foundation for the Blind, 15 West 16th Street, New York, NY 10011

9. American Heart Association, 44 E. 23rd Street, New York, NY 10016

10. American Lung Association, 1790 Broadway, New York, NY 10019

11. American Mensa, 1701 W. 3rd Street, Suite 1-R, Brooklyn, NY 11223

12. American Occupational Therapy Association, 6000 Executive Blvd., Rockville, MD 20852

13. American Physical Therapy Association, 1156 15th Street NW, Washington, DC 20005

14. American Printing House for the Blind, 1839 Frankfort Avenue, Louisville, KY 40206

15. American Psychological Association, 1200 17th Street NW, Washington, DC 20036

16. American Speech-Language Hearing Association, 10801 Rockville Pike, Rockville, MD 20852

17. Association for Children and Adults with Learning Disabilities, 4900 Gerard Rd., Pittsburgh, PA 15236

18. Association for Children with Retarded Mental Development, 902 Broadway, New York, NY 10010

19. Association for Education of the Visually Handicapped, 206 N. Washington Street, Alexandria, VA 22314

6-9. **Continued**

20. Association for Retarded Citizens, 2709 Avenue E. East, Arlington, TX 76011

21. Association for the Gifted, Council for Exceptional Children, 1920 Association Drive, Reston, VA 22091

22. Association for the Severely Handicapped. 7010 Roosevelt Way NE, Seattle, WA 98115

23. Association on Handicapped Student Service Programs in Post Secondary Education, P.O. Box 21192, Columbus, OH 43221

24. Canadian National Institute for the Blind, 1921 Bayview Avenue, Toronto, Ontario MG43E8

25. Center on Human Policy, 216 Ostrom Avenue, Syracuse, NY 13210

26. CHADD—Children and Adults with Attention Deficit Disorder, 499 Northwest 70th Avenue, Suite 308, Plantation, FL 33317

27. Chicago Institute for Learning Disabilities (social adjustment, language), University of Illinois at Chicage Circle, Box 4348, Chicago, IL 60680

28. Children's Defense Fund, 1520 New Hampshire Avenue, Washington, DC 20036

29. Clearinghouse on the Handicapped, Rm. 3106, Switzer Bldg., Washington, DC 20202

30. Closer Look, 1201 16th Street NW, Washington, DC 20036

31. Conference of Executives of American Schools for the Deaf, 5043 Wisconsin Avenue NW, Washington, DC 20016

32. Coordinating Council for Handicapped Children, 407 S. Dearborn Street, Rm. 680, Chicago, IL 60605

33. Council for Children with Behavior Disorders, Council for Exceptional Children, 1920 Association Drive, Reston, VA 22091

34. Council for Exceptional Children, 1920 Association Drive, Reston, VA 22091

35. Council for Learning Disabilities, Department of Special Education, University of Louisville, KY 40292

36. Creative Education Foundation, State University College at Buffalo, 1300 Elmwood Avenue, Buffalo, NY 14222

37. Division for Children with Communication Disorders, Council for Exceptional Children, 1920 Association Drive, Reston, VA 22091

38. Division for Children with Learning Disabilities, 850 Hungerford Drive, Rockville, MD 20850

39. Division for Early Childhood, Council for Exceptional Children, 1920 Association Drive, Reston, VA 22091

6-9. Continued

40. Division for the Visually Handicapped, Council for Exceptional Children, 1920 Association Drive, Reston, VA 22091

41. Division of Mental Retardation, Council for Exceptional Children, 1920 Association Drive, Reston, VA 22091

42. Division on Career Development, Council for Exceptional Children, 1920 Association Drive, Reston, VA 22091

43. Education Development Center, 55 Chapel Street, Newton, MA 02160

44. Educational Due Process Services, Box 57387, Washington, DC 20037

45. Epilepsy Foundation of America, 1828 L Street NW, Washington, DC 20036

46. ERIC Clearinghouse on Disabilities and Gifted Education, Council for Exceptional Children (CEC), 1920 Association Drive, Reston, VA 22091-1589

47. Gifted Child Society, Inc., 59 Glen Gray Road, Oakland, NJ 07436

48. Gifted Students Institute for Research and Development, 611 Ryan Plaza Drive, Suite 1149, Arlington, TX 76011

49. Institute for Research on Learning Disabilities (identification, assessment, and placement), 350 Elliot Hall, 75 East River Road, University of Minnesota, Minneapolis, MN 55455

50. International Association of Parents of the Deaf, 814 Thayer Avenue, Silver Spring, MD 20910

51. Latino Institute, Research Center, Project REACHH, 1760 Reston Avenue, Suite 101, Reston, VA 22090

52. Learning Disabilities Research Institute (attentional deficits) The University of Virginia, Department of Special Education, 152 Ruffner Hall, Charlottesville, VA 22903

53. Muscular Dystrophy Association. 810 Seventh Avenue, New York, NY 10019

54. National Association for Gifted Children, 217 Gregory Drive, Hot Springs, AR 71901

55. National Association for Parents of the Visually Impaired, 2011 Hardy Circle, Austin, TX 78756

56. National Association for Retarded Citizens, 2709 Ave E East, Arlington, TX 76011

57. National Association for the Deaf, 814 Thayer Avenue, Silver Spring, MD 20910

58. National Association for the Deaf-Blind, 2703 Forest Oak Circle, Norman, OK 73071

59. National Association of the Deaf, 814 Thayer Avenue, Silver Spring, MD 20910

6-9. Continued

60. National Center for Law and the Deaf, 7th Street & Florida Avenue NE, Washington, DC 20002

61. National Council for the Gifted, 700 Prospect Avenue, West Orange, NJ 07052

62. National Cystic Fibrosis Research Foundation, 3379 Peachtree Road NE, Atlanta, GA 30326

63. National Easter Seal Society, 2023 West Ogden Avenue, Chicage Il 60612

64. National Federation of the Blind, 1800 Johnson Street, Baltimore, MD 21230

65. National Information Center for Children and Youth with Disabilities (NICHCY) PO Box 1492, Washington, DC 20013-1492

66. National Network of Parent Centers, 9451 Broadway Drive, Bay Harbor, FL 33154

67. National Society for Autistic Children, 621 Central Avenue, Albany, NY 12206

68. National/State Leadership Training Institute on the Gifted and Talented, 316 West Second Street, Suite 708, Los Angeles, CA 90012

69. Office of the Gifted and Talented, U.S. Office of Education, Washington, DC 20202

70. Orton Society, Inc., 8415 Bellona Lane, Baltimore, MD 21204

71. PACER Center, Parent Advocacy Coalition for Educational Rights, 4701 Chicago Avenue South, Minneapolis, MN 55407

72. Parents Educational Advocacy Center, 116 W. Jones Street, Raleigh, NC 27611

73. Research Institute in Learning Disabilities (LD adolescents) University of Kansas, Room 313, Lawrence, KS 66045

74. Spina Bifida Association of America, 343 South Dearborn Street, Suite 319, Chicago, IL 60604

75. The American Association for the Gifted, 15 Gramercy Park, New York, NY 10003

76. The Association for the Gifted (TAG), Council for Exceptional Children, 1920 Association Drive, Reston, VA 22091

77. The Educational Resources Information Clearinghouse on Handicapped and Gifted, Council for Exceptional Children, 1920 Association Drive, Reston, VA 22091

78. The National Association for Creative Children and Adults, 8080 Spring Valley Drive, Cincinnati, OH 45236

79. United Cerebral Palsy Association. 66 East 34th Street, New York, NY 10016

80. United Epilepsy Association, 111 W. 57th Street, New York, NY 10019

81. Volta Speech Association for the Deaf, 1537 35th Street NW, Washington, DC 20007

6-10. SELECTED JOURNAL PUBLICATIONS ON EXCEPTIONAL CHILDREN

1. *Academic Therapy*
2. *Accent on Living*
3. *American Annals of the Deaf*
4. *American Educational Research Journal*
5. *American Journal of Art Therapy*
6. *American Journal of Mental Deficiency*
7. *American Journal of Occupational Therapy*
8. *American Journal of Psychology*
9. *American Sociological Review*
10. *American Speech and Hearing Association Journal*
11. *Analysis and Intervention of Developmental Disabilities*
12. *Applied Research in Mental Retardation*
13. *Behavior Disorders*
14. *Behavior Therapy*
15. *Behavioral Science*
16. *British Journal of Mental Subnormality*
17. *Bulletin of Prosthetics Research*
18. *Bulletin of the Orton Society*
19. *Career Development of Exceptional Individuals*
20. *Career Education Quarterly*
21. *Child Psychiatry and Human Development*
22. *Childhood Education*
23. *Day Care and Early Education*
24. *Developmental Psychology*
25. *Disabled U.S.A.*
26. *Early Years*
27. *Education and Training of Children*
28. *Education and Training of the Mentally Retarded*
29. *Education Forum*

6-10. Continued

30. *Education of the Visually Handicapped*
31. *Educational Horizons*
32. *Educational Medicine*
33. *Educational Researcher*
34. *Exceptional Children*
35. *Exceptional Parent*
36. *Focus on Exceptional Children*
37. *Gifted Child Quarterly*
38. *Gifted/Creative/Talented Children*
39. *Harvard Educational Review*
40. *Health Services Report*
41. *Hearing*
42. *Instructor*
43. *Journal for the Education of the Gifted*
44. *Journal of Abnormal Child Psychology*
45. *Journal of Abnormal Psychology*
46. *Journal of Applied Behavior Analysis*
47. *Journal of Career Development*
48. *Journal of Career Education*
49. *Journal of Consulting and Clinical Psychology*
50. *Journal of Creative Behavior*
51. *Journal of Experimental Education*
52. *Journal of Language, Speech, and Hearing*
53. *Journal of Learning Disabilities*
54. *Journal of Music Therapy*
55. *Journal of Nervous and Mental Disease*
56. *Journal of Personality and Social Psychology*
57. *Journal of Personality Assessment*
58. *Journal of Rehabilitation*
59. *Journal of Rehabilitation of the Deaf*

6-10. Continued

60. *Journal of Social Issues*

61. *Journal of Social Psychology*

62. *Journal of Special Education*

63. *Journal of Special Education Technology*

64. *Journal of Speech and Hearing Disorders*

65. *Journal of Teacher Education*

66. *Journal of the Association for Persons with Severe Handicaps*

67. *Journal of the Division of Early Childhood*

68. *Journal of Visual Impairment and Blindness*

69. *Language, Speech, and Hearing Services in the Schools*

70. *Learning Disabilities Focus*

71. *Learning Disabilities Quarterly*

72. *Learning Disabilities Research*

73. *Mental Retardation*

74. *Perceptual and Motor Skills*

75. *Personnel and Guidance Quarterly*

76. *Physical Therapy*

77. *Psychology in the Schools*

78. *Reading Research Quarterly*

79. *Rehabilitation Digest*

80. *Rehabilitation Literature*

81. *Rehabilitation Research and Practice Review*

82. *Rehabilitation Teacher*

83. *Remedial and Special Education*

84. *Research in Education*

85. *Review of Educational Research*

86. *Roeper Review: A Journal on Gifted Child Education*

87. *School Psychology Digest*

88. *Sign Language Studies*

89. *Teacher Education and Special Education*

6-10. Continued

90. *Teacher of the Deaf*

91. *Teaching Behaviorally Disordered Youth*

92. *Teaching Exceptional Children*

93. *The Creative Child and Adult Quarterly*

94. *The Deaf American*

95. *The Sight Saving Review*

96. *The Volta Review*

97. *Today's Education*

98. *Topics in Early Childhood Special Education*

99. *Vocational Guidance Quarterly*

PART 7

Definitions, Terminology, and Abbreviations

7-1. EDUCATIONAL TERMINOLOGY ASSOCIATED WITH SPECIAL EDUCATION

1. **Ability grouping**—The grouping of children based on their achievement in an area of study.

2. **Accelerated learning**—An educational process that allows students to progress through the curriculum at an increased pace.

3. **Achievement**—The level of a child's accomplishment on a test of knowledge or skill.

4. **Adaptive behavior**—An individual's social competence and ability to cope with the demands of the environment.

5. **Adaptive physical education**—A modified program of instruction implemented to meet the needs of special students.

6. **Advocate**—An individual, either a parent or professional, who attempts to establish or improve services for exceptional children.

7. **Age norms**—Standards based on the average performance of individuals in different age groups.

8. **Agnosia**—Child's inability to recognize objects and their meaning, usually resulting from damage to the brain.

9. **Amplification device**—Any device that increases the volume of sound.

10. **Anecdotal record**—A procedure for recording and analyzing observations of a child's behavior; an objective, narrative description.

11. **Annual goals**—Yearly activities or achievements to be completed or attained by the disabled child, documented on the Individual Educational Plan.

12. **Aphasia**—The inability to acquire meaningful spoken language by the age of three, usually resulting from damage to or disease of the brain.

13. **Articulation**—The production of distinct language sounds by the vocal chords.

14. **At risk**—Usually refers to infants or children with a high potential for experiencing future medical or learning problems.

15. **Attention deficit hyperactive disorder (ADHD)**—A psychiatric classification used to describe individuals who exhibit poor attention, distractibility. impulsivity, and hyperactivity.

16. **Baseline measure**—The level or frequency of behavior prior to the implementation of an instructional procedure that will later be evaluated.

17. **Behavior modification**—The techniques used to change behavior by applying principles of reinforcement learning.

18. **Bilingual**—Having the ability to speak two languages.

343

7-1. Continued

19. **Career education**—Instruction that focuses on the application of skills and content area information necessary to cope with the problems of daily life, independent living, and vocational areas of interest.

20. **Categorical resource room**—An auxiliary pull-out program that offers supportive services to exceptional children with the same disability.

21. **Cognition**—The understanding of information.

22. **Consultant teacher**—A supportive service for disabled children in which the services are provided by a specialist in the classroom.

23. **Criterion referenced tests**—Tests in which the child is evaluated on his or her own performance according to a set of criteria and not in comparison with others.

24. **Declassification**—The process in which a disabled child is no longer considered in need of special education services. This requires a meeting of the CSE and can be requested by the parent, school, or child (if over the age of 18).

25. **Deficit**—A level of performance that is less than expected for a child.

26. **Desensitization**—A technique used in reinforcement theory in which there is a weakening of a response, usually an emotional response.

27. **Diagnosis**—Identification of specific disorder(s) as a result of some evaluation.

28. **Distractibility**—Difficulty in maintaining attention.

29. **Due process**—The legal steps and processes outlined in educational law that protect the rights of disabled children.

30. **Dyscalculia**—A serious learning disability in which the child is unable to calculate, apply, solve or identify mathematical functions.

31. **Dysfluency**—Difficulty in the production of fluent speech, as in stuttering.

32. **Dysgraphia**—A serious learning disability in which the child is unable to write.

33. **Dyslexia**—A severe learning disability in which a child's ability to read is greatly impaired.

34. **Dysorthographia**—A serious learning disability that affects a child's ability to spell.

35. **Enrichment**—Providing a child with extra and more sophisticated learning experiences than those normally presented in the curriculum.

36. **Etiology**—The cause of a problem.

37. **Exceptional children**—Children whose school performance shows significant discrepancy between ability and achievement, and who, as a result, require special instruction, assistance, or equipment. Also includes gifted children.

7-1. Continued

38. **Free appropriate public education (FAPE)**—Used in PL94-142 to mean special education and related services that are provided at public expense, conform to the state requirements, and conform to the individual's IEP.

39. **Group homes**—Residential living arrangements for handicapped adults—especially the mentally retarded, along with several nonhandicapped supervisors.

40. **Habilitation**—An educational approach used with exceptional children that is directed toward the development of the necessary skills required for successful adulthood.

41. **Homebound instruction**—A special education service in which teaching is provided by a specially trained instructor to students unable to attend school. A parent or guardian must always be present at the time of instruction. In some cases, the instruction may take place on a neutral sight—not in the home or school.

42. **Hyperactivity**—Behavior characterized by excessive motor activity or restlessness.

43. **Impulsivity**—Nongoal-oriented activity exhibited by individuals who lack careful thought and reflection prior to a behavior.

44. **Individualized educational plan**—A written educational program that outlines a disabled child's current levels of performance, related services, educational goals, and modifications. This plan is developed by a team including the child's parent(s), teacher(s), and supportive staff.

45. **Inclusion**—Education of disabled children in their home school, with nonhandicapped children in the same classroom.

46. **Interdisciplinary team**—individuals from a variety of disciplines engaged in a collective effort to assess the needs of a child.

47. **Intervention**—Preventive, remedial, compensatory, or survival services made on behalf of a disabled individual.

48. **Itinerant teacher**—A teacher hired by a school district to help in the education of a disabled child. The teacher is employed by an outside agency and may be responsible for several children in several districts.

49. **Learning disability**—Severe discrepancy between ability and achievement in children with average or above average potential intelligence.

50. **Least restrictive environment**—The educational setting of exceptional children and the education of handicapped children with nonhandicapped children whenever realistic and possible. It is the least restrictive setting in which the disabled child can function without difficulty.

51. **Mainstreaming**—The practice of educating exceptional children in the regular classroom.

7-1. Continued

52. **Mental age**—The level of intellectual functioning based on the average for children of the same chronological age. When dealing with severely disabled children, the mental age may be more reflective of levels of ability than the chronological age.

53. **Mental disability**—A disability in which the individual's intellectual level is measured within the subaverage range and there are marked impairments in social competence.

54. **Native language**—The primary language used by an individual.

55. **Noncategorical resource room**—A resource room in a school that provides services to children with all types of classified disabilities. The children with these disabilities are able to be maintained in a regular classroom.

56. **Norm referenced tests**—Tests used to compare a child's performance with the performance of others using the same measure.

57. **Occupational therapist**—A professional who programs and delivers instructional activities and materials to assist disabled children and adults to participate in useful daily activities.

58. **Paraprofessionals**—Trained assistants or parents who work with a classroom teacher in the education process.

59. **Physical therapist**—A professional trained to assist and help disabled individuals to maintain and develop muscular and orthopedic capability and to make correct and useful movements.

60. **PINS petition**—PINS stands for "Person in Need of Supervision" and is a family court referral. This referral can be made by either the school or the parent and is usually made when a child under the age of 16 is out of control in terms of attendance, behavior, or some socially inappropriate or destructive pattern.

61. **Positive reinforcement**—Any stimulus or event, occurring after a behavior has been exhibited, that increases the possibility of repetition of that behavior in the future.

62. **Pupil personnel team**—A group of professionals from the same school who meet on a regular basis to discuss children's problems and offer suggestions or a direction for resolution.

63. **Pupils with handicapping conditions (PHC)**—Children classified as disabled by the Committee on Special Education.

64. **Pupils with special educational needs (PSEN)**—Students defined as having math and reading achievement lower than the 23rd percentile and requiring remediation. These students are not considered disabled, but are entitled to assistance to elevate their academic levels.

65. **Related services**—Services provided to disabled children to assist in their ability to learn and function in the least restrictive environment. Such services may include in-school counseling, speech and language services, and math remediation.

7-1. Continued

66. **Remediation**—An educational program designed to teach children to overcome some deficit or disability through education and training.

67. **Resource room**—An auxiliary service provided to disabled children for part of the school day. It is intended to service children's special needs so that they can be maintained within the least restrictive educational setting.

68. **Screening**—The process of examining groups of children in hopes of identifying potential high-risk children.

69. **Section 504**—Section 504 of the Rehabilitation Act of 1973 in which guarantees are provided for the civil rights of disabled children and adults. It also applies to the provision of services for children whose disability is not severe enough to warrant classification, but who could benefit from supportive services and classroom modifications.

70. **Self-contained class**—A special classroom for exceptional children usually located within a regular school building.

71. **Sheltered workshop**—A transitional or long-term work environment for disabled individuals who cannot, or who are preparing for, work in a regular setting. Within this setting the individual can learn to perform meaningful, productive tasks and receive payment.

72. **Surrogate parent**—A person other than the child's natural parent who has legal responsibility for the child's care and welfare.

73. **Token economy**—A system of reinforcing various behaviors through the delivery of tokens. These tokens can be in the form of stars, points, candy, or chips.

74. **Total communication**—The approach to the education of deaf students, which combines oral speech, sign language, and finger spelling.

75. **Underachiever**—A term generally used in reference to a child's lack of academic achievement in school. It is important that the school identify the underlying causes of such underachievement, since it may be a symptom of a more serious problem.

76. **Vocational rehabilitation**—A program designed to help disabled adults obtain and hold a job.

7-2. PSYCHOLOGICAL TERMINOLOGY ASSOCIATED WITH SPECIAL EDUCATION

1. **Affective reactions**—Psychotic reactions marked by extreme mood swings.

2. **Anxiety**—A general uneasiness of the mind characterized by irrational fears, panic, tension, and physical symptoms including palpitations, excessive sweating, and increased pulse rate.

3. **Assessment**—The process of gathering information about children in order to make educational decisions.

4. **Baseline data**—An objective measure used to compare and evaluate the results obtained during some implementation of an instructional procedure.

5. **Compulsion**—A persistent, repetitive act that the individual cannot consciously control.

6. **Confabulation**—The act of replacing memory loss by fantasy or by some reality that is not true for the occasion.

7. **Defense mechanisms**—The unconscious means by which individuals protect themselves against impulses or emotions that are too uncomfortable or threatening. Examples of these mechanisms include the following:

   a. **Denial**-A defense mechanism in which the individual refuses to admit the reality of some unpleasant event, situation, or emotion.

   b. **Displacement**-The disguising of the goal or intention of a motive by substituting another in its place.

   c. **Intellectualization**-A defense mechanism in which the individual exhibits anxious or moody deliberation, usually about abstract matters.

   d. **Projection**-The disguising of a source of conflict by displacing one's own motives onto someone else.

   e. **Rationalization**-The interpretation of one's own behavior to conceal the motive it expresses by assigning the behavior to another motive.

   f. **Reaction formation**-A complete disguise of a motive, expressed in a form that is directly opposite to its original intent.

   g. **Repression**-The psychological process involved in not permitting memories and motives to enter consciousness; they are operating at an unconscious level.

   h. **Supression**-The act of consciously inhibiting an impulse, affect, or idea, as in the deliberate act of forgetting something to avoid having to think about it.

8. **Delusion**—A groundless, irrational belief or thought, usually of grandeur or of persecution. It is usually a characteristic of paranoia.

7-2. Continued

9. **Depersonalization**—A nonspecific syndrome in which the individual senses that he or she has lost personal identity, that he or she is different, strange, or not real.

10. **Echolalia**—The repetition of what other people say, as if echoing them.

11. **Etiology**—The cause or causes of a problem.

12. **Hallucination**—An imaginary visual or auditory image that is regarded as a real sensory experience by the person.

13. **Magical thinking**—Primitive and prelogical thinking in which the child creates an outcome to meet a fantasy rather than the reality.

14. **Neologisms**—Made-up words that have meaning only to the child or adult.

15. **Obsession**—A repetitive and persistent idea that intrudes into a person's thoughts.

16. **Panic attack**—Serious episodes of anxiety in which the individual experiences a variety of symptoms including palpitations, dizziness, nausea, chest pains, trembling, fear of dying, and fear of losing control. These symptoms are not the result of any medical cause.

17. **Paranoia**—A personality disorder in which the individual exhibits extreme suspiciousness of the motives of others.

18. **Phobia**—An intense irrational fear, usually acquired through conditioning to an unpleasant object or event.

19. **Projective tests**—Methods used by psychologists and psychiatrists to study personality dynamics through a series of structured or ambiguous stimuli.

20. **Psychosis**—A serious mental disorder in which the individual has difficulty differentiating between fantasy and reality.

21. **Rorschach test**—An unstructured psychological test in which the individual is asked to project responses to a series of 10 inkblots.

22. **School phobia**—A form of separation anxiety in which the child's concerns and anxieties are centered around school issues. As a result he or she has an extreme fear about coming to school.

23. **Symptom**—Any sign, physical or mental, that stands for something else. Symptoms are usually generated from the tension of conflicts. The more serious the problem or conflict, the more frequent and intense the symptom.

24. **Syndrome**—A group of symptoms.

25. **Thematic Apperception Test**—A structured psychological test in which the individual is asked to project his or her feelings onto a series of drawings or photographs.

26. **Wechsler Scales of Intelligence**—A series of individual intelligence tests measuring global intelligence through a variety of subtests.

7-3. MEDICAL TERMINOLOGY ASSOCIATED WITH SPECIAL EDUCATION

1. **Albinism**—A congenital condition marked by severe deficiency in or total lack of pigmentation.

2. **Amblyopia**—Dimness of sight without any indication of change in the eye's structure.

3. **Amniocentesis**—A medical procedure done during the early stages of pregnancy for the purpose of identifying certain genetic disorders in the fetus.

4. **Anomaly**—Some irregularity in development or a deviation from the standard.

5. **Anoxia**—Lack of oxygen.

6. **Aphasia**—The inability to acquire meaningful spoken language by the age of 3 as a result of brain damage.

7. **Apraxia**—Problems with voluntary, or purposeful, muscular movement, with no evidence of motor impairment.

8. **Astigmatism**—A visual defect resulting in blurred vision, caused by uneven curvature of the cornea or lens. The condition is usually corrected by lenses.

9. **Ataxia**—A form of cerebral palsy in which the individual suffers from a loss of muscle coordination, especially those movements relating to balance and position.

10. **Athetosis**—A form of cerebral palsy characterized by involuntary, jerky, purposeless, and repetitive movements of the extremities, head and tongue.

11. **Atrophy**—The degeneration of tissue.

12. **Audiogram**—A graphic representation of the results of a hearing test.

13. **Audiologist**—A specialist trained in the evaluation and remediation of auditory disorders.

14. **Binocular vision**—Vision using both eyes working together to perceive a single image.

15. **Blind, legally**—Visual acuity measured at 20/200 in the better eye with best correction of glasses or contact lenses. Vision measured at 20/200 means the individual must be 20 feet from something to be able to see what the normal eye can see at 200 feet.

16. **Cataract**—A condition of the eye in which the crystalline lens becomes cloudy or opaque. As a result, a reduction or loss of vision occurs.

17. **Catheter**—A tube inserted into the body to allow for injection or withdrawal of fluids, or to maintain an opening in a passageway.

18. **Cerebral palsy**—An abnormal succession of human movement or motor functioning resulting from a defect, insult, or disease of the central nervous system.

7-3. Continued

19. **Conductive hearing loss**—A hearing loss resulting from obstructions in the outer or middle ear or malformations that interfere in the conduction of sound waves to the inner ear. This condition may be corrected medically or surgically.

20. **Congenital condition**—A condition present at birth.

21. **Cretinism**—A congenital condition associated with a thyroid deficiency that can result in stunted physical growth and mental retardation.

22. **Cyanosis**—A lack of oxygen in the blood characterized by a blue discoloration of the skin.

23. **Cystic fibrosis**—An inherited disorder affecting the pancreas, and salivary, mucous, and sweat glands that causes severe, long-term respiratory difficulties.

24. **Diplegia**—Paralysis that affects either both arms or both legs.

25. **Down syndrome**—A medical abnormality caused by a chromosomal anomaly that often results in moderate to severe mental retardation. The child with Down Syndrome will exhibit certain physical characteristics such as a large tongue, heart problems, poor muscle tone, and broad, flat bridge of the nose.

26. **Electroencephalogram (EEG)**—A graphic representation of the electrical output of the brain.

27. **Encopresis**—A lack of bowel control that may also have psychological causes.

28. **Endogenous**—Originating from within.

29. **Enuresis**—A lack of bladder control that may also have psychological causes.

30. **Exogenous**—Originating from external causes.

31. **Fetal alcohol syndrome**—A condition usually found in the infants of alcoholic mothers. As a result low birth weight, severe retardation, and cardiac, limb, and other physical defects may be present.

32. **Field of vision**—The area of space visible with both eyes while looking straight ahead; measured in degrees.

33. **Glaucoma**—An eye disease characterized by excessively high pressure inside the eyeball. If untreated, the condition can result in total blindness.

34. **Grand mal seizure**—The most serious and severe form of an epileptic seizure in which the individual exhibits violent convulsions, loses consciousness, and becomes rigid.

35. **Hemiplegia**—Paralysis involving the extremities on the same side of the body.

36. **Hemophilia**—An inherited deficiency in the blood clotting factor which can result in serious internal bleeding.

37. **Hertz**—A unit of sound frequency used to measure pitch.

351

7-3. Continued

38. **Hydrocephalus**—A condition present at birth or developing soon afterwards from excess cerebrospinal fluid in the brain; results in an enlargement of the head and mental retardation. This condition is sometimes prevented by the surgical placement of a shunt, which allows for the proper drainage of the built-up fluids.

39. **Hyperactivity**—Excessive physical and muscular activity characterized by extreme inattention, and excessive restlessness and mobility. The condition is usually associated with attention deficit disorder or learning disabilities.

40. **Hyperopia**—Farsightedness; a condition causing difficulty with seeing near objects.

41. **Hypertonicity**—Heightened state of excessive tension.

42. **Hypotonicity**—Inability to maintain muscle tone or an inability to maintain muscle tension or resistance to stretch.

43. **Insulin**—A protein hormone produced by the pancreas that regulates carbohydrate metabolism.

44. **Iris**— The opaque, colored portion of the eye.

45. **Juvenile diabetes**—A children's disease characterized by an inadequate secretion or use of insulin resulting in excessive sugar in the blood and urine. This condition is usually controlled by diet and/or medication. However in certain cases, control may be difficult and if untreated, serious complications may arise such as visual impairments, limb amputation, coma, and death.

46. **Meningitis**—An inflammation of the membranes covering the brain and spinal cord. If untreated serious complications can result.

47. **Meningocele**— A type of spina bifida in which there is protrusion of the covering of the spinal cord through an opening in the vertebrae.

48. **Microcephaly**—A disorder involving the cranial cavity, characterized by the development of a small head. Retardation usually occurs from the lack of space for brain development.

49. **Monoplegia**—Paralysis of a single limb.

50. **Multiple sclerosis**—A progressive deterioration of the protective sheath surrounding the nerves leading to a degeneration and failure of the body's central nervous system.

51. **Muscular dystrophy**—A group of diseases that eventually weaken and destroy muscle tissue leading to a progressive deterioration of the body.

52. **Myopia**—Nearsightedness; a condition that results in blurred vision for distant objects.

53. **Neonatal**—The time usually associated with the period between the onset of labor and six weeks following birth.

7-3. Continued

54. **Neurologically impaired**—Individuals who exhibit problems associated with the functioning of the central nervous system.

55. **Nystagmus**—A rapid, rhythmic, and involuntary movement of the eyes. This condition may result in difficulty with reading or fixating on objects.

56. **Ocular mobility**—The eye's ability to move.

57. **Optometrist**—A professional trained to examine eyes for defects and prescribe corrective lenses.

58. **Opthamologist**—A medical doctor trained to deal with diseases and conditions of the eye.

59. **Optic nerve**—The nerve in the eye that carries impulses to the brain.

60. **Optician**—A specialist trained to grind lenses according to a prescription.

61. **Ossicles**—The three small bones of the ear that transmit sound waves to the eardrum—malleus, incus, and stapes.

62. **Ostenogenesis imperfecta**—Also know as "brittle bone disease," this hereditary condition affects the growth of bones and causes them to break easily.

63. **Otitis media**—Middle ear infection.

64. **Otolaryngologist**—A medical doctor specializing in diseases of the ear and throat.

65. **Otologist**—A medical doctor specializing in the diseases of the ear.

66. **Otosclerosis**—A bony growth in the middle ear which develops around the base of the stapes, impeding its movement and causing hearing loss.

67. **Organic**—Factors usually associated with the central nervous system that cause a handicapping condition.

68. **Paralysis**—An impairment to or a loss of voluntary movement or sensation.

69. **Paraplegia**—A paralysis usually involving the lower half of the body, including both legs, as a result of injury or disease of the spinal cord.

70. **Perinatal**—Occurring at or immediately following birth.

71. **Petit mal seizures**—A mild form of epilepsy characterized by dizziness and momentary lapse of consciousness.

72. **Phenylketonuria**—Referred to as PKU, this inherited metabolic disease usually results in severe retardation. However, if it is detected at birth, a special diet can reduce the serious complications associated with the condition.

73. **Photophobia**—An extreme sensitivity of the eyes to light. This condition is common in albino children.

7-3. Continued

74. **Postnatal**—Occurring after birth.

75. **Prenatal**—Occurring before birth.

76. **Prosthesis**—An artificial device used to replace a missing body part.

77. **Psychomotor seizure**—An epileptic seizure in which the individual exhibits many automatic seizure activities of which he or she is not aware.

78. **Pupil**—The opening in the middle of the iris that expands and contracts to regulate light intake.

79. **Quadriplegia**—Paralysis involving all four limbs.

80. **Retina**—The back portion of the eye, containing nerve fibers that connect to the optic nerve on which the image is focused.

81. **Retinitis pigmentosa**—A degenerative eye disease in which the retina gradually atrophies, causing a narrowing of the field of vision.

82. **Retrolental fibroplasia**—An eye disorder resulting from excessive oxygen in incubators of premature babies.

83. **Rh incompatibility**—A blood condition in which the fetus has Rh positive blood and the mother has Rh negative blood, leading to a buildup of antibodies that attack the fetus. If untreated, can result in birth defects.

84. **Rheumatic fever**—A disease characterized by acute inflammation of the joints, fever, skin rash, nosebleeds, and abdominal pain. This disease often damages the heart by scarring its tissues and valves.

85. **Rigidity cerebral palsy**—A type of cerebral palsy characterized by minimal muscle elasticity, and little or no stretch reflex, which creates stiffness.

86. **Rubella**—Referred to as German measles, this communicable disease is usually of concern only when developed by women during the early stages of pregnancy. If it is contracted at that time, there is a high probability of severe handicaps of the offspring.

87. **Sclera**—The tough white outer layer of the eyeball that protects as well as holds the eye's components in place.

88. **Scoliosis**—A weakness of the muscles that results in a serious abnormal curvature of the spine. This condition may be corrected with surgery or a brace.

89. **Semicircular canals**—The three canals within the middle ear that are responsible for maintaining balance.

90. **Sensorineural hearing loss**— A hearing disorder resulting from damage or dysfunction of the cochlea.

91. **Shunt**—A tube that is inserted into the body to drain fluid from one part to another. This procedure is common in cases of hydrocephalus to remove excessive cerebrospinal fluid from the head and redirect it to the heart or intestines.

7-3. Continued

92. **Spasticity**—A type of cerebral palsy characterized by tense, contracted muscles, resulting in muscular incoordination.

93. **Spina bifida occulta**—A type of spina bifida characterized by a protrusion of the spinal cord and membranes. This form of the condition does not always cause serious disability.

94. **Strabismus**—Crossed eyes.

95. **Tremor**—A type of cerebral palsy characterized by consistent, strong, uncontrolled movements.

96. **Triplegia**—Paralysis of three of the body's limbs.

97. **Usher's syndrome**—An inherited combination of visual and hearing impairments.

98. **Visual acuity**—Sharpness or clearness of vision.

99. **Vitreous humor**—The jelly-like fluid that fills most of the interior of the eyeball.

7-4. TERMINOLOGY ASSOCIATED WITH OCCUPATIONAL THERAPY

Occupational Therapists in an educational setting should communicate their findings in a clear manner. The following definitions will help when documenting medically related terminology for the educational community. A therapist may continue to use medical terminology, but it should be defined in the body of the report. Definitions for these terms, wherever possible, may be written by an individual therapist in his or her own words.

1. **Abduction**—Movement of limb outwards away from body.

2. **Active Movements**—Movements a child does without help.

3. **Adaptive Equipment**—Devices used to position or to teach special skills.

4. **Associated Reactions**—Increase of stiffness in spastic arms and legs resulting from effort.

5. **Asymmetrical**—One side of the body different from the other (unequal or dissimilar).

6. **Ataxic**—No balance, jerky.

7. **Athetoid**—Child with uncontrolled and continuously unwanted movements.

8. **Atrophy**—Wasting of the muscles.

9. **Automatic Movements**—Necessary movements done without thought or effort.

10. **Balance**—Ability to keep a steady position.

11. **Bilateral Motor**—Refers to skill and performance in purposeful movement that requires interaction between both sides of the body in a smooth manner.

12. **Circumduction**—To swing the limb away from the body to clear the foot.

13. **Clonus**—Shaky movements of spastic muscle.

14. **Compensory Movement**—A form of movement that is atypical in relation to normal patterns of movement.

15. **Congenital**—From birth.

16. **Coordination**—Combination of muscles in movement.

17. **Contracture**—Permanently tight muscle or joint.

18. **Crossing the Midline**—Refers to skill and performance in crossing the vertical midline of the body.

19. **Deformity**—Body or limb fixed in abnormal position.

20. **Diplegia**—Legs mostly affected.

21. **Distractable**—Not able to concentrate.

22. **Equilibrium**—Balance.

7-4. Continued

23. **Equilibrium Reactions**—Automatic patterns of body movements that enable restoration and maintenance of balance against gravity.

24. **Equinus**—Toe walks.

25. **Extension**—Straightening of the trunk and limbs.

26. **Eye-Hand Coordination**—Eye is used as a tool for directing the hand to perform efficiently.

27. **Facilitation**—Making it possible for the child to move.

28. **Figure-Ground Perception**—To be able to see foreground against the background.

29. **Fine Motor**—Small muscle movements; use of hands and fingers.

30. **Flexion**—Bending of elbows, hips, knees, etc.

31. **Fluctuating Tone**—Changing from one degree of tension to another, e.g., from low to high tone.

32. **Form Constancy**—Ability to perceive an object as possessing invariant properties, such as shape, size, color, and brightness.

33. **Gait Pattern**—Description of walking pattern including:

- **Swing to gait**-walking with crutches or walker by moving crutches forward and swinging body up to crutches.
- **Swing thru**-walking with crutches by moving crutches forward and swinging body in front of the crutches.

34. **Genu Valgus**—Knocked knee.

35. **Genu Varum**—Bowlegged.

36. **Gross Motor**—Coordinated movements of all parts of the body for performance.

37. **Guarded Supervision**—When an individual is close to the student to provide physical support if balance is lost while sitting, standing, or walking.

38. **Guarding Techniques**—Techniques used to help students maintain balance, including contact guarding, when a student requires hands-on contact to maintain balance.

39. **Head Control**—Ability to control the position of the head.

40. **Hemiplegia**—One side of the body affected.

41. **Hypertonicity**—Increased muscle tone.

42. **Hypotonicity**—Decreased muscle tone.

7-4. Continued

43. **Inhibition**—Positions and movements which stop muscle tightness.

44. **Involuntary Movements**—Unintended movements.

45. **Kyphosis**—Increased rounding of the upper back.

46. **Lordosis**—Sway back or increased curve in the back.

47. **Manual Muscle Test**—Test of isolated muscle strength.

   normal: 100%

   good: 80%

   fair: 50%

   poor: 20%

   zero: 0%

48. **Mobility**—Movement of a body muscle, body part, or the whole body from one place to another.

49. **Motivation**—Making the student want to move or perform.

50. **Motor Patterns**—Ways in which the body and limbs work together to make movement, also known as praxis.

51. **Nystagmus**—Series of automatic back-and-forth eye movements.

52. **Organization**—A student's ability to organize himself or herself in approach to and performance of activities.

53. **Orthosis**—Brace.

54. **Paraplegic**—Motor and sensory paralysis of the lower half of the body.

55. **Passive**—Anything that is done to the student without his or her help or cooperation.

56. **Pathological**—Due to or involving abnormality.

57. **Perception**—Organization of sensation from useful functioning.

58. **Persevation**—Unnecessary repetition of speech or movement.

59. **Positioning**—Ways of placing an individual that will help normalize postural tone and facilitate normal patterns of movement, and that may involve the use of adaptive equipment.

60. **Position in Space**—Child's ability to understand the relationship of an object to himself or herself.

61. **Postural Balance**—Refers to skill and performance in developing and maintaining body posture while sitting, standing, or engaging in an activity.

62. **Praxis**—Ability to think through a new task which requries movement; also known as motor planning.

7-4. Continued

63. **Pronation**—Turning of the hand with palm down.

64. **Prone**—Lying on the stomach.

65. **Quadriplegic**—Total paralysis of the body from the neck down.

66. **Range of Motion**—Joint motion.

67. **Reflex**—Stereotypic posture and movement that occurs in relation to specific eliciting stimuli and outside of conscious control.

68. **Righting Reactions**—Ability to put head and body right when positions are abnormal or uncomfortable.

69. **Right/Left Discrimination**—Refers to skill and performance in differentiating right from left and vice versa.

70. **Rigidity**—Very stiff movements and postures.

71. **Rotation**—Movement of the trunk where the shoulders move opposite to the hips.

72. **Scoliosis**—C or S curvature of the spine.

73. **Sensation**—Feeling.

74. **Sensory-Motor Experience**—The feeling of one's own movements.

75. **Sequencing**—Concerns the ordering of visual patterns in time and space.

76. **Spasm**—Sudden tightness of muscles.

77. **Spasticity**—Decreased muscle tone.

78. **Spatial Relations**—The ability to perceive the position of two or more objects in relation to himself or herself and to each other.

79. **Stair Climbing**—Methods of climbing include

   mark stepping: ascending or descending

   climbing stairs one step at a time

   alternating steps—step over step

80. **Stereognosis**—The identification of forms and nature of object through the sense of touch.

81. **Subluxation**—A partial dislocation where joint surfaces remain in contact with one another.

82. **Supination**—Turning of hand with palm up.

83. **Symmetrical**—Both sides equal.

84. **Tactile**—Pertaining to the sense of touch of the skin.

7-4. Continued

85. **Tandem Walking**—Walking in a forward progression placing heel to toe.

86. **Tone**—Firmness of muscles.

87. **Vestibular System**—A sensory system that responds to the position of the head in relation to gravity and accelerated and decelerated movements.

88. **Visual Memory**—Ability to recall visual stimuli in terms of form, detail, position, and other significant features on both short- and long-term basis.

89. **Visual-Motor Integration**—The ability to combine visual input with purposeful voluntary movement of the hand and other body parts involved in the activity.

90. **Voluntary Movements**—Movements done with attention and with concentration.

7-5. ABBREVIATIONS ASSOCIATED WITH SPECIAL EDUCATION

1. ACLC Assessment of Children's Language Comprehension
2. ADHD Attention Deficit Hyperactive Disorder
3. AE Age Equivalent
4. AUD.DIS Auditory Discrimination
5. BINET Stanford-Binet Intelligence Test
6. BVMGT Bender Visual Motor Gestalt Test
7. CA Chronological Age
8. C.A.T Children's Apperception Test
9. CEC Council for Exceptional Children
10. C.P Cerebral Palsy
11. CSE Committee on Special Education
12. DAP Draw a Person Test
13. dB Decibel (hearing measurement)
14. DDST Denver Developmental Screening Test
15. DQ Developmental Quotient
16. DTLA-3 Detroit Tests of Learning Aptitude-3
17. ED Emotionally Disturbed
18. EMR Educable Mentally Retarded
19. FAPE Free Appropriate Public Education
20. fq Frequency Range (hearing measurement)
21. GE Grade Equivalent
22. GFW Goldman-Fristoe-Woodcock Test of Auditory Discrimination
23. HH Hard of Hearing
24. HTP House-Tree-Person Test
25. Hz Hertz (hearing measurement)
26. IEU Intermediate Educational Unit
27. IHE Institutions of Higher Education
28. IQ Intelligence Quotient
29. ITPA Illinois Tests of Psycholinguistic Abilities

7-5. Continued

30. LA Learning Aptitude

31. LD Learning Disabled

32. LEA Local Education Agency

33. LPR Local Percentile Rank

34. MA Mental Age

35. MBD Minimal Brain Dysfunction

36. MH Multiply Handicapped

37. MMPI Minnesota Multiphasic Personality Inventory

38. MR Mentally Retarded

39. MVPT Motor-Free Visual Perception Test

40. NPR National Percentile Rank

41. PHC Pupils with Handicapping Conditions

42. PIAT Peabody Individual Achievement Test

43. PINS Person in Need of Supervision

44. PLA Psycholinguistic Age

45. PPVT Peabody Picture Vocabulary Test

46. PQ Perceptual Quotient

47. PR Percentile Rank

48. PS Partially Sighted

49. PSEN Pupils with Special Educational Needs

50. PTA Pure Tone Average (hearing measurement)

51. SAI School Abilities Index

52. SCSIT Southern California Sensory Integration Tests

53. SEA State Education Agency

54. SIT Slosson Intelligence Test

55. SRT Speech Reception Threshhold (hearing measurement)

56. TACL Test for Auditory Comprehension of Language

57. TAT Thematic Apperception Test

58. TMR Trainable Mentally Retarded

59. TOWL Test of Written Language

7-5. Continued

60. TWS Larsen-Hammill Test of Written Spelling
61. VAKT Visual/Auditory/Kinesthetic/Tactile
62. VIS.DIS Visual Discrimination
63. VMI Beery-Buktenica Developmental Test of Visual Motor Integration
64. WAIS-R Wechsler Adult Intelligence Scale–Revised
65. WISC-R Wechsler Intelligence Scale for Children–Revised
66. WISC-III Wechsler Intelligence Scale for Children-III
67. WPPSI-R Wechsler Preschool and Primary Scale of Intelligence–Revised
68. WRAT-R Wide Range Achievement Test–Revised